The Vortex

Arthur and me Volume II

Ann Treherne

The Vortex

ISBN-13: 978-1-8383855-3-8

ASIN: B0CBNYS362

Cover design by: Art Painter

Dedication

This book is dedicated to Gill and George the remaining two members of our Thursday Group, for their commitment, loyalty, trust and dedication.

Gill has been a member of the Group almost from the beginning in 2006 and has witnessed some of the incredible physical phenomena that we encountered soon into its existence - she remains a most valued and trusted member today.

George joined the group ten years ago in 2013 and reminds me that most spiritual circles usually dissipate after a couple of years at most, and he has remained even although he was not witness to those early years. He remains a valuable asset to the Group to this day.

So, the longevity of The Thursday Group is just one of the over-riding facets of this Group - the other, of course is its people and I simply couldn't have asked for better.

With love and appreciation for all that you do.

Contents

Foreword
Gary E. Schwartz, PhD

In 2019, Ann Treherne published an extraordinary book titled Arthur and me: The true story of Arthur Conan Doyle communicating from beyond the grave, culminating in the foundation of The Sir Arthur Conan Doyle Centre in Edinburgh. Ann's book included a brief Foreword by Professor Chris A. Roe, President of the Society for Psychical Research in London, and Professor of Psychology at the University of Northampton. Professor Roe wrote *"Some of the phenomena Ann describes are truly incredible, such that even direct witnesses may come to doubt their own senses."* And he ended his Foreword speaking to the survival of bodily death hypothesis by stating *"This metaphysical question seems to fall outside of the scope of science, but surely nothing could be more important to science than exploring the full nature of what it is to be a human being and to recognize the fundamental properties of consciousness."*

Volume II continues this incredible story with additional real-life evidence of Sir Arthur's apparent continued commitment to establishing that life after death is real. The extraordinary events that Ann shares in this book are as inspiring as they are challenging. In

Volume I, the book's editor Professor Lance St John Butler, formerly of University of Stirling, attested to Ann's integrity by stating *"I have personally been able to verify the transcripts of spirit communication recording in this account with the original tape recordings of the actual events and can vouch for their authenticity and accuracy."*

If anyone – real or fictional – appreciates the need for accuracy of information and interpretation in making valid discoveries, it is Doyle's detective Sherlock Holmes. In Volume I, Ann quotes Holmes, *"When you have eliminated the impossible, whatever remains, no matter how improbable, must be the truth."* In Volume II, I would like to quote one of my favorite examples of Holmes' wisdom, *"It is a capital mistake to theorize before one has data. Insensibly one begins to twist facts to suit theories, instead of theories to suit facts."* Ann appreciates Doyle's commitment to accuracy in reporting and interpreting details as well as celebrating the wonders of life. As Holmes understands, *"Life is infinitely stranger than anything which the mind of man could invent."*

As yet I have only met Ann Treherne in a virtual capacity as we have not had the opportunity to meet in person. However, I have conducted an impromptu test of Ann's mediumship and she impressed me by revealing information about some of the experiments I have been conducting in my laboratory at the University of Arizona that have been kept under strict confidentiality conditions. Ann states that she works with Doyle and sometimes receives evidential information from scientists like Einstein and Tesla. The information she provided during and following our virtual session is consistent with her controversial claims. Consequently, I have invited Ann to serve as a consulting research medium on the Soul-Phone Project in my Laboratory for Advances in Consciousness and Health (https://lach.arizona.edu/survival-consciousness-hypothesis)

My agreement to write this brief Foreword for Volume II was partly based on Professor Butler's endorsement of Ann's commitment to accuracy and truth, and her integrity which was affirmed by Professor Roe. For example, in my 2021 book titled *Extraordinary claims require extraordinary evidence: The science and ethics of truth seeking and truth abuse*, I expand upon Professor Carl Sagan's extraordinary claims quote and document how accuracy of information and interpretation is a prerequisite for human survival, health, and evolution. Ann's commitment to truth seeking is illustrated by the list of visionary scientists who have participated in the Tuesday Talks Series sponsored by the Sir Arthur Conan Doyle Centre in Edinburgh which she founded.

In this book Ann takes us on an adventure of personal discovery, mystery, insight, and gratitude. Her writing style is as entertaining as it is illuminating. My prediction is that after you finish reading Volume II, you will find yourself wishing for a future Volume III.

Gary E. Schwartz, PhD.

Professor of Psychology, Medicine, Neurology, Psychiatry, and Surgery, The University of Arizona, and Director of the Laboratory for Advances in Consciousness and Health. Schwartz has more than 500 scientific publications, including six in the journal Science. His books include The Afterlife Experiments, The Sacred Promise, and Extraordinary Claims Require Extraordinary Evidence.

Introduction

Dr Adam Reed

In her first book, *Arthur and Me*, Ann Treherne outlines how a dramatic premonition, and its subsequent realization, changed her life. Ann was traumatised by that event. Indeed, it was the prompt to self-transformation. As that first book relays, Ann left a high-powered career in the corporate, financial world and began a new spiritual journey, which included research and investigation of the paranormal. She also set up a home circle to sit for Spirit. Known as the Thursday Group, that circle and its extraordinary experiences forms the narrative heart of *Arthur and Me*. And as the title of that book suggests, so do the circle's communications with Arthur Conan Doyle.

Over the five-year period covered by the first book, Arthur guides the Thursday Group in their development and understanding of the paranormal. He also leads Ann and the rest of the circle members to locate a certain building in Edinburgh – to be named after him. That building was found in December 2010 and opened the following year as Scotland's premier centre for holistic well-being and as a centre of excellence for mediumship training and development as well as studies into consciousness and parapsychology. The Sir Arthur Conan Doyle Centre was born.

I first met Ann in 2022 after coming across and reading Arthur and Me. And as a consequence of that meeting, I also visited the Centre and eventually also met some of the other members of the Thursday Group, with whom I have had the pleasure of sitting in circle on a number of occasions since then. Although I remain very much a novice, the experience has been immensely rewarding as well as highly stimulating in terms of my own academic interests (as an anthropologist absolutely concerned with contemporary intersections between religious and literary life). As well as a force of nature, Ann has been an extremely generous and lively interlocutor. I always look forward to our conversations and the questions they throw up, partly because of Ann's open-mindedness and driving desire to open new fields of inquiry.

It is no surprise therefore that I was excited to learn of the imminent publication of a second book, Arthur and Me, Volume 2, which picks up events again and explores the first ten years in the history of The Sir Arthur Conan Doyle Centre. But when I finally read the new book, I quickly realised that this was no ordinary history. Indeed, as well as continuing the story of the Thursday Group, its communications with Arthur and the spiritual mission of Ann, Volume 2 offers us something different and original: the paranormal story of a building, and more expansively of a wider Scottish landscape. In short, it's a great read! Ann probably won't thank me for saying so, but by the end it left me full of anticipation for the next episode in this story, a Volume 3. Whether Ann chooses to write that book or not, I feel sure that the paranormal adventure that first started back in 1996 will continue unabated. For, as Sherlock Holmes would say, and I know that Ann would echo: *'When you have eliminated the impossible, whatever remains, however improbable, must be the truth.'*

Dr Adam Reed

Reader in Social Anthropology,
University of St Andrews
Literature and Agency in English Fiction Reading: a study of the
Henry Williamson Society. Manchester University Press [New
Ethnographies]/ Toronto University Press [Studies in Book & Print
Culture] Papua New Guinea's Last Place: experiences of constraint
in a postcolonial prison. Berghahn.

Chapter 1

The man on the stairs

By 2009, the Thursday Group, which I had put together at the request of Spirit[1] was becoming frustrated. Directed for a number of years by Arthur Conan Doyle, our circle remained unsure how to interpret the continual instruction from Arthur to find a building. We were accustomed to his repeated clues as to what this building might look like but as to where it was, this was still a mystery to us, and our frustration was turning to annoyance. Why didn't he just tell us where it was? Early in that year we accepted an invitation to sit in Gill's house and Gill had offered to put on a supper for us afterwards. As we sat in her lounge after our session and enjoyed her home-cooking, we discussed this instruction that once again had been received to find this elusive building. That night for some reason our frustration seemed particularly poignant. Little did we know that we were actually sitting in the same street (Palmerston Place) where the building was situated, but that was not to be discovered until the following year.

When in December 2010 I eventually found the derelict building that would become The Sir Arthur Conan Doyle Centre, I took the Group members to see the building that had so clearly been foretold to them. As I opened the wide wooden door and they walked inside, they too felt the same energy that had greeted me just a few months before.

'Ooooh yes', said Mairi.

'This is incredible. I can't believe that staircase; no wonder they [Spirit] told us it was like *'Gone with the Wind.'* Gill was smiling as she looked at the dilapidated grandeur of the place.

Jim just seemed to be looking around with awe and wonder, whilst Gordon was busy walking in and out of all the downstairs rooms surveying the scene. 'I've agreed that I get a room for myself', I said, 'so that will be our room – we'll have to pay to hire it – but it will be exclusively for us, for the Group, just as Spirit has directed us. We just have to decide which one we want, and it'll have to be one of the smaller rooms so it does not cost too much to hire.'

'Okay, can we go upstairs', asked Gordon, 'I want to dowse for it'.

'Yes, let's go upstairs. But I'll warn you the place gets worse as you get higher up'. We climbed the stairs whilst listening to various gasps and exclamations from Gordon as his pendulum responded to the energy in the stair. After much assessing and comparing of the energy in various rooms Gordon pronounced that a room on the very top floor right in the corner of the building had the best energy for our Group. Gill and Mairi concurred and so the Group had found their room – Room 403.

The building was eventually purchased in July 2011, so we didn't get to sit in our room right away. For there was a delay to the intended purchase date of May 2011. The building had been derelict for the previous four years and following the financial crash of 2008 it had been repossessed by the bank. It had previously been operating as a rather downbeat back-packers hostel, although designated a hotel for planning purposes. It now required to be re-designated as a place of worship if it was going to become a new spiritual Centre in Scotland.

My husband Iain and I had already been ear-marked to handle

the refurbishment and we had drawn up a project plan for the work to ensure it was completed in time for the planned opening of the building to the public at the end of October; some five months after the expected purchase date. What no-one banked upon was an objection to our planning application; this meant our project plan was effectively delayed by two months from what was already a very ambitious timetable.

Faced with this delay, Iain and I quickly re-assessed our plan and postponed all the trades that had been lined up ready to commence work on the building. We were in limbo. The estate agent had allowed me to keep the keys as the potential new owner and indeed they also paid for the locks to be changed as a reassurance that no-one else had keys to the building. This was done as a goodwill gesture because of the building's previous use as a hostel. So, I said to Iain, 'I've got the keys so we could at least start to tidy the place up and throw out all the junk. No-one is going to object to that if the purchase falls through. It will just mean we would have done that work for nothing but at least it will not have cost us anything, just our own time?'

Iain agreed although he did say, 'What if someone catches us doing this work?'

'We could hardy make it any worse than it is just now, Iain.'

'That's true.'

Iain is a very fast worker and within a couple of days he had cleared the building of all the assorted rubbish. He remarked as he did this that he began to wonder if someone had previously started to repair or refurbish the building and had suddenly stopped as he was finding food wrappers, lunch boxes and flasks, bottles of coke that were only half drunk. There was a radio and some pieces of clothing like a sweatshirt that someone had taken off ready to put back on again on the way out and shoes. I had noticed this too but perhaps not to the same extent, since it was Iain who was collecting all this stuff. He said it was like the Marie Celeste, as if everyone who had been working there had just disappeared mid-shift, even leaving their half-eaten lunch and personal belongings behind them. We did think this was strange. It was as if they had left in a rush. This thought was to revisit us when our own painters were in situ but for now, we thought it nothing more than curious.

'It's a pity we can't do more.' Iain said. I was feeling the same thing.

'We could start work on building the apartment?' We had planned to create a self-contained apartment on the second floor of the building for visiting speakers and mediums to use when they were working at the Centre and that required creating a new kitchen where there wasn't one before. Iain and I were adept at fitting kitchens. I reckoned we could make a start on that. 'I know it will cost us money this time but if we buy a flat-packed kitchen from Ikea it'll not cost much and again if anyone objects or if the sale does not go through then someone has got a new kitchen for free?'

Iain agreed and we set about measuring and planning out the space for this new kitchen in the second-floor apartment. We collected the flat packs from Ikea a couple of days later and carried them up the two flights of stairs and stacked them on the landing. The following day we set about our work. We started off in the apartment preparing the space for the addition of the new units and then begun building up the flat packs. We were both kneeling on the floor of what was to become this new apartment whilst building one of the units, when we both stopped and looked at each other as we heard the sound of footsteps on the stair. This was the distinctive sound the sole of a shoe makes as it scuffs on the surface of each stone step – someone was climbing the stairs towards us. We hardly had time to process that thought when it was followed up with the sound of a door opening and being allowed to slam shut with the force of the self-closers which were installed on all the doors as a safety precaution. It sounded as if it was the door from the back stairs into the corridor on this floor. 'Quick', I said to Iain, 'you go down the main staircase and I'll go down the back stairs and one of us will meet whoever it is who is on the stairs. It's probably the estate agent; maybe someone has reported seeing us bringing in the flat packs. He's probably just checking it out. We need to reassure him that we're not doing any structural work, just building flat packs.' At that, Iain headed off towards the main staircase and I headed along the corridor towards the door that we had heard banging shut just a moment before. I was sure I was going to find the estate agent whom I knew well by this time on the other side of the door to the back stairs but there was no-one there. I proceeded down the two flights of stairs to the bottom where I opened the door to the ground floor reception where Iain was already standing at the bottom of the main staircase waiting for me with a questioning expression on his face. 'Nothing', I said.

'No-one on the main stairs either, so I was sure he was going to be on the back stairs?'

'No', I said. Iain checked that the front door was still locked shut. 'Maybe he's gone further on up the stairs?'

'Why would he go up the stairs?'

'I don't know', I said, 'but let's check because someone is in this building.' Automatically we both returned up the stairs in the same way we had descended. There were two staircases in this old building: the main grand staircase and the back staircase, which would have originally been used by the servants of the house. I climbed this right to the top of the building where once again I met Iain. 'Nothing?'

'Nothing,' Iain said as we looked at each other and wondered what we had just heard and why we could find no explanation to these distinctive sounds. Slowly and reluctantly, we descended the stairs back to the second-floor apartment and our screw-drivers. We resumed our job of building the new kitchen units with our thoughts still contemplating what had just happened. One by one I carried a flat pack from the pile on the landing through to the apartment, where Iain was building them up. When I went back through to the landing to pick up the next pack from the pile, my eyes glanced through the balustrading towards the stairs and there looking back at me was a man. I shrieked with the shock of seeing him and instantly dropped the flat pack, which fell back on to the pile with a loud bang. Iain came running, 'What's wrong, what's wrong?'

Pointing a finger towards the stair I said, 'There was a man on the stair.'

'Where? Where is he now?' I could hear the urgency in Iain's voice as he looked across the balustrade to the stairs and then down-wards to the floors below.

'Oh, he wasn't a real man. He disappeared almost as soon as I saw him.' I could see the relief on Iain's face that this was someone from the Spirit World; interesting that this was more acceptable to him than being found out by a real person. Iain was accustomed by now to hearing of some of my mediumistic encounters over the years and he was now a firm believer, although did not want to be involved personally. 'What do you think he wanted?'

'I don't know; it was probably a previous owner, just letting us know he was here. He was letting me know it was his house and he was watching us.' I had received this information from the man in the few seconds in which our eyes had met through the balustrade. It wasn't a threatening challenge, just the sort of thing anyone would do who had workmen in their house. But it was a firm message; he was keeping an eye on us. As I recounted this message to Iain, I realised we had just created one of the criteria that makes a location particularly conducive to paranormal phenomena – we had just started refurbishment in a building that had previously been quiet, indeed empty for the last few years. I wondered what else might happen, especially since the major refurbishment work had not yet started. The answer was yet to unfold.

I was to encounter the man on the stairs again. This time it was after the refurbishment works were completed and we were getting ready to open the building to the public. An opening ceremony had been planned for 23rd October 2011 and the president of the Spiritualist National Union was due to attend to perform the ceremony. All the redecoration works were now complete, the new carpets had been fitted and the place was looking resplendent and back to its former glory. I had created several floral displays for our opening ceremony and placed them on the grand staircase, in the vestibule and in the Sanctuary where the service would take place. As I was walking round the building alone on the Friday evening prior to the planned opening event, I was taking one final look at the place to make sure everything was looking good for the Sunday when suddenly the man appeared again. He was just as before, as solid as you or me and back on the stairs in exactly the same place where I had seen him several months before. But this time he was above me. I was on the first-floor landing and so looking up at him. He looked down at me and this time his demeanour was kinder, caring and appreciative. He was dressed as before with his top hat and dress-coat together with waistcoat with a gold watch chain and a cane in his hand; he was very much the Victorian gentleman. And he had the same distinctive long grey beard. The man touched the rim of his top hat, as if doffing his hat to me. At the same time there was a small bow of the head in my direction and in that moment he conveyed to me that he was pleased with what had taken place. I got the impression he was thanking me, saluting me. I was pleased. I left the building that night thinking that whoever this man was he was letting me know that he was happy that his house was looking good again and that he liked the work we had done.

Chapter 2

Snakes and Ladders or Hide and Seek?

O nce the planners waived through the change of use, Iain
and I sprang into action to rework the project plan to get
us back on schedule. The contractors that had previously been put on hold had all been informed of the prospective
start date and so the work on the building could begin straight away.
The first jobs were to make the building wind and water-tight so the
roofers were brought in first, followed by the window contractors;
there were 43 windows in this building and they were all pretty
draughty and ill-fitting, so they required an overhaul. At the same
time, we planned to do much of the internal remodelling work
ourselves in repairing missing or broken floor-boards throughout the
building, building another kitchen, repairing the toilet blocks and
bathrooms on all six floors and make various repairs to walls and ceilings where the plasterboard would have to be renewed. We esti-
mated that once this work was completed we could move on to the
cosmetics of the building before bringing in the painters and decora-
tors and laying the floor coverings.

The roofers worked quickly, even working over the weekend to
meet our timescales. They could access the roof from inside the

building so there was no need for scaffolding and that was a real bonus; they were in and out in no time. This was quickly followed by the window contractors and they put four men on the job so that they could work in pairs on two floors at the same time. Iain and I were there each day too working through our schedule, but always ensuring that our work did not interfere with theirs so we didn't get in their way. Everything was working swimmingly until one of their men said that they had seen someone in one of the ground-floor rooms – a man. Initially this workman just came to find where Iain and I were working and said, 'There's a guy downstairs.' He just seemed to be reporting that someone had arrived at the building and he was letting me know. I went downstairs but found no-one there. I climbed the stairs again to where the window guys were working and said, 'There's no-one there? Who was he? And what did he want?'

'Dunno,' the window guy said nonchalantly as he continued working on the window, 'I just saw him as I was walking past the open door to that big room downstairs.'

'What was he doing?'

'Just standing there and looking around the room.'

'Okay, well I don't know who he was but he's not there now.' I went back to my work and thought nothing more of it until it happened again a few days later. This time his colleague came to tell me that someone was waiting for me downstairs. Again, I downed tools and went down to the ground floor. There was no-one there. 'Maybe it was just a passer by taking the chance to be nosey; you should make sure the front door is kept closed when you go outside to get things out of your van,' I said to the window guys.

'I wasn't at the van. The door was shut. I was just getting more draught-excluder from the reception.'

Because of the difficulty in parking outside due to the traffic the men had off-loaded all their equipment from their van when they had first arrived and created a stock of tools and supplies on the ground floor. 'What did he look like?' I asked.

'I don't know, just a man. Dark clothing – a coat, I think.'

'That's the man I saw the other day,' said his colleague as they looked at each other disconcertedly.

The next day we were two men down; the two who had encountered the man never returned.

As the work continued, John the president of the Spiritualist Church at that time said that he would like to have stained-glass windows in the sanctuary; this was the room that had been earmarked for the Spiritualist Church and coincidentally also the one where *the man* had appeared. John and I discussed his ideas of having trees depicting the seasons and he had done some initial sketches. I added the idea of framing John's sketches in gothic-shaped arches to make them look more like church windows and together we took these initial sketches to the offices of the window firm to see if they could come up with a plan where these could be incorporated. We were introduced to their chief designer, a large burly man with huge hands which belied his artistic abilities. He said he would work up a plan to scale up these drawings to fit the windows and have the stained-glass designs put on to secondary glazing that could be fitted to the existing windows. He wanted to come to the building to measure up the three windows involved so he could get an accurate scale. I agreed to meet him at the building first thing the following morning.

The next morning I was running late. As I eventually drove along Palmerston Place my car was stopped at the traffic lights just opposite our building. I could see this big burly chap standing on the doorstep looking out for me along the pavement in either direction. When the lights changed I drove across the road and stopped my car immediately outside the front door where he was standing. I put the car window down and stretched out my hands holding a big bunch of keys, 'Here's the front door key. You make a start. I'm just going to park the car and then I'll be with you.'

'You've got to be joking,' came the immediate response. I was perplexed. As he saw the puzzlement in my face he said, 'I'm not going in there without you – I'm not going in on my own – it's too spooky.'

I couldn't quite believe what I was hearing. This guy had never been in our building before and yet he was too scared to go in on his own – and how I was supposed to protect him was beyond me. I smiled to myself but told him I was off to park the car; he said he would wait. As I walked back from the car-park, I was mulling over with faint amusement how and where this big guy had come up with this notion that the building was spooky. I could only deduce that his colleagues who had worked there earlier and who had encountered *the man* must surely have had a discussion about this back at the office and that this was sufficient for their chief designer to be scared to be there on his own. Little did I know that this spooky building was to reach a whole new level when the painters arrived.

The building was now wind and water-tight and the major works had been completed so now was the time to bring the painters in to get the main function rooms completed in time for the opening. As a charity we had obtained three estimates and gone with a firm of respected painters who were experienced in handling the very high ceilings and ornate cornicing of a buildings of this type. We contracted them to paint the main function rooms on the ground and first floor as well as the grand staircase. These were the rooms that had the highest ceilings; we would paint the remainder of the building ourselves to keep the costs down. There were three guys – the boss, Cameron [pseudonym], and his two employees.

They stored their paint, brushes, rollers, etc, in a ground floor room but their ladders were so tall they were stationed at the foot of the grand staircase until they were needed. The interior was beginning to take shape and we were beginning to see what a grand building this was. Cameron had been a professional footballer in a past life and so he, Iain and the other guys would regularly start 'work' on a Monday morning by first analysing the performances of their various teams from the weekend. There was always a bit of friendly banter that just added to the positivity of the atmosphere.

One evening as we were packing up for the day, Cameron, Iain and I were standing on the second-floor landing discussing the plan for painting the main staircase, when Cameron said, 'There's a strange feeling in this building.'

'What sort of feeling.' Iain asked him.

'It's quite a nice feeling and I hear someone singing.'

'Oh.'

'I've never said that to the guys – they'd think I was mad – but it sounds like a woman singing and I think she's singing in the stair-way. It sort of echoed up the stairs. I actually asked the guys to switch off the radio today because I thought it was coming from a crossed signal. But when I realised it wasn't and that they couldn't hear it I just asked them to switch it back on again. They think there's something wrong with my ears. Have you ever heard it?'

'No.'

'I can hear it now,' he said.

'What can you hear Cameron? What is she singing?' I asked.

'It's not a song that you would recognise. It's sort of haunting, like what they say about mermaids but its angelic somehow – it's really nice – I feel I could fly or float away and join her.'

I didn't like the sound of that last comment especially whilst we were standing overlooking the balustrading of the second floor and a drop of about forty feet. 'Okay, let's go now and come back tomorrow.' I said. I wanted him to come down the stairs.

'I'm not here tomorrow. I'm going to work on another job. But the guys will be here.' And with that we were all off home, with us wondering about what Cameron had just told us.

We had given a spare key to the painters so they could get an early start the next day but when we arrived they were in the tearoom arguing with each other. They had indeed come in early only to find that their paintbrushes had disappeared and they were accusing each other of taking the tools. (The painters had a routine where at the end of each night they would return to the ground floor tearoom with their paintbrushes and rollers and there they had an industrial sized roll of cling film which they would use to wrap their brushes and rollers so that they were kept air-tight for use the next day. This is a well-known practice of painters which means they don't have to clean their equipment each time. But now the brushes were gone.)

'Maybe Cameron's taken them?' I said in an attempt to stop the bickering.

'Naw, Cameron wouldn't take them. We all have our own brushes. He's taken them,' the painter said pointing at his colleague. The younger man who seemed to be the apprentice was perhaps being accused of a prank. He was shaking his head and saying that his brushes had disappeared too. He was also making the point that it wasn't him but his colleague who had the keys.

'We were here last night and we left with Cameron,' I said, 'so if he didn't take them maybe you've left them somewhere else?'

'Naw,' came the indignant response. I could tell he was now trying to figure out where they could possibly be.

'Okay, they can't be far away. Let's look.' We all headed off to look for these paintbrushes – and we found them – lying all still wrapped in their cling-film but up on the top most floor of the building where no painting works had been contracted nor started. This was three floors above where they had been working and so the older guy had another go at the apprentice asking him if he thought that this was funny and making the plea that they had lost the first hour looking for paintbrushes that were not where they had been left. After much gnashing of teeth, they both went back to work.

The two painters were working on the first-floor function room.

This was our largest and most impressive room, with very high ceilings and ornate cornices. Painting these cornices was pain-staking work and involved using very tall A-frame ladders with a couple of equally long planks straddled between the A-frames to provide a working platform from which the two painters could stand to reach the ceiling. The size and length of this equipment meant that quite a long section of cornicing could be completed before the ladders and planks had to be moved – again quite a task for our two painters.

When we walked in the following day, we were once again faced by angry shouts and accusations, this time coming from the first-floor function room. The air was blue with the sound of the painters cursing and swearing at each other. It was so aggressive Iain immediately ran upstairs and into the function room. I followed just a little behind him not being too eager to enter the fray.

'What's going on?' Iain said.

'This little shit thinks this is funny.' the painter said about his apprentice. The apprentice was looking fearful of the increasingly aggressive tone of his work colleague but equally he displayed the sheepish look of someone being unfairly chastised.

'What's happened?' Iain said, 'have the paintbrushes disappeared again?'

'Just look around you,' the painter said, 'what do you see?' Iain and I looked around the room but nothing drew our attention. It was just an empty room. There was no mess or damage that could possibly have caused the amount of angst that the painter was displaying. Realising he wasn't getting through to us he said, 'What *don't* you see?'

Ah, something's missing I thought. If it's not the paintbrushes then it must be the paint but a quick glance showed that they had both brought their brushes and pots of paint upstairs with them from the tearoom where they had left them the night before.

'Where's the fucking ladders.' The painter's exasperation had overflown into anger. Iain and I stood open-mouthed. Strange how you miss something so obvious as huge, great big ladders and staging planks but they were gone. Iain and I looked at each other in disbelief and the apprentice looked at us for some sort of sympathy whilst his colleague continued to berate him.

'Hold on a second,' I said, 'you both left at the same time last night so he can't have taken the ladders.' The apprentice who was keeping quiet throughout most of this acknowledged this reasoning with a nod of the head that seemed to gesture *I told you so* but didn't dare open his mouth for fear of another onslaught from his colleague. His colleague was now beginning to calm down a little as I said to him, 'Cameron is working on another job just now. Could he have come and taken them?'

Without saying anything, the painter put his hand in his pocket and pulled out his mobile phone and pressed a button, 'Hello Boss did you come back here last night to pick up the ladders?'

We couldn't hear the answer but the painter followed up by saying, 'no I've got the keys here,' at which point he pulled the keys from his other pocket as if to demonstrate the fact. Cameron was clearly pointing out that he did not have keys to access the building and perhaps he was asking him if he had given the keys to anyone else. At this the painter quickly finished the call telling the boss he would report back to him later. He probably realised from the exchange that it was only he who had access to the building since he was the only one with keys, so if any accusations were going to be thrown they would likely fall in his direction. He quietened down as this thought sunk in.

'Okay', Iain said, 'before we report them as stolen let's just search the building to make sure that they're not here and also look for any means of forced entry to the building.' This course of action seemed to calm him down as he now seemed to accept a possible explanation for the disappearance of the ladders. The two painters set off up the stairs to check out the rest of the building whilst Iain said to me, 'I'm going to the basement. It's the only possible explanation. You can't take ladders out of a window that's forty feet off the ground and the windows up the stairs are even higher. Someone has maybe broken in from the back.' That sounded plausible to me so I joined Iain as we headed down to the basement. Iain went to check the back door and I went to check the basement windows to the front. When I saw them I remembered they all had wrought iron fixed bars. Iain returned, 'All the windows are barred.'

At that moment, we heard more shouting from upstairs. We both rushed upstairs because the shouting had suddenly returned to its previous levels of volume and abuse. The noise was coming from the second floor. As we rounded the corner at the top of the stairs following the direction of the sound, we entered a second-floor room. Room 205 had previously been two rooms which at some point in the building's history had been knocked into one. The result of this was that the opening that had been created between these two rooms was relatively small and certainly not big enough to create one big room. This had created a sort of ante-room, with an opening no bigger than a wide doorway to the other room which was the larger of the two. And there lying on the floor were the ladders and the planks neatly stacked.

The sight of this equipment lying on the floor triggered the painter into further abuse of his apprentice, accusing him of pranks and time-wasting. This aggression soon diminished when they couldn't figure out how to get the ladders back out of the room. The ladders were so tall that they couldn't be stood upright in the room as these ceilings were much lower and the space where they were positioned was so tight it was really difficult to manoeuvre them. It took all four of us to balance the ladders at an angle to get them round the corner from the main room into the ante-room, then through the doorway and back to the staircase. Once we did this, the two painters were able to carry them between them back downstairs and back to the first-floor function room from whence they had come.

It was clearly impossible for any one individual to have moved these ladders from the function room up to this second-floor room and then to position them in such an awkward location. These ladders had been brought in specially because of the height of the ceilings in the main function rooms on the ground and first floors. The second-floor rooms did not have high ceilings and these ladders were heavy, wooden, A-frames so this added to the difficulty in getting them back out. Indeed we actually damaged the walls in the manoeuvring operation of trying to get the ladders back out of that room. No painting work had been contracted for the second floor; there was no need to take them there.

After this incident the painters handed back the keys and refused to enter the building without us being there. Whether that was to guard against unfair claims of tomfoolery or because the key-holder would be the one held responsible for any missing equipment is unclear, but my own view and the reason I thought the painter was being so aggressive to his apprentice was because he was scared.

Conversely the next contractor took a completely opposing position. As we worked through this schedule of works we contracted a plasterer to put a fine skim of plaster on to the new plasterboards we had erected whilst we moved on to the kitchens and bathrooms. We decided to instal another new kitchen. The existing kitchen in the basement had previously served as the hotel kitchen when the building functioned as a hostel and it was buried in several inches of dirt and grease as well as mouse droppings. We hauled the whole thing out and started a re-build of a new kitchen. The plasterer was working his way up the building floor by floor. When we stopped for a lunch-break I said to Iain that I would go and find the plasterer and see if he wanted a cup of tea and wanted to join us since he was working on his own. When I found him he was up his ladder plastering the wall of one of the small rooms on the first floor. 'How are you getting on?' I asked.

'Fine', he said, 'but there's a wee lassie running around here.'

'Really?' I couldn't think how there could possibly be a child in the building but if there was that was dangerous. 'I'll go and have a look around.' I said, 'maybe the door's been left open.' I phoned Iain – we had got used to using our phones to communicate in such a large building – and asked him to check that the front door was closed even though I knew it was, since I had just passed it on the way up the stairs. I walked the building but nothing or no-one was to be found. I returned to the kitchen to continue my work telling Iain of what the plasterer had just said. By this time we were becoming familiar with strange happenings in the building and had adopted a policy of keeping quiet about them; we didn't want to lose any more workmen.

We finished the kitchen and moved on to the bathrooms; there was a bathroom on every floor and there were six floors, so there was a lot to do. We were working on the ground floor this day when I again went to find the plasterer to tell him it was lunchtime. He was on the second floor when once again he said, 'That wee lassie's here again.'

'I searched the whole building the other day and couldn't find anyone – what does she look like?' I asked.

'I don't know', he said, 'I just hear her running and playing and giggling. Then when I turn around she's gone. It's like she's playing hide and seek.'

'Okay, well come and have your lunch and then I'll do another search afterwards.' The next time it happened he had reached the top floor and so the last of his work. As I climbed to the top of the stairs to get him this last time he said to me, 'That wee lassie isn't real, is she?'

'What do you mean?'

'I mean she's a wee ghost girl?'

'I don't know – I've not seen her. What makes you say that?' I asked.

'I've got a friend who does this stuff and sometimes I get some stuff too when I'm with her and I think that wee lassie is a ghost and she's from the past. She's not from this time.'

'I really don't know. There's only you who has seen her. I know that I've searched the building and couldn't find anyone but maybe you just heard something from outside, out on the street?'

'No,' he said indignantly, 'I saw her this time. She wasn't on the street she was here wi me.'

'Are you okay? Has that scared you?'

'Naw, she's just a wee lassie playing – hide and seek I think – making me turn around and each time I do she runs away. I think she's just lonely, looking for someone to play with.' At that, he had his lunch then finished his work and left the building.

Chapter 3

The Volunteers

Once the external contractors had completed their works to the main function rooms, Iain and I were able to continue with the works required to the upper floors ourselves. These rooms were not so critical in terms of timescale as these floors would not be accessed by the general public and therefore the rooms would not be seen, nevertheless we were keen to do what we could to complete the works before our opening date; we were aware that this work would be much more difficult to achieve once the building was open for business.[1]

Now that the upper floors had been repaired and prepared for painting, we put a call out for volunteers to come and help us with the painting. We figured that this would be a safe call since the main function rooms had been redecorated by the professional painters so these little rooms on the fourth and fifth floors were safe enough to allow the volunteers to handle since they were small with low ceilings and since these floors would not be open to the public, they didn't demand a professional finish. We were pleased to receive an answer to our call from some of the men from the church, namely Alex Harrison, Bill McGregor and Ewan Irvine. Ewan was working, so his time was restricted. But Alex and Bill were both retired gentleman and very fit, active and eager to help. We set Alex and Bill a room each to paint giving them rollers and trays, paintbrushes and a tin of emulsion paint each. It was amusing to see the difference in technique between these two. When we called them down to the tearoom for a break, Alex was just as he was when he started and hadn't a spot of paint on him, whilst Bill was covered in paint splashes covering most of his face, hands and clothes. We were amused by the polite rivalry between these two. They were both of a similar age where chivalry and gentlemanly conduct was the order of the day. When they used to turn up for church each Sunday it was difficult to tell which was the smarter dressed as they both looked as if they had just stepped out of a tailor's window with sharply pressed trousers, shoes so polished you could see your reflection in them and jackets, shirts and ties that were immaculate. Now in their old clothes they seemed enthused to be helping out and seemed to enjoy the friendly rivalry and company of Iain and I as they worked their way along the little rooms of the third floor. One day I particularly remember was when Bill had moved on to start work on one of the rooms on the top floor. This had previously been a bedroom in the old hostel and had an en-suite shower-room which we had repaired ready for painting. Iain and I were working on the ground floor when suddenly Bill came running down the stairs grabbed his bag from the tearoom and ran out of the building. I ran out of the building too to see him running along the street and although I called after him he didn't turn around as I watched him disappear out of sight.

As I was preparing to write this book and looked at my notes of all the happenings that took place in the building back then I was reprimanding myself for not having asked Alex and Bill for written statements of their experiences at the time. Now I knew that Alex had sadly passed away and I wasn't sure what had happened to Bill. I hadn't heard from him in all that time and now I was kicking myself at this lost opportunity for independent corroboration for some of the events recorded in this book. You can imagine my surprise when the very next day I received an email forwarded to me from the Centre's email address asking if I knew this man who had contacted them – Bill McGregor – looking for me. At first I thought it must be a scam but I soon realised Bill was answering that psychic call that I didn't even realise I had made. Here is his email:

Hello Ann,

Bill McGregor here, I loved your book, I have written a journal starting when I was 3 years old up to the present day of my experiences with Spirit including when we were refurbishing the Sir Arthur Conan Doyle Centre prior to the Grand Opening in 2011.

Ann would it be possible that you could read this journal it is not for publication but for my Family, my address and phone number is on file at the Centre.

Please say hello to Iain. Hope to hear from you Ann, all the best

Bill McGregor

So not only had Bill got in touch just when I needed him but miraculously his email stated that he had just written his testimony of the happenings whilst refurbishing the building; sometimes Spirit is just too clever by half! I wrote back to Bill and he very kindly allowed me to copy his journal and to include this excerpt:

'I am a Spiritualist and a member of The Sir Arthur Conan Doyle Spiritualist Centre and Church. We moved our church from Morrison Street to the new building officially on 23rd October,

2011 *but prior to the opening a great deal of remedial work had to be carried out.*

As a volunteer I was on the main staircase from the ground floor where the stairs turn 180° heading towards the first-floor landing. I was halfway up this part of the stairs when I happened to look between the banister upright spindles as movement had caught my eye. I was looking at a number of chiffon scarves, about 5 or 7 all multi-coloured and all held in one hand (did not see hand). They were being waved as if by someone in a happy carefree manner as they ran up the stairs. I received the impression that this someone was a young family member, a girl of teenage years. I did not see anyone, just the scarves. They were being waved at about shoulder height. I was held in amazement. I do not ever say, 'wow', but I did that day but under my breath. I watched as they reached where the stairs started their upward turn towards me when they just disappeared.

The stairs are well lit for their full extent from the ground floor to the second floor even when the room doors on the landings are closed, due to the large skylight set in the roof space directly above the stairs. The scarves made my day. I do feel blessed that I am allowed to see what I do see.

The next day I thought that I would start work on the top floor It was a very pleasant room so I laid down the ground sheets, switching on my CD Player and started to listen to some easy listening. It must have been an hour or so later that I stopped for a break when I noticed two figures. These figures were not solid as I could see the wall and the door behind them. Both were girls about 15/16 years of age and both were wearing long pale night-dresses. They were about six feet in front of me and looking at me for about 30 seconds. I felt comfortable in their company as they seemed in mine until I said, 'hello' they turned and were gone. I was sorry that they had gone. I would have spoken to them.

The next day I continued with my painting on the top floor

and on one of my rest periods I thought that I would inspect the next rooms to be painted on this floor. I entered the second bedroom. It was en-suite so I first of all gave the bathroom a good check on what I would have to do, on leaving the en-suite I entered the bedroom and received a massive shock because standing in front of me was a black figure about five feet in height but was three feet across at the shoulder. It was ten feet in front of me. A figure yet not a figure. I am not easily frightened but this thing scared me it was really out of this world. I could not utter a sound/speak/shout/manly scream as I felt as if my throat was being compressed and I was cold, very cold. Somehow I backed out of the room and ran down the stairs. I kept looking back. I am surprised that I did not fall. On reaching the ground floor I grabbed my belongings and exited the building at speed. I did not return for a week then I told my fellow workers of my experience.'

— Bill McGregor

For more info and a profile of Bill McGregor – see Appendix 1.

Chapter 4

We're Open

The Centre opened on 23rd October, 2011. The service of dedication was conducted by David Bruton, president of the Spiritualist National Union (SNU) and was attended by amongst others, Kathryn Grundy, Simone Key and Janet Parker. All three were tutors/mediums from Stansted (Arthur Findlay College), who had been booked to run our first workshops at the Centre with dates agreed for the following year (2012). Because of the delay involved in getting the planning permission, most of the SNU Tutors were already booked up for 2012 and so had no availability in their diaries. Thankfully Kathryn came and ran a healing workshop, Simone did trance and Janet re-arranged an existing couple of courses she had planned for Swiss/German and Swiss/French students and swapped her planned venue to come to us. I wanted to ensure that where tutors were unable to offer us dates for 2012, that they gave us dates for the following year, as I knew we had a big challenge to meet in generating the funds necessary to keep this grand old building functioning. Our 2013 programme included: Eamonn Downey, Chris Drew, Thelma

Frances, Kathryn Grundy, Paul Jacobs, Simon James, Simone Key, Judith Seaman, Tony Stockwell, Bill Thomson, Brian Robertson, Gordon Smith and James Van Praagh – an impressive line-up in anyone's eyes but for now we would have to think of more innovative ways to bring in much needed income.

Arthur Conan Doyle had led me and my Group to this building and so now I had to make it work. My mission was to follow his aim to get the message over to people that there was life after death. I knew too that he wanted to get this information to as many people as possible so I would have to consider my strategy carefully. I was well aware that Spiritualism generally received bad press. At worst people thought that mediums and psychics conned the public out of their hard-earned cash or preyed on the vulnerable and bereaved. At best they thought it was all a load of rubbish and that these mediums were deluded. I knew I'd have to work hard to change this perspective. In truth, the majority of mediums provide a service to the bereaved that cannot be accomplished by any other means; a service that is often unpaid. Therefore, mediumship and private sittings would be ubiquitous in this new building but what else and how to change that image? Firstly, I wanted to ensure that the image presented to the public was a professional one; the building largely did this as it dominated its corner site on one of Edinburgh's prestigious streets. Secondly, we would have to differentiate ourselves from the usual offerings and give the public something different, something that they saw as safe and normal, something that would encourage them to come in through the door even if it wasn't for Spiritualism or mediumship. I also wanted to ensure that we included a psychical investigation unit and a lecture programme; these had been instrumental in my own education in the paranormal world and so I felt it imperative that these be included in the new Centre. The inclusion of a lecture programme allowed me to invite the scientists, the academics, the university professors and the researchers to come and talk and be part of what we were doing. I've always used the mantra, *'if you don't believe me, believe them'*. Equally, John Blackwood, a fellow trustee was keen to include art and music and I wanted to include healing in its many forms as well as holistic therapies. This together with the option to use the Centre for social and community-led activities we felt would give me the scope as chairman to get the message across to the public and encourage them to come and visit this new Centre.

I recruited my previous partner in psychical investigations and past vice president of the Scottish Society for Psychical Research (SSPR), Archie Lawrie, to head up the psychical investigation unit at the Centre and Tricia Robertson, past secretary of SSPR, to help me with the lecture programme. As a further example of our programme the speakers included Andy Thomas on crop circles, Dr Peter Fenwick on Near Death Experiences (NDE's), Prof Erlendur Haraldsson on mediumship, Dr Cal Cooper on telephone calls from the dead, Professor Bernard Carr on quantum physics, Dr Alan Sanderson on Spirit Release, Nigel Peace on precognition, Nick Kyle, president of SSPR on physical mediumship, Dr Caroline Watt, chair of the Koestler unit of Edinburgh University on the psychology of apparitions, Dr Roger Straughan from Reading University who purported to be in communication with ACD – something I was intrigued to hear – and Dr Ciaran O'Keefe the sceptic from the television programme Most Haunted.

I owe both Tricia and Archie a debt of gratitude for all that they did in those early years to help me get the Centre on the map with a line-up of distinguished speakers and of course they too spoke regularly at the Centre as both have wide experience in the field of paranormal research and both are authors of their own books on related subjects.

Other early actions I took to help generate income and fill some of the tiny rooms on the top two floors that would previously have served as the servants' quarters was to hire them out as artists' studios. I was surprised and pleased at how quickly these rooms were filled as I realised that Edinburgh had a high demand for such spaces. There was also a high demand for room hire from yoga teachers and very soon we had a regular programme of the many different types of yoga from three different tutors as well as classes in Qigong and Tai chi from a master tutor. Whilst these early interventions were helpful in filling some of the 26 rooms housed in this grand old building it was not attracting the general public into the building. I wondered what could be done to address this. One day travelling into the Centre from home I noticed an advertising banner outside one of the many churches in Edinburgh. It was promoting an art exhibition. Great, I thought, we can do that. We even had the artists already in the building. In the spring of 2012, I put out a request to all our newly found artists now occupying the rooms on the upper two floors to say that I planned to run an exhibition of their art; this surely would bring them to the meeting. It worked. I had a full turnout and I explained to them that I had no budget for advertising but I needed to let the people of Edinburgh know that we were here, we were open and wanted to welcome them into the building. My theory was to attract the public in for one thing – in this case art – and then once inside the building they would see that there was a Spiritualist church, talks and demonstrations of mediumship that they might then be encouraged to try. In practice, this was a little bit of cross-selling, a blast from my past. The artists were delighted they were going to get a free exhibition of their art in our lovely big function room and all they had to do was organise it, hang their works of art and help promote it to their own database and email lists. They also informed me that it was customary to have a private viewing prior to the exhibition opening to the general public, where the artists could invite their friends and family – this usually involved some wine and canapés – so I agreed I was happy to do this too. I left the artists to get all of this arranged and promoted over the next couple of months and meantime I wondered what other events

I could organise like this that might attract the general public into the building, events that would be seen as safe or normal i.e., not Spiritualism or mediumship. I figured the autumn would probably be the best time. If the art exhibition was to take place in the summer, then the autumn would be a good time for the next event when people usually started to think about evening events as the nights started shortening towards winter. So, maybe September or October. Then it struck me, October would be the first anniversary of our opening. Why not run a first anniversary concert. Music had been one of our aims in our corporate objectives and as yet I hadn't worked out how I would be able to introduce music into the building. But this would be a good incentive to myself to try to find a musician or a group of musicians who would be able to put on an anniversary concert. This idea would have to wait meantime and be a challenge for another day, as for now we were about to host our private art viewing.

We had seven artists in residence – Colin Wilson, Annie Broadley, Jennifer-Rose Bruce, Georgina Parkins, Christine McSorley, Sally-Anne Mochrie and Charlene Nelson. Each had a different style and subject matter, which gave us an interesting array of art and in various formats. I had also recruited the services of my niece Alison Hogg, also an artist, who did beautiful sketches of Edinburgh architecture and was a great help to me in getting the art exhibition organised. Each artist had been allocated an area of wall space to hang their own pieces so now our main function room was looking resplendent. In the middle of the room, we had placed two long banqueting tables end to end covered with white linen tablecloths, on which the canapés, nibbles and several bottles of wine, bubbly and soft drinks were available. Each artist had met and greeted their invited guests and were each busy showing people around their own area of the exhibition and then that of their neighbours. All I had to do was mingle and keep people topped up with wine; things were going swimmingly. Sally-Anne Mochrie, whose subject matter was usually birds depicted in the greatest of detail and often using gold-leaf in her designs, walked across the room to where I was standing. 'Come and meet my dad', she said. I had already met her husband a couple of months earlier as he was a cabinet-maker and made all of the frames for her paintings. But now she wafted a hand towards this tall, slim gentleman and said, 'This is my dad. Dad, this is Ann Treherne. She's the chair of the Centre.'

'Good evening,' I said, 'I'm very pleased to meet you', as I shook his hand.

'I must say, you've done a marvellous job on this place.' He looked around the room and upwards at the ceiling, cornicing and large chandelier,

'Well thank you, that's kind of you to say so. It was a massive effort. The place was pretty dilapidated, and we were on a tight timescale to get it finished in time for opening but we made it.'

'I hardly recognise the place. It didn't look like this before,' he remarked.

'You were here before?' I asked.

'Yes, I used to work here when it was the music school – I was a music teacher'.

'Oh, we're hoping to have music back in the building again sometime. I'm hoping to find some musicians to help me do that.'

'I can help you do that', he said.

'Really,' I said, 'That would be great.'

'What sort of music do you want – I know a lot of musicians.'

'Oh well I hadn't really thought about what *type* of music. I had only hoped to have an anniversary concert to mark our first year in the building.'

'An anniversary concert – why don't I compose a special piece of music for that?'

'You can do that?'

'Yes, that's what I do,' he said, as if it was something as ordinary as going for a pint of milk.

'We don't have any money – we can't pay you,' I said, quickly thinking he had suddenly seen an opportunity to earn a grand fee.

'That's not a problem. You commission me to write a piece of music to commemorate your first anniversary and I'll make sure it's done, and I'll find some musicians to play it for you. You'll probably have to pay *them* something though, just for their time.'

I was stunned. Was I really hearing this? Through a casual conversation here was someone who was offering to compose a piece of music specially for us and not only would it be free but he would also organise the musicians to play it. I couldn't believe that my aimless thoughts of possibly having an anniversary concert had suddenly materialised before my very eyes and without any intervention by myself. Talk about synchronicity[1]. I thanked him profusely for his kind offer. He asked me when our anniversary was and when I told him 23rd October. He said that this date would be tight but that he could make it and in the meantime he would be in contact with the musicians.

The next day I was still revelling in the coincidence, although I don't believe there is such a thing. Had Arthur or those in Spirit arranged for this to happen? Then another thought struck me. Could he actually do this? Was he any good? All he had told me was that he had been a music teacher. I was aware that the building had previously served as the music school to St Mary's Cathedral, our neighbours just across the road. There was a plaque in the vestibule that told me so but that was all I knew. Who was this man? Had he simply created some amateur junior school concert? I checked him out on the internet:

'One of the leading French Horn players of his generation, in orchestral, chamber music, jazz, film and commercial music, who is now a writer composer and conductor. Terry Johns during a 45-

33

year career as a player worked with the composers, Benjamin Brit-
ten, William Walton, Leonard Bernstein, Andre Previn and with
John Williams on the Star Wars trilogy, Superman and the Indiana
Jones films. In the London studios he worked with many of the
great singers of his day including Tony Bennet, Barbara Streisand,
Shirley Bassey, Jack Jones and Peggy Lee.'

I decide he might be quite good.

Chapter 5

The Violins

Once I realised that Terry Johns was for real and this giant of music who had played on the film soundtracks of Star Wars, Indiana Jones and Superman was offering to compose a piece of music specially for us, I decided I should just leave him to get on with it and wait and see what happened. As time moved on and I hadn't heard from him I began to wonder if it was just something that is said at parties. Was he too busy? Had he forgotten? And although his daughter Sally had her studio up on the third floor of our building, I didn't think it fair that I should ask her to intervene. Maybe it was all just too good to be true. Until one day he strode purposely into our building. He was a tall, thin man with long legs and was wearing a long dark raincoat even though this was mid-summer. He seemed to cover the distance between our vestibule door and our reception desk – some 20 feet or so – in about three strides, his coat flapping around him like Batman's cape as he arrived at the reception desk. 'Just thought I'd bring you up to date with where I've got to', he said.

'Great,' I said, trying not to sound too relieved that he'd actually returned.

'I've spoken to Allister and he's willing to do it and he'll get the guys together because we need four you see – there has to be four.'

'Who is Allister? And who are the guys?'

'Alastair Savage. He's a fiddle-player. He works for the BBC Scottish Symphony Orchestra and so he'll get together some of his pals, so that we have a string quartet.' I was trying to take in this most recent pronouncement, especially since I had presumed that the musicians were most likely to come from St Mary's School, probably a mixture of teachers and students I had surmised. Now we were getting classical musicians from Scotland's Symphony Orchestra. Sheesh!

As I was processing this latest news, he continued. 'I've decided to base it on *The Sign of the Four* – you know Conan Doyle's second Sherlock Holmes story?' He didn't wait for an answer but instead produced a well-thumbed book from somewhere inside this voluminous raincoat, almost like a magician would produce a rabbit. As he quickly opened it at a book-marked place, he said, 'See here. It says, *Sherlock Holmes took his bottle from the corner of the mantelpiece and his hypodermic syringe from its neat Morocco case. With his long, white, nervous fingers he adjusted the delicate needle and rolled back his left shirt-cuff. For some little time his eyes rested thoughtfully upon the sinewy forearm and wrist, all dotted and scarred with innumerable puncture-marks. Finally, he thrust the sharp point home, pressed down the tiny piston, and sank back into the velvet-lined armchair with a long sigh of satisfaction.... It is cocaine.....'*

I looked at Terry Johns in disbelief. I couldn't believe that the passage chosen to demonstrate how he would compose a piece of music to celebrate our first anniversary was going to be about the mighty Sherlock Holmes as a drug addict. I wondered if he was aware of what we did here. Our whole ethos was about the well-being of the mind, body and spirit; I didn't think this subject matter would be beneficial to any.

As he caught my look of disbelief, he said, 'It's got to be dramatic you see. And not many people know that Sherlock Holmes dabbled in drugs; it's not the sort of thing they show on the telly.'

'And I can understand why,' I said.

'Everyone knows the Sherlock Holmes stories, so I was trying to go for something completely different and I think this is it. You said you needed to get people into the building. People will come to hear an excerpt read from the stories that they've probably never heard before. Don't worry it'll be good', he said as he strode off out into the Edinburgh sunshine again, that long coat still flapping around his legs.

I sat there in disbelief wondering how I had got myself into this one, and how was I going to get out of it. I couldn't possibly tell this maestro who had so graciously volunteered to compose a piece for us that I no longer wanted it or that his chosen piece was not acceptable. I reminded myself that this intervention had seemingly been put in place by those in Spirit; so, I'd just wait and see what happens. I got a sense that something else was to come.

A couple of weeks later, I was travelling by bus into the Centre which by now was simply known to us as Palmerston. I had picked up *The Metro* newspaper and was aimlessly leafing through it as the bus wound its way slowly through the streets of Edinburgh towards the West End. I turned another page and there was Arthur Conan Doyle's face staring right back at me. It is funny but after having encountered him in the way that I did he was now instantly recognisable, so much so that it felt like a close friend or relative was appearing in the newspaper. What was this article about? The Dunedin School for children with learning difficulties had a tree that had to be taken down in their grounds because it had become dangerous. Nothing newsworthy there, I thought. But it went on to say that they had discovered that young Arthur had stayed there as a child and played in that tree. When the school discovered this, they commissioned a local instrument maker to create a violin out of the tree in commemoration of Conan Doyle and his love for the violin.

The instrument-maker, Steve Burnett, had created a magnificent concert violin and christened it The Sherlock. It was created to celebrate the 150th anniversary of Conan Doyle's birth in 2009. So, just when I was thinking that this news was a bit late appearing now in 2012 the article followed up by telling us that Steve Burnett had since gone on to make a further violin, a viola and a cello from the same tree to form the Conan Doyle Quartet. I couldn't believe it – a string quartet – just what we needed for the concert and named after the great man himself. We had to have them. I couldn't wait for the bus to get to Palmerston Place. I skipped off the bus, grabbing a second copy of this free newspaper and as I walked along the pavement towards the Centre I quietly thanked Arthur for pulling all these elements together.

When I got to the Centre I phoned Terry Johns to tell him about my recent discovery of these instruments. He was surprised that he hadn't heard of them before but agreed with me that they would make a fitting addition to our planned concert. 'Why don't you phone this Steve Burnett fellow and just ask if you can borrow them for the concert?' said Terry.

'Why would he give them to me? I have no background in music whatsoever – he's more likely to agree to lend them to you?', I said.

'Okay', said Terry, 'I'll give him a call'.

And so in October we held our first anniversary concert featuring the Conan Doyle Quartet of instruments played by four musicians from the BBC Scottish Symphony Orchestra including Alistair Savage their lead violinist playing 'The Sign of the Four', a specially composed piece of music to commemorate our first anniversary composed by internationally famed musician and composer, Terry Johns. You couldn't write this stuff.

The press picked up on it, I think because of the violins and because it was a specially composed piece of music, thankfully; rather than the fact that Sherlock Holmes was a drug addict. And Terry was right. The piece was very dramatic. He narrated sections of the book whilst the quartet provided the dramatic background music. It was just like watching a film except there were no visuals. You had to fill in those blanks in your own mind – mind-blowing – literally. The concert was a sell-out and the public loved it. Arthur was helping in getting the message across.

Notes:

By the end of the year we issued a press release as Terry offered to help us bring more music to our beautiful building.

See copy press release and some of the press coverage at Appendix 2.

Chapter 6

Iain's Experiences

That first full year (2012) after opening Iain and I had settled into a pattern of working. These were long hours and there were only the two of us for most of the time. We devised a rota where Iain would start early in the morning and get the building up and running. He'd do the cleaning and setting up rooms for the evening activities. I would arrive around 4pm. Iain and I would have a hand-over period and then I would take over and work the evening shift. The building was always much busier during the evenings as that was when most classes, talks and events would be running – we were often full – so my job was really to administer all of this and look after our many visitors. Evening events were supposed to finish at 9pm but it was usually about 9.30pm by the time everyone had left the building. I'd do whatever tidying up was required, switch off all the lights, close the doors and head home and we would start the process over again the following day. On the weekends where we had events running we would draft in some volunteers to help us but for the most part Iain and I were managing the building on our own.

In the past Iain had always kept anything to do with the Spirit

World at arms-length – initially telling me that it was nonsense – then over the years when hearing some of the evidence I'd received he'd become more interested to hear what was going on but never wanting to get involved himself. He was now a reluctant believer but retained his sceptical objectivity. And so it was with surprise that he started to tell me about things he was experiencing at the Centre whilst in there on his own. He told me that when he was sitting at our reception desk, which was situated at the bottom of our grand staircase under the domed-ceiling, he had a feeling of a presence and become aware that someone was staring at him. As he looked up from his paper-work he saw a child, a young girl in the library (the doorway to which was adjacent to the desk) peeping her head round the open doorway as if hiding from him. When he looked up at her, she ducked back inside the room in a playful way.

He said she was dressed like an urchin rather similar to the promotional image from *Les Misérables* the musical. He also saw someone who could have been her mother who would walk across the floor between the library and the door to the servant's staircase, which was right in front of the reception desk where he was sitting.

This description was remarkably similar to the sighting described by the plasterer when he had described his little ghost girl playing hide and seek. I had become aware of her too from time to time but as the evenings were usually very busy times it was Iain who saw her most often. As Iain would relay these encounters, he would tell me with a sense of wonder and enthusiasm that is often present in those who experience the Spirit World for the first time. I wondered if sitting in the quiet of this great building on his own for long periods of time had helped create the conditions that allowed Iain to witness these things, or was it the building itself that was host to these phenomena and we were simply witnessing them? Only time would tell and we didn't have long to wait.

Another day when I arrived to take over from him and to start my shift, I asked him what had been happening and he told me, 'It's been really busy in here today.'

'That's great,' I said, 'we must be attracting more people into the building;' for whilst evening classes and events were busy it was usually quiet during the day.

'No. Not real people,' he said. 'They're ghosts – lots of them and they've been marching up and down the stairs all day.' When I asked him what these people were like he said, 'Legionnaires – they were like Roman soldiers with breast-plates, like gladiators with domed helmets with nose-plates. There were dozens of them and they marched down the stairs in formation one behind the other whilst another column of soldiers marched upwards. When they reached the bottom of the stairs they would just turn around and march back up again – this went on all day.' I was dumbfounded. This was a very visual and unusual description but I couldn't think why a building built in the late 1800's would have any connection with Roman legionnaires or why they would be marching up and down our staircase for no apparent reason.

Another day Iain reported seeing a man in the basement; I had seen this man too but it was Iain who saw him first. When descending the stairs from the reception area to the basement the corridor at the bottom of the stairs leads directly to the kitchen at the opposite end to the stairs. To the left of that corridor there are two doors which lead into the dining-room. It is a long rectangular room with twin windows at one end which look out into the outside area, the space between the building and the pavement but below ground level. The room had been set-up with rows of rectangular tables with four chairs set around each table, two either side. This configuration allowed for the greatest capacity of diners, some 60 covers. The doors to the dining-room were always left open and Iain said that as he walked along the corridor past the first open door he saw a man sitting at one of the tables at the far side of the room facing the window. He described him as a big man, bulky, wearing dark clothing; he only saw his back view. A week later in almost a repeat of this scenario, I too saw this same image of a man, a big man who seemed to be wearing something like a Donkey Jacket and he was sitting forward in his chair leaning his forearms on the table, the way you would do if you were sitting over a coffee or a newspaper, with his head down so I couldn't see his face. He was in the same position sitting at the same table. Both Iain and I saw him as we walked along the corridor past the open doorways. Iain is a fast walker and by the time he had registered that someone was sitting in the room he had passed the first open door and was heading to the next door (also into the dining-room) but when he got to it, expecting to confront the man, he had gone. My experience was very similar but I reversed back a couple of steps when I saw him sitting there and looked again through the first open doorway but he was gone. (Some of the volunteers who had been helping us at weekends had also witnessed this man.)

Up until this point the ghostly apparitions had been just that – or perhaps even residual energy[1] – an imprint of past events. I put the numbers of sightings down to the fact that we had created one of the known criteria which is conducive to creating these types of phenomena i.e., we had just undertaken major refurbishment of a building that had remained empty for the last four or five years. I expected it would calm down again as the energy in the building settled to its new occupiers. I was wrong.

Although the majority of the refurbishment work had been completed there was another large room in the basement which was originally intended to be rented out to a private business as an office space; we had hoped this would have added to our much-needed rental income. The business in question had asked if they could bring in several large office desks, swivel chairs, cabinets and those screens that are used as room-dividers in open-plan offices. They did so even though we hadn't yet painted the room. All this furniture of course was now creating obstacles for the painting process, so when

Iain was ready to give the room several coats of white emulsion ready for its new occupants, he first of all had to spend the morning piling all this furniture up at one end of the room and covering it with dust sheets to avoid splashes of paint. The room now prepared, he went to the store room to pick up his roller, tray and paint and returned to the basement only to find the furniture – all of it – back where it had come from and in its original position.

These were large, heavy desks and chairs, filing cabinets, etc; indeed, Iain had spent the first hour and half manoeuvring them across the floor and into a stack at one end of the room and as he was on his own this was a labour-intensive task. Imagine his surprise when all of this furniture was back its original position within an instant; he had only gone to the storeroom at the end of the corridor and back. After he had come to terms with the shock of seeing this, he said he got the feeling that someone was making fun of him. Someone thought this was amusing. Someone was watching. He moved the furniture once more but this time did not leave the room until the paint job was completed otherwise he felt that the moving of the furniture might be repeated. In the end that business decided not to proceed with the renting of our basement room.

Things gradually took a more sinister turn. Iain described what happened as follows:

'Well, I was attacked three times. The first time was when I was filling up the urn that sat in the tearoom. I had taken the inner water tank out of the urn and down to the basement kitchen to fill it with water. [The inner tank was just like a large cylindrical stainless-steel bucket but with no handle just a slim rim around the top. It held about 20 litres/5 gallons of water.] Once filled it was very heavy and so I was holding it in front of me and trying to walk as quickly as I could when carrying this weight. As soon as I started to climb the stairs from the basement I had only taken a few steps when suddenly a force took the urn from my hands and upturned it over my head; I was soaked. I had to take my t-shirt off and put it over the radiator to dry. Thankfully I was on my own in the building so no-one saw me looking like a drowned rat.

The second time was when I was putting the rubbish out for collection. I had four black bin-bags full of rubbish, two in each hand, and I was taking them out from the basement exit door and up the outside steps to place them on the pavement for collection. When I got to the top of the stairs, I was stuck fast to the top step. I couldn't move my legs and no matter how hard I tried I couldn't budge them. It was as if my feet were glued to the step. Then a force propelled me forward through the air right over the pavement and I landed in the road with my knees in the gutter and my feet behind me on the kerb of the pavement, still holding the bags of rubbish. This was a difficult position to get out of but I could at least now move my legs. I got up and ran back into the building through the front door. I threw the bags at the fence, grabbed my keys and drove home. I got a real fright.

When it happened the third time, I had a witness. When Jim Cleary was appointed a Trustee of the Centre he took it upon himself to come in each day to help me in any way he could, usually with hoovering or mopping the floors, doing the dishes or just generally helping out, and he was a great help. We were setting out a few rows of chairs in the library for a small function that was due to take place in the room that evening and we were chatting as we worked. We had just finished, when I felt a strange sensation in the room – I can't quite describe it – but when I looked at Jim his face had changed it was deformed and he started speaking to me but it was not his voice. It was as if someone else was speaking. Suddenly I was lifted off the floor by a force that threw me over the rows of chairs that we had just set out and I landed in a heap on the floor at Jim's feet. Jim was shocked but not as much as I was. Even though it had happened before, I was glad to have someone else there. Like me, Jim didn't know what had just happened but I remember him saying he was glad to have witnessed it and didn't think he'd see anything like that in his lifetime. I would've been pleased if I hadn't either!'

— Iain Treherne

Jim Cleary's Testimony:

'As a Trustee of The Sir Arthur Conan Doyle Centre, I always tried my best to help out as much as I could. I was no computer whiz-kid so I couldn't help Ann with the website or answering emails but what I could do was help Iain with the manual work and so I would go into the Centre most days. I usually helped with the hoovering and cleaning the toilets sometimes, doing the dishes or mopping the floor – whatever was needed. Being retired but still very fit and healthy I enjoyed helping out and Iain and I had a routine where we split this work between us then after all the cleaning duties had been performed we would stop for a coffee and then move on to setting up the rooms for the evening classes. I remember that day distinctly. Indeed it will stay in my mind forever because I've never seen anything like it. We were both in the library setting the room up for a meeting. It was to be set up with three rows of chairs running length-wise along the room and a small table was to be placed at the front for the speaker. The chairs were usually stacked under the staircase in the vestibule, so Iain and I did a relay back and forth carrying chairs until the three rows were established. I was standing at the front where the speaker would normally stand – although I hadn't put out the small table yet – and Iain was standing behind the three rows with his hands on the backs of two chairs as we stood there discussing football. Iain and I supported opposing sides so there were always a friendly rivalry when discussing the performance of our respective teams. As we chatted, I became aware of a change in the energy in the room. It began to feel strangely heavy and I remember Iain saying, 'something's happening,' so he clearly felt it too, which I remember thinking was strange since Iain doesn't involve himself in anything spiritual or psychic. But the next thing, Iain was catapulted over the seats head first and landed clumsily on the floor. He had crashed down on the front row of seats and sort of bounced off them and landed at my feet. I didn't know quite what had happened and I asked Iain if he was alright. I remember he was really shaken – as was I – and he said that a force had thrown him.

I've never seen anything like it but feel privileged to have seen it.'

— Jim Cleary, Retired Trustee,
The Sir Arthur Conan Doyle Centre.

Chapter 7

Ann's Experiences

W hen Iain had begun to recount to me his early experiences in the Centre, they seemed to start in a very natural way and in a manner that I was very familiar with both from my own experiences in developing my mediumship and in helping others develop theirs when conducting classes and workshops. (Although his legionnaires still had me puzzled.) His experiences however seemed to increase in frequency and intensity, a fact that I had not quite recognised as he would regularly tell me of what had happened each day. I would simply recognize it as Spirits making themselves known to him (like the little girl) and I would not put any particular emphasis on it. I put his ardour to tell me of his experiences down to the fact that this was a new experience for Iain – to sense Spirit – and I thought it was nothing more than that, until the day of his second attack as he has referred to it in the last chapter.

I remember that day very well for I was shocked too and I wasn't even there. By the second half of 2012 we had recruited some volunteers to help staff the reception desk on some of the evenings, thereby allowing me to have a night off and for Iain and I to have dinner at home together, which had been a rare occurrence at that time. I was at home preparing our meal when Iain arrived back from the Centre, earlier than expected and he seemed very shaken. I was standing at the sink preparing vegetables when he said, 'A really strange thing happened today at the Centre.' This was a familiar statement to me now as he regularly told me of his experiences. I suppose I was only half listening and half thinking of the meal I was preparing as he was standing in the doorway to the kitchen telling me of this force that had propelled him over the pavement. But when I heard the fear in his voice, I stopped and turned to hear what he had to say. Instead of continuing speaking he too stopped and with hands still shaking he pulled the belt of his trousers to unbuckle it and allowed his trousers to fall to the floor around his ankles. 'Look!' he said. His legs, his knees and particularly his shins were all cut, bruised and bloodied from where he had landed in the gutter. The blood had been running from his knees down the fronts of his legs. 'Now will you believe he,' he said.

I realised I had not been giving his testimonies the attention they deserved but now he had my undivided attention. As I thought about what he told me, I was calculating that the pavement was around 2 metres wide – no-one could jump that from a standing start, not even when pushed and certainly not whilst carrying 2 bags of rubbish in each hand. And the fact that he had been thrown into the road made me realise that he could have landed further into the road, perhaps in front of a lorry or car. This was becoming dangerous. If this force he experienced could throw Iain who would weigh-in at around 12stone, plus his rubbish bags – another couple of stone – then they could do this to anyone.

I pondered on this and wondered why? What was the purpose of this? I was of the opinion that everything to do with Spirit happens for a reason. It has purpose, there is an intelligence there. So why throw Iain into the road? I also knew from experience that Spirit can do things which are designed to get our attention. This ranges from simple coincidence (or synchronicity), used to make us sit up and take notice and to realise there is something more going on, to the amusing and down-right annoying e.g., taking things (usually familiar possessions like keys, wallets, phones, etc) and either putting them in the most unlikely positions or putting them back in the place that you have just checked a few minutes before. It can also include poltergeist activity, where things are thrown or moved right in front of you. All of these things can usually be explained when a medium is used to intervene and make contact with the Spirit-being concerned. In my experience there is normally a message that they are trying to convey and when it is articulated they simply disappear, move on and the phenomenon stops, as they have achieved their objective. What were they trying to get across to Iain?

I had had my own experiences in the building. I had seen the little ghost girl playing hide and seek and could hear her giggling, particularly when in some of the upstairs corridors where the plasterer had originally confronted her. I had seen the big hulk of a man who sat at the table near the window in the basement dining-room and I had seen the man on the stairs who had let me know very early on that this was his house. I had wondered if it could have been he who was now directing attention at the new man of the house – Iain – but I considered this to be unlikely since he had seemed pleased, indeed proud of the fact that the building was now back to its former glory. Indeed Iain had now taken to shouting, 'Goodnight ghosts,' when he left the building for the evening and uncannily he would get a response of two knocks or bangs from somewhere high up in the main staircase. Later, when some of our volunteers witnessed this, they too would adopt the same scenario.

I had also encountered more physical phenomena. One evening when I was closing the place for the night, I had done my usual walk around the building closing doors and switching off lights before leaving and I was walking along Palmerston Place towards the bus stop when something made me turn to look back at the building and there it was shining like a beacon with the lights burning brightly in all of its 43 windows. I decided to leave it to the ghosts. One day I left a wet tea-towel that I had just used to dry dishes on a serving table in the kitchen. As I returned to the basement with a fresh, dry tea-towel from the laundry room, and walked into the kitchen, the wet tea-towel flew through the air above head-height towards the window and landed in the sink. I stopped still in my tracks and stood there wondering how that had just happened. The window was not open so there was no draught. Even if there had been, it made no sense that the tea-towel would travel towards the window, as it was heavy and wet. I concluded that someone was letting me know that they were there.

I was also now accustomed to walking into the library on the ground floor, which was now nicely shelved with library books behind glass doors along one wall and books, CDs, cards and other items for sale on the open shelves on the other wall. Almost every time that I walked into the room some of these items would fly off the shelves, and I don't mean just drop to the floor with possible movement or vibration from either me walking on floor boards or perhaps the passing traffic on the road outside. I mean I would walk in and no sooner than I'd crossed the threshold the books and CDs would fly off the open shelves and land in the Centre of the room approximately two meters from their starting positions. It was such a regular occurrence that I had got used to it and didn't take much cognisance of it. When it happened in the presence of others, it would be they who would often be a bit spooked by this phenomenon.

On another occasion, in the evening after everyone had gone home, I was setting up one of the rooms for a class that was due to take place there the following morning. I thought this would make it a bit easier for Iain if it was set-up in advance. The room was on the second floor and was now referred to as the boardroom mainly because it had a boardroom table in the ante-room section. I knew from the booking that this was a dieting class and the teacher had asked for the seats to be set up as two straight rows of chairs against the two opposite and longest walls. After setting-up the room, I stood at the open doorway to the main room and admired my perfectly lined-up chairs. As I turned back towards the ante-room I gave the boardroom table a little polish with my duster and was just about to leave when I glanced back into the main room to notice that one of the chairs was out of line. It was forward from the other chairs by about one foot (30 centimetres). I immediately thought this was strange since I had just been admiring my handiwork, so I pushed it back into position, lining it up with the other chairs immediately either side of it and walked to the door. At the doorway I turned again and there it was standing out from the line but this time by the full chair's width, as if someone was really making their point. I walked back to the chair and once again pushed it back into line and because I was tuning-in to the fact that someone was playing with me, I responded and left my duster on the chair as if to say, 'you can't move it now, it's too heavy.' Once again, I turned my back and walked back to the doorway. When I looked around this time, the chair had stayed in place with the duster still on the seat. But then I watched the chair slowly and gently move forward of its own accord till it was once again standing proud of the others in the line. At this, I decided it was time to exit the building.

Whilst some of the phenomena referred to can come as a bit of a shock to one's normal sense of equilibrium, especially when the universally accepted laws of physics are being circumvented in this way, I had never felt in real danger. Having investigated some poltergeist cases in the past, I was aware that even when heavy objects were being thrown, they tended not to hit people, even changing trajectory mid-flight. In most cases, those witnessing the phenomenon were not hurt. Yet now Iain had shown me his injuries, the result of being thrown into the road – thankfully only into the gutter and not further. What was I to make of this?

It is strange but even when confronted with these visual images of physical harm to another human being, it can never be as impactful as it would be if it had been experienced personally. I had sympathy for Iain. I was concerned for him as he was clearly in shock because of his experience but somehow I had reasoned that it wasn't a serious injury. He'd be okay, maybe a little wary of the happenings in the building but he'd survive. This thinking allowed me somehow to compartmentalise my feelings, move on and get on with managing the building – until it happened to me.

That night I was on the evening-shift as usual. The building had been busy but the last class of the evening – a yoga class -had cancelled at the last minute. The tutor had phoned to tell me that she had been delayed in Glasgow and had contacted all her students to let them know that the class would not now be going ahead tonight.

An early night. Great, I thought, I'd get home early. All I had to do now was the usual walk around the building switching off lights and closing doors and then I'd be off home. I tidied away everything that I had been working on at the reception desk and put the paper-work away. I got my jacket from the coat rack, retrieved my handbag from the bottom drawer, fished out my car keys and put them in my coat pocket. I laid both the jacket and my bag on the desk and locked the desk ready for the off. There was always a decision to be made in a building of this size, whether to check the building starting from the top and work downwards or start from the bottom and climb to the top. As I was already on the ground floor, I decided I'd pop down to the basement, start there and then walk up the stairs, switching off lights and closing doors as I went. I went downstairs to the base-ment. I walked into the first room on the left, the dining-room. As I stood just inside the door, I scanned the room checking for anything that might have been left switched on, like lamps or CD-players but there was nothing there. I switched off the lights and closed the door. I next walked to the kitchen which was adjacent to the dining-room. I again scanned to ensure all appliances were switched off. I switched off the lights and closed the door. I walked further along the corridor passing two rooms, one on each side of the corridor which were used as offices. I pushed a hand against each of these closed doors, just to ensure they were locked and I moved on to the last room in the basement, at the far end of the corridor. I knew it hadn't been in use that night but the door was ajar, so I glanced in and looked to the side of the room where the electrical sockets were situated. I could see from this half-open door that there was nothing there. I firmly closed the door and began walking smartly back along the corridor, focusing on getting round the rest of the building as quickly as possible, so I could get home early.

The corridor in the basement is actually shaped like a squared off 'U' shape, it turns back on itself, and no sooner had I turned the second corner in the corridor than I was suddenly aware that someone or something was coming behind me at a great speed. In those split seconds my mind whirred. There must have been someone hiding in the back basement room, probably behind the half-open door waiting for everyone to leave the building, waiting to rob us or at least spend the night there and I had just disturbed him by banging the door as I closed it. I figured that he was now making his escape. He had been found out and now he was going to get out as fast as possible. These thoughts ran through my head in an instant. I had probably only taken about another two or three steps when I knew he was going to catch up with me and no doubt knock me out of the way in his panic to get out without being caught. As I sensed this force making the turn in the corridor behind me, I suddenly realised that the speed with which this thing was coming along the corridor towards me was far faster than any human could muster. It felt a little like the whoosh of displaced air that you experience in the London Underground when a train is approaching at speed. It felt as if it had the same power and speed as a train too. I instinctively jumped to the side, my back slammed up against the wall of the corridor in the hope I didn't get crushed. As I did that, the thing stopped – it was right up close beside me – at my face. It was awful, disgusting, strong, powerful and aggressive. It was up near my neck and I thought I would be throttled at any moment.

Much later I would describe it to someone as slime. I realise that is not a very accurate description but whatever it was it had no skeletal structure, no vertebrae, no defined body or form. Yet it was occupying a space as tall as a man but much wider in every direction and yet its fluidity made it difficult to define. I was terrified! I was very aware of the strength of power of this thing and that I could be crushed in an instant. I didn't think I was going to make it out alive that night or at the very least I was in danger of being very seriously injured. This intensity of fear and the proximity of the entity probably lasted just a few seconds and then it was gone – instantly – as if it had just dissolved into the floor. I didn't wait around for a second chance. I rushed up the stairs from the basement, bursting through the door to the reception area, slamming the door firmly behind me and standing with my back up against the door in some faint hope that I could possibly stop this immense force from coming through the door behind me. I stood there, still with my weight firmly forced against the door in a semi spread-eagle stance. I breathlessly looked around. The building was lit up with just about every light burning in the main part of the building, including the grand staircase which was still fully illuminated but it would just have to stay like that, as I was certainly not going to be venturing any further in this building nor switching the lights off tonight. I just wanted to get out. I looked across the floor to the reception desk where my bag and jacket were still lying ready to be picked up and I wondered whether I could risk running across to grab them before heading for the front door or whether if I did so the thing from the basement would burst through the door and attack me before I made it out the front door. I decided that although I didn't really need my bag, I did need the car keys if I were to get home. I went for it, running as fast I could to the desk, sweeping up the strap of my bag and my jacket in one movement as I flew past and turned to head for the front door still running as fast as my legs would carry me. I charged through the front door, pulling this mighty big wooden door behind me, and as I heard it slam shut, the chub automatically locking it in place, I collapsed on the doorstep. My legs could carry me no further.

I think the adrenalin must have kept me going up until this point. For now I was shaking uncontrollably in a crumpled heap on the doorstep, with my bag and jacket squashed somewhere beneath me. I was aware of the shock my body was experiencing at that point and I tried to slow my breathing as I was aware of my heart racing and the thought did cross my mind that I might have a heart-attack, sitting on the doorstep, and no-one would know why. I needed to warn people of the dangers and this thought helped me regain some composure and eventually to get to my feet.

When I eventually made it home Iain took one look at my face and asked what was wrong. When I told him what had happened, he said, 'Now you know what it feels like – to be attacked.' I was feeling really dejected by this response. I was expecting sympathy after this almighty trauma and all I got was the *I told you so* response. But he was right. I had been listening to what he had been telling me about his encounters at the Centre but I had not really appreciated the ferocity of these incidents, the immense power being demonstrated and the abject fear of something unknown and so powerful that you know your life could be in danger, until I had experienced it myself.

'So, what are you going to do about it,' Iain asked.

'I don't really know. No-one will believe us – I didn't think this was possible.'

'You didn't believe me,' sounding a little bumptious that he had got there before me.

'I'll phone John. He'll probably know what to do.' John Blackwood was my fellow trustee but also president of the Spiritualist Church at that time and he had been brought up in Spiritualism, man and boy. He's bound to have encountered such things and know what to do, I figured. But when I called John and told him, I could tell that although he knew me well and trusted me, he was having difficulty understanding this scenario. He kept asking me if I was sure and if I could have imagined it.

Sure I was sure. I had sat in a heap at the front door waiting for my legs to stop shaking so I could drive home. Indeed, a couple had walked past when I was in this state and the woman did a double-take looking back at me and I thought she was going to give me some money thinking I was a homeless person making a bed on the doorstep. 'So, no John, I'm sure it is not my imagination.' When I told him I was scared to go back into the building, he began to realise the extent of my fear. I asked him if he knew of anyone who could help rid us of this powerful entity in the basement; did the Spiritualist Church train its ministers to deal with such things? No, came the answer, and he didn't know anyone who could help.

I felt a bit let down by this answer, not because it came from John - he was a friend and still is to this day - but because the Spiritualist Church was unable to help. They did not deal with such things, as they didn't believe they existed. That seemed rather naive to me and still does to this day. I'd have to look elsewhere for help. The only other source of authoritative knowledge on these types of subjects that I knew of was the Scottish Society for Psychical Research (SSPR), where I had undertaken much of my early learning on the paranormal myself. I called Nick Kyle, the president. He too knew me well and knew I was not prone to sudden flights of fancy or of exaggeration, so he listened intently to what I was saying and then surprised me by saying, 'Can I come and stay – I'd like to experience it?'

'You've got to be joking – you really – *really* – don't want to experience this.'

'Yes, I do and I'd be happy to come through and stay in the building – if that's okay with you – and see what I can experience.'

This was not what I expected Nick to say but he knew me well and as a fellow paranormal investigator he knew I had experienced some strange phenomena over the years but never anything like this, so he was keen to experience it too. I arranged for him and his wife Sarah to come to the building and stay overnight. Nick's statement of what happened when he and Sarah visited is noted at the end of this chapter. (Note: They encountered an entirely different experience since they were stationed on the second floor but they brought some investigation equipment with them that would seem to register some strange phenomena.)

This was the first of many subsequent overnight vigils and investigations by the SSPR and others. In my initial conversations with both John and then Nick I swore them to secrecy as I could not afford this news to leak out. At first my thoughts were to warn people of the dangers but on reflection I realised that this would result in polarising the view of the general public. There would be those who wanted to come to experience the phenomenon and that might lead to false claims and expectations. There would be the others who would say that this was a lot of nonsense and I'd be ridiculed as the medium who was afraid of ghosts or some other such thing. I was after all trying to encourage the public into the building; I did not want anything that could detract from that aim. I decided to keep it all confidential and instead see what could be done to control, remove or at least minimise the threat to visitors to The Sir Arthur Conan Doyle Centre.

As I write this chapter now, I am still at a loss as to why that happened and why my Spirit Team and indeed Arthur Conan Doyle who had led me to this building would allow this to happen. Why would he want us to come to a building where there is such a malevolent force that could put our lives in danger – for that's how it felt.

I have been re-visiting these thoughts as I write this book and was asking Iain again how he felt at the time – the answer, 'Scared – really scared.' I was asking myself again why and how I could return to the building to work when that experience was so utterly frightening. The answer – I trusted what I had been given from Arthur over the preceding five years or so. I knew without a doubt that this was the building to which we had been led. I knew we were supposed to be here. So fearful as I was, I knew I had to go back and continue his work. It was an act of faith.

As coincidence would have it (you know what I think of coincidence by now) I had been pondering over these happenings again, when a collection of books subsequently arrived at my house which were given to me as a donation to the Centre's library. This box of books has been sitting on my kitchen floor during lockdown [pandemic of 2020] until I was able to get them into the Centre. And all that time I've been feeling that they needed to stay together as one collection rather than be distributed and amalgamated into our library. Indeed there has been one book on the top of the pile that has been calling to me and I knew I needed to read it but had said to myself that I'd do so after I've finished writing this book. When I eventually got the box into the Centre, George, a member of the Thursday Group whom I've yet to introduce you to said, 'You need to read the book now.' And so I took it back home again. The book is called *Spiritual Pilgrims by John Welch, O.Carm.* and the Foreword explains:

> '*Although the book purports to be a study of the psychology of Carl Jung and the spirituality of Teresa of Avila, it is far more. It is a personal journey into one of the most important writings of St Teresa, The Interior Castle, on which the author was given great help through an understanding of the human psyche and soul*

provided by the great psychiatrist... Baron Von Hugel showed that the only way to study mysticism was to study mystics and then follow their example. Fr. Welch has done just that. He has looked at the lives and writing of two people who have spent their entire lives on the religious quest into their own interior castles [souls/self – referred to as the Centre or depths in their references]. *He shows clearly the dangers which beset the traveller on this inner journey and he provides a clear image of the goal of the journey which spurs us to make the voyage.'*

Although I read only the first two chapters, I had been drawn to a random section of the book and to this reference:

'As a religious experience this cocoon time of alienation has been called "the dark night of the soul". St John of the Cross, another Carmelite Spanish mystic and friend of St Teresa, used the image of the night to express the Christian journey in faith. More vividly than Teresa, John's writings emphasized the cocoon phase of transformation through union with God. The dark night stands as a symbol of purification experienced by Christians.'

It goes on:

'The night of the spirit, midnight in the journey of faith, is a more intense experience still. All support systems are found wanting, and only a naked faith sustains the pilgrim. In the darkness of this cocoon experience the contrast between the polarities is stunning. "The brighter the light," John writes, "the more the owl is blinded." It is as though the plunge into the depths, the movement towards mystery which is at the Centre, evokes this question: Are these depths, is this Centre, trustworthy? Is the Centre for me, sustaining and life-giving? But no answer is given, and the trust itself must become its own reason. John's images for this experience parallel

Teresa's cocoon image. He compares the experience by being swallowed by a beast, being tried in a crucible, being in the depths of the sea, being the sepulchre of death, and peering into hell.'

And when referring to Jung on this subject the author writes:

'Entry into the cocoon of tense confusion, and groping for a way out, is a painful process which attends any growth of consciousness. It feels like dying. Jung wrote: "The dread and resistance which every natural human being experiences when it comes to delving too deeply into himself is, at bottom, the fear of the journey to Hades."

And going back to St Teresa the author writes:

'It is the night of the spirit and the trustworthiness of the Centre is in doubt. Teresa writes: "The Lord, it seems, gives the devil licence so that the soul might be tried and even be made to think it is rejected by God..."

Whilst I had never considered myself to be on a pilgrimage, the similarities were now obvious. I had spent the last five years religiously, if you pardon the pun - following the clues and direction from Arthur Conan Doyle to find a building that was planned to bring enlightenment to the general public. Having found it, refurbished it and got it ready to open and do its job, the very people who were going to be managing it were being tested. It would have been very easy at this time for Iain and I to decide this was a step too far and far too risky and frightening to be putting our efforts into something that wasn't really going to benefit either of us either financially or personally – it wasn't *our* goal.

This tenuous form of explanation was the only one I had back then, further investigations have taken place subsequently [see

Chapter 12], but whatever it was, the force in the basement seemed to dissipate after this crescendo. Whist we were aware that the physical energy remained in the building, it had diminished considerably from these frightening times and seemed much more tolerable. The positive energies being generated by the activities in the building (mediumship, healing, divine services, etc) may have helped too to mitigate the negative.[1]

I had been made aware in the past whilst our Group was sitting in the Theosophical building of the power of evil with the manifestation of Aleister Crowley, (which is outlined in detail in, *Arthur and me,*) but this was completely different. He was a man who had dabbled with the occult. This was an entity without form. It had never been human. There was some intelligence but none that I felt could be communicated with, yet it had such immense power it could destroy life in an instance and then disappear without leaving a trace.

Perhaps we had passed the test.

Testimony by Nick Kyle:-

'In 2012 Ann telephoned me to tell me about a frightening paranormal encounter that she had in the basement of the Centre. My immediate response was to offer support from my wife, Sarah, and me. We suggested that we could visit and give Ann a second opinion on what might be going on.

The following weekend, we met Ann in the Centre one evening, and she took us on a quick tour of the building. The building had a strong sense of 'presence' in the basement and on the second floor. I expect that many large homes might have basements that contain a 'presence.' Perhaps it's the impact of architecture, temperature and lighting on our psychology, but the feelings that I had in one basement room was that we were being watched. I *was aware that the entire building had an atmosphere of grandeur from its sweeping central staircase and décor, with a history from its former days as a music school and a family home before that. I was intrigued by reports of strange noises coming from the second floor, and that's where the apartment was, which was used by visiting mediums. It had an entrance hallway leading to a lounge/kitchen, bathroom and double bedroom, so we settled ourselves in the lounge, knowing that we were alone in the Centre.*

Before going to bed that evening, I set up four pairs of infra-red security alarms in the area outside the apartment:

   - one pair at the entrance to the flat

   - two pairs at opposite ends of the second-floor landing

   - one in a short corridor leading to other meeting rooms.

These devices were battery-operated transmitter-and-receiver pairs, linked by an infra-red beam inches from the floor that would trigger an alarm if the beam was broken, such as by a foot walking across it. The batteries were new, and the devices had never malfunctioned and given a false alarm when used before.

First alarm: *a few hours later, after we retired to the bedroom, the corridor alarm that was furthest away sounded and we went to check on it and reset it. There was no obvious reason for the alarm being set off; we checked for anything that might have broken the beam, perhaps a rodent or a moth or something falling from the wall, but we found nothing. I checked that the alarm was working by deliberately breaking the beam, then resetting it, and we returned to the bedroom.*

Second alarm: *minutes later, the same alarm sounded and, before we left to check it, another adjacent alarm on the far side of the landing went off. Nothing could be seen to explain these alarms and they both worked when I reset and triggered them by breaking the beams. We removed both pairs, leaving one pair already set up on the landing, and another inside the locked door to our apartment.*

Third and fourth alarms: *shortly after returning to our bedroom for the second time, a pair of alarms went off outside our apartment. Again, we saw nothing to explain it, but we removed the pair on the landing, leaving only a pair of alarms in the locked hallway of our apartment. When the apartment hallway alarm sounded shortly afterwards, and we checked around, I removed that pair too.*

Fifth alarm: *we decided to set up a pair of alarms across the floor of our bedroom, and as you may predict, they sounded too, shortly after we got into bed.*

We felt as if we were being followed into our bedroom. There was a strong sense of 'presence,' but no other phenomena. These alarms have worked perfectly well since that night on several other occasions.

Sarah and I don't think that moths or rodents that were not seen provide an explanation, especially in the sequence observed, getting closer to us in turn.

Follow-up: *We returned with a team from the Scottish Society for Psychical Research, who held an overnight vigil where each participant completed an individual survey of their experiences before there was any sharing or discussion. Video camera footage of orbs was captured that night in the basement.*

We would recommend that environmental monitoring equipment is used in another overnight vigil at the Centre, with infra-red and heat thermal recording equipment operated simultaneously and remotely from the targeted locations.'

— Nick and Sarah Kyle, 09.08.21

I believe that the presence of so many spiritual people doing spiritual work in the Centre has helped dissipate this energy; their collective good seemingly able to triumph over the negative intent prevalent in the basement. I remember too in 2012 we had a lot of yoga classes in the building and in particular there was a regular group who practiced Kundalini Yoga which was quite new to Edinburgh at the time. (Kundalini Yoga has the intent to awaken the 'sleeping serpent' represented by a snake that is the kundalini energy coiled at the lower spine and in most people is inactive. Kundalini Yoga attempts to awaken this energy by pranic breathing and chanting as well as yoga exercises.) The group would stay over weekends starting their practice at sunrise – often 4am in the summer – and when they did this they would invite one of the highly advanced Yogi Masters to take these sessions. Hari Hadji travelled the world as she was one of the few devotees who had reached the level of Kundalini Master. She was a highly intuitive spiritual master. She had a serenity about her and a hidden knowingness. I remember her telling me whilst we were standing in the basement that there was a dark energy in the building. When I asked her why this should be when what we were doing was spiritual work of good intent she said, 'The brighter your light, the longer the shadow you cast.' Now I was never quite sure what that meant and was concerned that the meaning might be that the more good one does the more darkness is attracted; that sounded scary to me, and unfair. But if I go back to the book and St John of the Cross:

> 'In the darkness of this cocoon experience the contrast between the polarities is stunning. "The brighter the light," John writes, "the more the owl is blinded." It is as though the plunge into the depths, the movement towards mystery which is at the Centre, evokes this question: Are these depths, is this Centre, trustworthy? Is the Centre for me, sustaining and life-giving? But no answer is given, and the trust itself must become its own reason.' [2]
>
> Spiritual Pilgrims by John Welch, O.Carm. Paulist Press p145.

For further info on investigations into this phenomenon see Appendix 3

Chapter 8

The experiences of others

Those early traumatic experiences of Iain and I happened in 2012, the first full year of operations. And it really challenged us. We had witnessed the painters' ladders being moved the year before and other items and pieces of furniture either moving or disappearing and reappearing and we could now count several people, either workmen or volunteers, who had left the building never to return. So we knew we had an 'active' building. None of this had fazed Iain and I. We just took it in our stride. I knew we had been directed by Spirit to this building, so I knew it was the right place to be. I trusted Spirit and Iain trusted me. But this most recent experience had shaken us to the core and that would be reflected back to me ironically at a Spiritualist Church service.

When I was not chairing the Sunday church service I would normally sit at the very back of the congregation near the open door so I could see the reception area in case anyone popped in. One Sunday morning the visiting speaker had brought along a trainee medium. This happened every now and then to allow trainees the experience of being on the platform and working with a live audience rather than their classmates. When the trainee started to work she was doing particularly well giving various messages to members of the congregation and then she said she had a message for me. I'm normally naturally wary when mediums want to give me a message as most know me but of course this newbie didn't.

'You run your own circle?' she said. I was underwhelmed. This was less impressive than the earlier messages she had been giving. Since she was standing in the midst of a Spiritualist Church it was not a great leap to suggest that most of those present at one time or another would have run their own circle. However I responded in the positive.

She then said 'And it's a physical circle.'

At that utterance I heard the sharp intake of breath collectively from the congregation and many turned around to see how I was going to respond. At this time physical mediumship[1] was extremely rare (and still is). There were only literally one or two exponents of the craft known to be working; most of the physical mediums had long since gone after the heydays of the Victorian period. Also no-one knew my Group existed, let alone that we were experiencing physical mediumship. But I had to answer her.

'Yes', giving always as little information as possible. But her next statement stunned me.

'You got more than you bargained for.'

As I slowly and gingerly nodded my head wondering what else was about to be revealed she issued some vague platitudes about her not knowing the details of what had happened but that I had got a fright. She then went on to say that I should know that those in the Spirit World were looking after me; this statement taking her back into the usual familiar territory of love and light of Spiritualism.

This technique of using new trainee mediums to bring me information – often publicly – was to be employed again. But for now I had escaped what could have been a public exposé of my experience in the basement. Thankfully it remained confidential, only known to two other people -until now. What she had done of course was firstly give me confirmation – if ever I needed it – that the Spirit World was aware of what had happened and its effect on me. Secondly, she had informed the congregation that I had a physical circle so I had a few enquiring questions to dodge after the service to ensure that the Group too would remain confidential (as previously instructed by Spirit).

In my last book, I described meeting Aleister Crowley as the most frightening thing I had ever encountered, and at that time that was true but this experience in the basement topped it by a mile. I had never felt in fear of my life before as I did that night and I believe Iain felt the same. Despite this, we resolved to carry on and isn't it strange that once you have experienced the ultimate in paranormal phenomena everything after that paled into insignificance – for us – but not for others who were experiencing it for the first time.

Thankfully the physical energies in the building seemed to have peaked with those experiences of Iain and I and now seemed to have returned to previous levels. I was aware that there was a different energy below ground (in the basement) to that above ground but you could feel that it was there - both positively and negatively - and sometimes it was stronger than other times, which may have had something to do with the number of people in the building at any given time. We were now running workshops and demonstrations of mediumship regularly and consequently there were more people in the building and therefore more chance of others experiencing this, especially if they were in training to develop their psychic and mediumistic abilities.

Paul Jacobs

We began to get reports from students of being pushed on the stairs. Some students did not want to go into the basement where their teas and coffees would be served at break time and we had one volunteer receptionist who downright refused to go into the basement for any purpose.

Of course we downplayed all of this, never revealing what had gone before but there was no denying some of the experiences that many of our visitors had. One such occasion was in June of 2012, when Paul Jacobs had been booked to run a workshop over the weekend starting with a demonstration of mediumship on the Friday evening. I welcomed Paul to the Centre on the Friday afternoon and showed him to the apartment on the second floor where he would be staying for the weekend. He seemed pleased to be here and we were happy to have him. Paul is a medium of international acclaim as most of our mediums were but he had been trained by one of the masters of mediumship Gordon Higginson, so his skills were renowned as one of only a handful who could claim this pedigree.

We were not disappointed. His demonstration went very well and the audience loved it. It was around 10pm by the time we had cleared the building of all the people who had wanted to thank him for their messages and maybe get a selfie. I then just asked Paul if he was comfortable enough in the apartment and had everything he needed – he said he had – so we wished him goodnight and said we'd see him in the morning and that we would be in early to set up for the workshop.

The following morning as we got off an early morning bus and walked along Palmerston Place towards the Centre I could see Paul standing on the doorstep having a cigarette. As Iain and I approached, I said, 'Good morning Paul. Did you sleep well?'

'No I did not. I don't know who was in the building last night or what they were doing but whatever they were doing there were doors banging all night. I hardly got a wink of sleep. And there must have been a few of them because it wasn't just one door that was banging, it was as if they were going back and forward into all the rooms on the floor above me. At one point I was going to go up and tell them that someone was trying to sleep down here.'

As he finished his tirade, Iain and I just looked at each other in silence.

'What?' he asked as he looked at our puzzled faces.

'There was no-one in the building Paul – you were here alone.'

He was visibly shaken by this revelation and his anger at what he had thought was a wild party going on in the rooms above changed to one of foreboding as the realisation hit him that he was going to be spending another night in the building on his own.

That evening I had arranged for us to have dinner with John Blackwood after the workshop as Paul and he were old friends. We met in a local Chinese Restaurant where Paul once again relayed his story to John. John could hardly have missed the deep concern in Paul's voice as he stated again that he was fearful of having to stay another night in the building following these experiences. By this time John had been regularly disregarding my feedback about the physical phenomena in the building but I felt sure that he would listen to his old friend and his personal experiences, but John remained unconvinced.

I asked Paul at the time if he was willing to complete a question-naire which had been left by the SSPR after they had run one of their first vigils. The SSPR asked that I give these to people who witnessed strange events in the building by asking that they be completed and forward to the SSPR for collation and analysis. Paul completed the questionnaire – this is what he said:

'I could hear movement and noise and banging in the rooms above where I was sleeping. It went on for quite a while. I thought of going up to ask them to be quiet then I realised I was the only person staying in the building that evening.'

— Paul Jacobs, 30 June 2012.

June Field

Another of our professional mediums to have encountered a paranormal event whilst staying at the Centre was June Field. June gained the title of 'World's Greatest Psychic' after participating in and winning 'International Battle of the Psychics' where over 70,000 Psychic Mediums from all over the world took part, so we were delighted to welcome her and have her working from the Centre. As was customary with visiting mediums, she stayed in the flat on the second floor. This is her statement:

'I stayed at the Centre and myself, Sam my student and Ann went to the Italian restaurant round the corner for dinner. Ann had just had the psychical research institute in the Centre conducting a vigil and investigation the week prior to my course and so I asked a student if she wanted to stay with me in the flat.

After the meal we all went back to the flat and had a cup of tea. We were talking about imps and I felt a presence and asked for the conversation to be changed to another topic. After our blether, Ann left for home and I heard the front door of the building slam shut behind her. Sam and I did not leave the flat.

I felt very uneasy and sensed Spirit right outside the door to the flat as if they were right up against it.

I reluctantly went to bed. At 2am the fire alarm went off. I knew there was no fire and that that entity just wanted me to come out of the flat. I woke Sam and told her I didn't think there was a fire but we had to leave the flat.

I called Ann but it went to answer phone, so I sent a text hoping she would get it.

We opened the door and I felt a sense of evil all around me. We made our way downstairs switching the lights on as we went. Sam felt panicked and wanted to run but I instructed her to walk. Once downstairs we called the number on the alarm panel and informed the man on the other end which zone was lit up.cHe said it was the basement and to go down and check.

I knew instantly they just wanted us down there. I refused and asked if he could reset the alarm remotely - if there was a fire I was not going down there. Once he did that. We made our way back upstairs leaving all the lights on. We got into the flat and put the Kettle on to make tea as we were both shaken. I felt an evil presence but did not tell Sam as she was afraid and I reassured her it was fine. Then, as we were sitting in the living room having a cup of tea (this was now about 3.30am) the flat door was being pushed back and forward as if someone was trying to get in. Sam was terrified. Then the bin lid in the kitchen started to swing back and forth on its own. That's when I got angry and asked it to leave and called on my own Spirit Team. We sat up for a few hours and all went quiet but the feeling never left me and the following morning I told Ann what had happened.

I will never stay in the Centre over-night again. It was an evil presence that was much bigger than me.'

— June Field, Medium

Manon Arnold

Another of our visiting mediums to the Centre was Manon Arnold from the Netherlands. Manon had been booked to do private sittings but phoned me to tell me that she had been so scared whilst staying in the Centre that she packed her bags and left; contacting a nearby hotel where she had stayed before to see if they could accommodate her. I remember her telling me that the receptionist there spent some time helping to calm her down after her frightening experience. She seems to now think that she should have been braver! Here is her testimony:

73

'I was at the Arthur Conan Doyle Centre for a day of private readings. As I come from The Netherlands the Centre offered me a room for the night on the fourth floor of the building during my work there.

When the last sitting was finished, I decided to go for a quick visit into town before the shops were closing. When I came back to the Centre it was dark inside and clear that the employees had left the building to celebrate the start of a relaxed weekend.

Not knowing that my weekend would be far from relaxed, I opened the door and switched on the lights in the hallway and went up the stairs to my room. The doors of the Helen Duncan room were open and by seeing a glimpse of the piano I thought it would be nice to sing a few notes just for fun. After doing so I left the room and walked towards the door, which led to the staircase. When my hand reached out to grip the doorknob, I heard downstairs in the hallway the swing door closing slowly with a grinding sound as only you hear in a movie. Then I heard footsteps walking from the middle of the hallway in the direction of the tearoom. They sounded kind of heavy, like a man's leather shoes.

Then the sound suddenly stopped, which was quite strange logistically speaking, because you expect a person to be walking to the tearoom, the toilets or the office, but not standing still in the middle of the hall for a longer time.

"Hello, is someone there?" I called, while figuring out who it could be. No answer. I walked down the stairs again expecting to see somebody from the staff who probably had forgotten something. But the hallway was empty but with a bit of a strange feeling. I went up to my room to grab my book and some comfy shoes to walk into town. This time for some food.

When I came back, I had the same ritual as I did the two hours before. I switched on the lights again, went to the door on the first floor and as my hand was on the door-knob to open it I heard the same grinding sound from the swing door, heard the same number of footsteps. I counted three of them, which stopped in the middle of the hall without reaching any of the rooms. And again, I checked to find nobody was there.

However, in my inner eye I saw a well-groomed looking man in a suit, clearly not from this time. I was quite impressed by it all. The energy and sounds both from the door together with the footsteps were so physically present that I knew I would have difficulties getting my own mind in a quiet state during the night.

This story ends with a confession from my side. As much as I love my job as a medium and as curious as I was to discover and experience other activities that night, sharing that big empty building for a whole night long with this remarkable man, who I am sure didn't want to frighten me – but did - was a bit too much to ask.

I packed my suitcase, booked a hotel close to the ACD Centre, (lucky me there was one single room left!) trying to get out as fast as I could going down the stairs, meanwhile thinking my behaviour was quite pathetic, switched out the lights and closed the front door behind me.

A corner away from the Centre, in a cosy single room at the Ritz Hotel I wished the well-groomed looking gentleman a very good night, apologies for my sudden stormy departure, together with the promise by my next visit in the Centre I will behave like a braver medium!'

— Manon Arnold - The Netherlands

George Inglis

The following year, 2013, I first met George when I was doing private sittings (of mediumship) and as with all our mediums I made sure that no information was divulged between the receptionist taking the booking and the medium who would be undertaking the sitting. This practice ensured that the medium could not be accused of having information on the sitter before they arrived. That day there was a full afternoon of bookings in the Centre's diary for me. As always I was just given a list with the first names and the times of all those who had booked and would be coming to see me that afternoon. All was going well. I knew because I'm my own worst critic and always liked to check with my sitters that they were happy and that they got what they wanted, or more often it was that they got what they needed, two different things.

I used Gordon's Room for my sittings. (This is the one that my good friend Gordon Souter had doused for intending to use it for his own work at the Centre but in practice he never did since by this time he was in the hospice suffering from terminal cancer and I was visiting him regularly.) It made me feel close to him by sitting in his room surrounded by his stuff and he was right, the energy was good in that room.

The next name on my list was George at 3pm. At the allotted time there was a knock at the door and the receptionist ushered in a man. He was short and well-built in stature and quiet in nature. I guessed him to be around 60ish. I invited him to take a seat opposite me. I did the usual preamble, making sure that he was comfortable with what I was about to do and told him that I would sit in silence for a few minutes just to tune in. When I did that, I could feel the energy of this man. George had a laid-back nature but even so I could feel that his energy was a bit low. It was as if he was lacking in physical energy. Although I knew it was improving, it felt as if he had suffered a blow to his well-being somehow and he was slowly regaining his strength. His emotional and mental energy was also at a low ebb understandably and I could tell he had endured a period of ill-health and was on the slow road to recovery. As I made this connection with him, I felt sorry for him and what he must have been feeling – but not showing – as Scottish men do. And at that I felt the Spirit World come close to me and I felt the energy of a man from Spirit. That was all I needed. I knew I had made my connection with someone from Spirit who wanted to connect with George and that when I started to speak they would give me the words they wanted to convey.

I opened my eyes and gave George the feedback about his physical wellbeing. He responded by telling me that he had had an operation for prostate cancer and that he had just finished a course of treatment (radiotherapy) and was trying to rebuild his strength.

I then said, 'There's a man here from Spirit who wants to speak to you. He's your dad and he's here asking for forgiveness.'

'I don't want to speak to him,' was the surprising response. George's nature suddenly changed from the laid-back person who had walked into the room to someone who was suddenly strongly animated as he held an open hand up towards my face and said, 'No. I don't want to speak to him.'

'Okay, that's fine but you should know that he will keep on trying as he needs this – there is unfinished business.'

'Oh I know,' said George but that's up to him. I've moved on with my life – I've had to.'

'Okay, you don't have to speak to anyone you don't want to; it is your prerogative. I'll move on too and see if there's someone else here to speak to you.' No matter how hard I tried after that, nothing worked. I got some vague information about his grandfather but other than that I kept getting random information that meant absolutely nothing to George. I wondered what had happened and why. Strangely enough, George said that he'd prefer to just have a chat with me rather than hear from the Spirit World. I thought this odd given he had paid for a sitting and I said, 'You can chat to me anytime, you don't have to pay to do that.' But he seemed keen just to spend the remaining time talking together, which we did. It was amazing there was such synchronicity between us and he had such a depth of knowledge of the Spirit World and many different religions and practices, many of which he had been involved in personally.

He had a strong affinity with the Shamanic traditions and was a skilled and knowledgeable healer in multiple disciplines. This complimented seamlessly with his career in the material world as a surgical theatre manager in Edinburgh's main hospital. As I absorbed all of this and felt the innate spiritual nature of this man and his need to help others, it was as if I was sitting here speaking to Gordon and in his room too. I knew at that moment that George had been sent to me. That is not to be boastful or arrogant; I had learnt by this time to take cognisance of synchronicity. He was sent to be part of our Thursday group.

George joined our Group the following month – April 2013 – and he remains a most valuable and knowledgeable member today. In the time since then he has unconsciously taken over from Gordon as the person who would lead the invocation, lead the healing meditations and bring his knowledge – particularly his shamanic knowledge – and skills into our practices (even though he had never sat with Gordon and didn't know him and therefore was totally unaware that it would be Gordon who would have carried out these functions in the Group prior to George's arrival).

As I type this piece now, and look back at my notes to ensure my dates are accurate, I've noticed another interesting fact. I've already mentioned that Gordon was in the hospice at this time but I now realise that this sitting with George took place on a Thursday afternoon (March 21st) and Gordon died just a few days later on the 25th – was he handing over the baton?

When I relayed this most recent information to a friend, he reminded me too that that date in March was the Spring Equinox, a time of renewal and new growth following the death of most plants and vegetation during the winter months.

And in a further strange coincidence, when the Group later visited Roslin for further experiments with the energy in that place, I soon noticed that George was being particularly successful in using one of our pendulums (I took along some extra equipment – dowsing rods and pendulums – for the Group to use). It was as if he and the pendulum were one and every time he asked a question of it the pendulum would respond before George had even finalised his question.

'This is great, this pendulum. It works really well.'

'I can see that. It's obviously meant for you, George. You should keep it – it's yours.'

'Are you sure – where did you get it?'

'Yes, I'm sure it's working well for you and I've never used it, so it was obviously meant for you,' I said. And where did I get it? I inherited it from Gordon. He had left me a lot of his spiritual things and I was pleased that it should go to George.

George was soon well ensconced in the Group and he would volunteer to help us out at the Centre by taking a turn in staffing the reception desk when we needed it. On one such occasion he too left the building by running down the stairs at speed and out the front door. Here's what he later wrote in our notebook that we kept for the purpose:

'I was checking the building was clear before locking up on a Thursday night. I became aware of an energy surrounding me on the second floor. As I walked down the stairs to the first floor, this energy became more powerful and I could see a vapour surrounding my head and neck. I continued to walk down the stairs and when I was in the section between the first and the ground floor I felt this presence building strongly, becoming more intense and I experienced a strong pressure on my neck and I began to choke. I also began to feel that I was being pushed forward and I grabbed the banister in order to regain my balance. This was an intense experience which left me in shock, spaced out and feeling sick.'

— George Inglis

Ciaran O'Keefe

In June of 2013 we were delighted to welcome Ciaran O'Keefe and his partner to stay. Ciaran was giving a talk on Tuesday, 4th June and he and his partner arrived on the Monday and they stayed two nights in the apartment. Ciaran's talk was entitled *'Researching the Weird and the Wonderful' An exciting journey of the psychics, ghosts, exorcisms and miracle blood.* As you might imagine, we had a full house for the resident sceptic of the popular TV show *Most Haunted.* However when they left on the Wednesday they too had experienced some of the strange energies in the building and I remember that his partner was none too happy to return.

Roger Straughan

Another speaker arrived in November 2013, Roger Straughan. I was looking forward to hearing his talk as he too claimed to be communicating with Arthur Conan Doyle but using a most innovative method – his bookshelf of books. These were used as the divination tool. Dr Straughan would pose a question and the response would come by him being influenced to pull a random book off the shelf allowing it to fall open at any page and for his eyes to fall upon that page and receive the answer. From Dr Straughan's talk and his book, this method seemed uncannily accurate. The book is called, *'A Study in Survival: Conan Doyle Solves the Final Problem'* (O Books).

Roger Straughan stayed the night with us following his talk and for some reason (there must have been others staying in the building that night) we had to put him in the bedroom on the top floor. What he didn't know was that just a couple of months before this, I had encountered another strange phenomenon in that room.

We had hosted quite a large workshop over that weekend which meant I could look forward to spending most of the Monday changing all the bedrooms and taking the washing to the launderette.

I started in the apartment, cleaning it and changing the bedding and towels and moving on upstairs to the next bedroom on the third floor. When I got to the top floor, I had taken with me the fresh laundry which was still in its polythene bag from the launderette. I opened the door with the key and walked into the bedroom en-suite. This was a double room and it had built-in cabinets fitted against the walls on either side of the bed. These cabinets were used as storage for extra bedding but were even more useful as worktop surfaces, as on one side we had placed a small fridge, kettle, toaster, a tray with cups, bowl, plate, cutlery, breakfast cereals etc. This made the room self-contained for anyone staying overnight. We were able to stock the fridge with milk, butter, jam, etc so that the visitor could make their own breakfast. On the other side of the bed, those cabinet tops held a fruit bowl, a mirror, a box of tissues and a bedside lamp all at arms-length from the bed. In this way, we hoped we had provided the visitor with everything they needed; it was a long way down to the ground floor if something was forgotten.

On the day in question, when I got to the top floor my usual routine was to drop the fresh linen – still in its polybag – on the floor outside the room. This gave me a free hand to open the door with the key and then start stripping the bed. So that morning I dropped the new linen outside the door as usual and stripped the bed putting all the dirty linen and towels in a bin bag. I opened the door to the corridor stopping the self-closer from shutting it completely with my foot as I dropped the full bin bag on the floor and picked up the polybag with the new linen. But when I turned and walked back into the room, I was stunned to see all the items that had been on the cabinet tops on both sides of the bed now on the floor. All the items were neatly placed between the cabinets and the bed. The worktops were completely bare of all items. I was shocked. Not a sound had been heard. I had only turned my back for a moment – a few seconds at most – and yet everything was now on the floor. I threw the bag with the new linen on the bed and walked out closing the door behind me; that could wait for another day - I was not going back in there today. (See photos of this room at the end of this chapter.)

Now in November this was the room that Roger Straughan would be staying in. As usual and throughout this whole time we managed to keep all of these phenomena confidential. We had divulged nothing at all, only acknowledging those that had had experiences by asking them to complete a questionnaire and noting the details in our notebook. Other than that no-one knew about these happenings. We wanted to keep it that way.

Roger Straughan arrived and we showed him to his room, apologising that it was up on the top floor. He was happy to be in the Sir Arthur Conan Doyle Centre, especially since he had an affinity with the man and prepared to give his talk later that evening. The talk went very well and was very well received. Roger sold some of his books and we bought a supply for our shop. We said goodnight to him and wished him a pleasant evening. The following morning as usual I asked if he had had a good night's sleep. He said that he had but that something strange had happened. I felt a twinge of trepidation as I wondered what he was going to tell me, although he seemed unperturbed.

Roger's account of what happened, recorded shortly after his visit, was as follows:

'I did a bit of reading before going to sleep that night, using my reading glasses and putting my distance glasses in a case on the surface by the bedside (near the lamp). In the morning I put my reading glasses on before reaching for the case – which wasn't there! Thinking I'd absentmindedly put it somewhere else, I searched every possible place without success.

I then spent a further 10 minutes or so combing **every-**

where – surfaces, floor, bed etc – before giving up. I would swear it was nowhere visible. I even looked outside the door to the room, then came back in to find the case lying in full view exactly where I had remembered leaving it the night before by the lamp!

I was astounded at this, as I couldn't possibly have overlooked it in my searches – my senior moments aren't that senior!'

Roger Straughan provided me with a testimony for my last book which I have reproduced here just for completeness. Dr Straughan knows nothing of what went on before him staying in that room and will only know on the publishing of this book.

'This is a remarkable book about a remarkable man. I have a particular interest in it for two reasons:

Firstly, I have myself experienced what I believe to be psychic communications from Conan Doyle over a period of many years. These are described in detail in my book and suggest that the creator of Sherlock Holmes is still ready and willing to continue his mission of spreading the word about the reality of life after death. His methods of doing so seem as various and ingenious as his plots!

Secondly, I was invited by Ann to speak about my book at the ACD Centre a few years ago, and while staying the night at the Centre I had an experience which I was quite unable to account for other than as a psychical phenomenon. This was totally unexpected as I knew nothing at the time about the results obtained by Ann's circle.'

> — Roger Straughan, Ph.D, Author, 'A Study in
> Survival: Conan Doyle Solves the Final Problem'
> (O Books). Reader in Education at the University
> of Reading (retired). 13/07/2019.

Roger Straughan's name would figure again but not for another couple of years after this. For now, I conclude this chapter by adding some testimonies from others who have had experiences in the building:

Testimony of Ewan Irvine

'These are my recollections and you will see that I have copied in Susan who will be able to add hers in or expand on the info I have given. I am just going by memory of a few instances.

I remember the mornings I used to go in and would say ' Hi guys' and there would be immediate tappings from the top floor at the corner banister. I was always aware of children at that part. Equally I used to say goodbye at night when locking up and the same thing would happen.

When Ann and Iain were away on holiday a few years ago, it was a Friday afternoon and Susan and I were the only ones in the building. We had carried out a clean of the stairs and rooms etc and had decided to take a short break with a cup of tea before finishing off hoovering the main ground floor hall and then mopping it. Henry the Hoover was sitting in the middle of the floor and we were each seated on the armchairs. We both watched the hoover travel along the hall as if someone was pulling or pushing it. Both of us saw this and there simply was no explanation. We both just sat there in silence watching this hoover travel along the hall.

I also saw the [Spirit] lady on the back stairs albeit a very quick glimpse. I seem to remember her being in red and black and that she was simply walking downstairs.

In the downstairs dining room, I recall being in there and starting to feel very uneasy and then became aware of what I recall was a very powerful unpleasant presence. I never experienced it again just that one time.

One notable occasion was when I was president of the church and went down to the church office in the basement after a Sunday service. I put the yale key in the lock and opened the door but the door was forcibly pushed shut on me. I assumed that someone was behind the door as it is a small office, but when I asked if it was ok to come in there was no reply. I opened the door again and this time the door opened without any forced pushing of it back and there was no-one in the office.

I also remember folk talking about things that would disappear and reappear. I remember this happening to me when I was using an old cassette tape for meditation. It used to always go back in the drawer at the desk and I do remember one night when in the hall someone from the group said it was really nice music and I said it was one of my favourite ones to use for meditation. I remember locking it in the drawer and it then completely disappeared. I always meant to ask if it ever did reappear but forgot.

Susan had experiences with the lights going on when no-one was in the building and also with a cd flying off the shelf at her.

I remember speaking to Ciaran O'Keeffe when he was here with his wife and I think she had a few experiences.'

— Ewan Irvine, past President of Spiritualist
Church, Medium and volunteer at
The Sir Arthur Conan Doyle Centre.
www.thescottishmedium.com

Testimony of Susan Cohen

'I can think of a number of inexplicable things that happened during times I spent in the Conan Doyle Centre:

- The account Ewan gives above of us both watching Henry the Hoover move on its own is something I very clearly recall. We were having a lovely chit-chat, both sitting in the reception area when we became aware at the same time of some movement in the Centre of the tiled floor. We both turned to look at what was happening and then looked at each other, both asking 'did you see that?' as if questioning ourselves and what we just witnessed. For my own part, what I witnessed was Henry the Hoover moving on its wheels in the hallway. It was moving away from the desk towards the door, with nothing touching it and no force being applied to anything attached to it.

- One Thursday evening, after I was the last one to leave the building, I was standing on Chester Street and was on my mobile phone talking to Ewan. During the conversation, I saw lights come on inside the building. I know this as I distinctly remember saying to Ewan, 'I've just seen lights switch themselves on but I'm too scared to go back inside and turn them off'.

- I have had repeated experiences in the tea room of the Centre during which I played CDs on the Centre's CD player at a volume I set on a manual dial. After a time – sometimes after minutes, sometimes after more than an hour – the volume increased. This happened a number of times over a period of weeks. The volume was never turned down, it was always turned up.

- One of the most notable incidents for me came during my early days at the CD Centre when I rented what affectionately became known as 'the cupboard' as an office in the basement of the building. I was sitting with my back to the exterior wall and the window to my right. My computer was in front of me and I was facing the door. I was reading a book and had a pen in my right hand, a piece of paper flat on the desk ready for notes. Suddenly, I felt what can only be described as an energetic force lift my arm off the desk. I clearly remember watching my right arm being raised until my elbow was level with my shoulder, my right hand outstretched. As I type this, I can remember this very clearly – the muscles of shoulder, upper and lower arms were not being used. At first, I remained silent but as the seconds passed, and I realised that a part of my body was being moved by some sort of invisible force, I actually started to cry out. I left the room and in truth, I didn't return to it for several days after that incident.

- Weeks later, a colleague of mine arrived to spend the day working with me in 'the cupboard'. He was sitting with his back to the door, facing the exterior wall. I had left the room to make two cups of coffee. Before he had arrived, I had told him that I was experiencing strange things – the lifting of my arm was just one of these – but he was very sceptical. My colleague is a very matter-of-fact empirical person and genuinely had no interest in my 'stories'. As I entered the room carrying two cups of coffee, my colleague turned to me and unmistakably appeared shaken. He told me that a noticeboard which had been propped up on the desk had toppled over and knocked a glass of water over the keyboard of his computer. I did not witness this myself but I did see that the noticeboard had fallen over and the keyboard was wet. That noticeboard had stood in the same position for weeks. It was not precariously balanced. My colleague is a very careful person, not prone to mishaps – this was not something he had done clumsily.

- I cannot honestly say that I have not seen any kind of figure in the CD Centre but I will take to my grave the time I spent with the lovely Jim who changed before my eyes into someone else whilst I sat in the foyer at the reception desk. I was sitting in the chair behind the desk and Jim was sitting a little behind me to my right, as I was facing the front door, and by the fireplace. I had a conversation with this person – who was absolutely not Jim – for more than ten minutes and during every second of those minutes,

I was conscious of experiencing something I did not understand but something which was authentic, calm and strangely comforting. Jim's facial features and body posture had changed substantially yet during the transformation, Jim himself was somehow able to convey to me that I shouldn't be afraid. What's more, I have to say that this different person who appeared knew a lot about me, telling me things about myself that Jim* could not possibly have known and telling me things about my life which have turned out to be prophetic.

As I write this email, I feel a great warmth and affection for the time I spent at the Conan Doyle Centre. I met some truly amazing people and spent some very happy times there, for which I'm grateful.'

— Susan Cohen, Author and publisher,
Director of The Wee book Company Ltd
www.theweebookcompany.com

* Jim – Refers to a member of the Thursday Group.

Testimony of Hector McLeod

Early encounters at ACD

'When my elder son Ruairidh was about 14 years old, he was a student at St Mary's Music School, which was about 300 yards from ACD Centre. Ruairidh had clear psychic gifts.

At St Mary's Ruairidh became conscious of a strange and unaccountable light image on his bedroom wall. This troubled him as he could not find any source. He also had an encounter with a small female ghost who would sing along as he practised piano in one of the outhouses. Later he also saw through the window of the dining hall the figure of a man in 1950s clothing and hat, who looked in before disappearing. This he knew immediately to be spectral. It was when he started hearing voices that Ruairidh became alarmed. He thought he was perhaps schizophrenic or having some other disorder. Knowing his psychic abilities, my wife and I felt that there may be a spiritual explanation. I approached ACD Centre one afternoon and described to Ann Treherne the situation. Ann asked me to bring Ruairidh to see her which I did. There was a clear and immediate linking between Ann and Ruairidh. She felt he was trying to communicate telepathically and felt he had serious mediumistic gifts. Over the next hour or so, she taught Ruairidh to "close down," when he didn't want to encounter the Spirit communication and provided him with helpful reassurance that he was not mad as he had feared.

Sometime later Ruairidh suffered from an episode of depression panic and anxiety and I asked Nick Kyle a friend to see whether teaching Ruairidh meditation would help. The venue for this was to be ACD Centre. Ruairidh and Nick went to the basement area. When I returned both gave accounts of the events that had transpired. Nick told me that what appeared to be Ruairidh's grandfather had 'come through,' as a protective entity, whilst Ruairidh said that he had 'seen' an impressive figure of a Victorian gentleman in a top hat.'

Hector's recollection of the SSPR Stakeout:

'It was a Saturday night when a group from the SSPR held a vigil at ACD. The team was split up into individuals who would sit in specific areas within sight of one another (for the most part.) After some 30 minutes, each person would move to another position. There are several memories of this vigil which I recall; one position on the first floor looking up the spiral staircase to the top floor, I had a very strange feeling about the upper left curve before the stair-head. I felt that there had been a death here, perhaps a suicide. There was a very sinister feeling about that particular portion of the stair which I could not substantiate. There was no manifestation, sound or whatever, just a very strange and unpleasant feeling. Nearly all the other vigil positions were uneventful from my perspective, save that of a room in the basement where I had no line of sight of any other participant. Here I was most uncomfortable, having a feeling that I was being watched. I confess I was relieved when that was over. I also confess that I could not sit in one position but would 'stretch my legs.' I was distinctly ill at ease. Again there was no particular manifestation sound or the like, just an oppressive atmosphere. When the vigil ended, one of the guests showed me a photograph she had taken on her mobile phone of a chair in the library. There was a clear manifestation of a translucent bluish blob about 14-16" and sausage shaped that bent to follow the contours of the chair. It was obviously not a speck of dust or the like, but a very convincingly supernatural phenomenon.'

— Hector McLeod

Hector is a retired Hong Kong solicitor specialising in matrimonial and common law damages claims. He became a member of SSPR in 2012 and a committee member later the same year. Hector says, 'I have spent a lifetime studying the paranormal and particularly Second Sight. I have relatives in Tiree who have this ability and from childhood were aware of various incidents of this sort.'

Testimony of Yvonne Craig:

'I attended a weekend course at the Arthur Conan Doyle Centre, which was being held in the basement. We were coming up the stairs to the tearoom, when I was pushed from behind by someone using both hands on my back. I immediately turned and was saying be patient there's no need to push me and as I turned a young female dressed in a maid's uniform rushed up past me. This most definitely was a Spirit form.

On another occasion, after an evening class in the sanctuary, I was crossing the reception hall when I saw a tall slim built gentleman coming downstairs towards me. He was wearing a long black jacket with tails and top hat. He was very smartly dressed and he had a beard.

Again this was definitely a Spirit person.'

— Yvonne Craig, President,
Edinburgh Association of Spiritualists

Testimony of Jim Cleary

Jim Cleary, Trustee and Director of The Palmerston Trust, (the charity which runs the The Sir Arthur Conan Doyle Centre,) who witnessed Iain being thrown by 'the force', gave his testimony at Chapter 6.

Testimony of Annie Broadley

In November 2011 I moved into my studio on the top floor of the Centre shortly after it opened. A few months later at the request of Ann and Iain I hung a few of my paintings in the Mary Duffy Room.

One of them, *Sea Voices*, was a large, square canvas depicting fossils through the ages, from the earliest Cambrian period up to the advent of humans who left evidence of their existence in the form of carvings on cave walls. To do this I used alternating layers of glue mixed with pigment and glue mixed with whiting powder which is called gesso. The glue + pigment resembled water and the gesso was the rock into which I carved the fossils. I finished with runes which I used to represent early humankind. Inspired by George Mackay Brown's poem *A Work for Poets*

Here is a work for poets -
Carve the runes
Then be content with silence

I wrote 'content with silence' in runic form across the surface of the work.

One morning soon after my work had gone up I walked into the Centre and was met by Iain who I remember thinking seemed rather perturbed. He took me to the Mary Duffy Room where I saw that the upper right corner and the lower left one of *Sea Voices* were twisting about six inches /fifteen centimeters away from the wall placing the canvas under a huge strain. It really looked as though it was doing its utmost to get away. Once we took it off the wall it went back to normal but the torsion that it had undergone had caused huge cracks across the surface which meant that the painting could not be sold.

Initially I put what had happened down to the fact that a lot of glue had gone into this painting and thought that perhaps that and the sun had caused the whole thing to contract. However, because it was no longer saleable I took it home where it has stayed ever since. It has been hanging on my wall, in a room with a large sunny window, for over ten years and nothing untoward has happened. At 144cm square it is not a small work. As well as that the canvas was pasted onto a hardboard backing and fixed to a wooden frame which means that a lot of force would be needed to warp it in the way it was warped when Iain and I saw it in the Mary Duffy Room that day.

After a friend told me more about runes and mentioned that they can be used as tools of divination I began to wonder whether by using them I had inadvertently managed to stir up something which was in some way, challenging or disturbing to an energy which was present in the building at the time.

— Annie Broadley, Artist.

Annie Broadley is an accomplished artist having exhibited in London, the Scottish Borders, McTear's in Glasgow, and in galleries in Edinburgh including the Doubtfire Gallery, Leith Gallery, the Torrence Gallery and also at The Sir Arthur Conan Doyle Centre where she has her studio.

The Thursday Group:

My own Group had sat several times seeking an explanation of some of the phenomena but none was given. On one occasion we had encountered the large hulk of a man who had previously been seen multiple times in the basement. He had overshadowed me when my Group sat in the basement and he made me aware that he had been a worker on the roof of the building – either when it was first being built or when the roof was extended some four years later. His initial approach was to ask me to put flowers on his grave to remember him by. When I asked where his grave was, he indicated under the ground in the foundations. He let me know that he had fallen to his death and the incident had been covered up and his body had been concealed in the foundations.

As usual I set about trying to confirm these details but none could be found. A research assistant I contacted for help told me that an incident such as this would likely be hushed up and not reported upon. I had given up trying to find the evidence when I received confirmation from the most unexpected source. The building had once housed St Mary's Music School and I was contacted out of the blue by a previous student of the school who happened to be back in Edinburgh (from his home town in England) to visit the Edinburgh Festival, when he saw that his old school had been turned into a Spiritual Centre he dropped me an email. I had emailed him back as he had stated in his opening email that: '*Some people (while it was a school) remarked on the unsettling undercurrents of energy, as it were, that they detected (or witnessed), notably on the second floor, and in the basement.*' and I wanted to know more of what had been experienced. It was another seven years before he responded, but he did, just at the time that I was looking for evidence of the builder who had fallen from our roof. Here's a segment from his email:

Dear Ann,

I see it has taken me several years to reply to your email but felt motivated to reply now; thanks for your time and attention. I wonder whether you discovered more about the history of 25 Palmerston Place? I'd be interested to hear of the building's connections with Conan Doyle.

There were a few instances of unsettling occurrences in my time as a student. A fellow student was practising a major-league piece of music on a dark evening in the warren of practice rooms that were in the basement, and he fled from his session after he'd seen a door open slowly by itself; yet the rooms were empty. He seemed profoundly distressed after this, and lost motivation to practice.

I had an unsettling experience when in one of the second-floor boarding rooms in Palmerston Place. The roommate was away and I woke up in the night with a total sense of disorientation that went on for about two minutes. I got very scared but the feeling passed. Perhaps I was unwell, but a friend who is a priest who also knows the building described the feeling as 'oppression', a technical term used by clergy who are trained in blessings, 'deliverance' and so on.

In my first year there I asked one of the staff whether the building was haunted, as I'd heard tapping sounds repeatedly against the wall in a top-floor room. Again there is probably a rational explanation but a day or two later the woman came back and told me about a builder dying in an industrial accident while installing the large dome in the roof.

One of the staff at the school claimed she was in fear of a baleful energy in the front stair area, near where a portrait of Menuhin used to be displayed. The students and others laughed at the time, but I wouldn't have been too hasty.

Finally I was interested to hear of your book and will aim to read it.

Anyway, thanks for bearing with this email, unexpected I'd imagine. I wish you all the best in these challenging times we have.

Kind regards

Dr A. Taylor

And so these physical phenomena continue in The Sir Arthur Conan Doyle Centre still to this day although it is much reduced in intensity and frequency from when we first started work on the building in early 2011. It seemed to reach its peak in 2012 with the 'attacks' that Iain and I suffered and some of the strong physical reactions felt by Bill MacGregor, George Inglis, Susan Cohen, Ewan Irvine and others. (I have included their testimonies as independent witnesses – none of whom were aware of what Iain and I had encountered – and who will continue to remain unaware until this book is published.)

Was it meant to get the message across that we are all insignificant against the greater power of the Spiritual World or universal consciousness? We think we are in control and that the material world is the real world – this shows, it is the unseen world that is far greater, stronger and in control.

I also believe that we are able to manipulate or utilise this energy by our own thoughts – as can the etheric world – both positively and negatively. I knew that whatever it was that I encountered in the basement it was not an entity that could be communicated with i.e., it was not Spirit or a Spirit-being in the normal sense of the word. This thing had never been human but it did have some intelligence. I knew or could sense the intention – which was to hit me at speed propelling me onto the stairs. It was only my own senses that prevented this – so was someone or something manipulating this power, utilising or controlling this power? And if so, can the positive intention of those who use this building help dissipate the negative? The following chapters may suggest so.

Chapter 9

Meanwhile back at the Ranch

I 've spoken about the energy in the Centre and how it manifested itself in different ways and in different locations in the building even getting physical. This energy remains to this day although the physical elements I'm pleased to say have reduced considerably from what had gone before. I've also given a couple of examples of some of the interesting but strange cases of paranormal anomalies that happened back then, and I have more to tell you but let me return to practicalities and the actual running of this new Centre, and what would appear to be the more positive aspects of this phenomenon.

Returning to 2012 for a moment – our first full year of operations – I've made mention already that most of the mediums were already booked elsewhere; their diaries filling more than a year in advance, so we booked them for the following year, 2013. We were most grateful to those who made a special effort to help us out by fitting in extra workshops in 2012 and some like Janet Parker who changed venues to be able to support the Centre. But by mid-summer I was aware that this level of activity was not going to sustain us – we needed to do much more – and perhaps even more importantly these activities were not reaching the general population, where I had set my sights.

It was July 2012. July is the traditional holiday month in Scotland, so all our regular weekly classes had stopped for the summer. They would resume in September. I looked at the diary. We had just run a very successful evening of mediumship followed by a weekend workshop with Tony Stockwell (who would later become a Trustee of the Centre), but there was nothing else in the diary. The building was quiet as I sat at the reception desk and pondered – what else could we do? And how could we get the general public into the building? We had already made a name for ourselves with the opening publicity of the previous year and so those in the spiritual and holistic fraternity knew of us and we were getting record crowds to our mediumistic events which would all sell-out in quick succession. People used to queue outside and around the building on the pavement waiting to get in when we hosted these events and we had to start a waiting list of those who had failed to get a ticket but lived in hope of someone cancelling. This was all great and there was a real buzz about the building when these events were running. But I was very aware that the general public didn't even know we existed. We were not hosting events that would interest them. We *were* looking forward to our first anniversary concert with our specially composed piece of music and the Conan Doyle violins that was due to take place in October but that was a one-off. It was designed to bring in the general public, but as I contemplated that I wondered how we would let them know about it. We had no advertising budget; indeed, we had very little resources at all. I'd have to call on Terry Johns, the composer, and Allister Savage, the violinist from the BBC Symphony Orchestra to use their connections and because of their presence perhaps try to get some advanced publicity in the local newspaper. And in working through that scenario in my head it brought me back to my original conundrum – how on earth were we going to draw the general public into the building when we were not running enough events to attract them? That question was complicated by the fact that we had no budget to advertise such events.

I knew about running marketing campaigns from my business days and I knew the size of a budget needed for a name-awareness campaign, which wasn't designed to bring in any income just to let people know you were there. I understood that it could be a huge on-cost, often with no tangible return. These thoughts were running through my head as I sat at my desk in the quiet of the building that sunny afternoon in July when I saw someone coming into the building. The sun was streaming through our front door which always stood open to welcome anyone in, so I could only see the silhouette blackened against the sunlight. As he walked further into our vestibule but still on the outside of our glass vestibule door, he started looking at some of our leaflets and the posters we had there to advertise our events. I could see then that this was a young man – indeed a teenager of around 16 – not our usual clientele. He'll soon realise he's in the wrong place I thought to myself. (Not that he wasn't welcome. He most definitely was. But I knew that our subject matter was not generally attractive to the young, something that I'm pleased to say has changed dramatically since then.) So, I was surprised when the vestibule door gently opened, and this young man walked in. He immediately looked up at the staircase and domed cupola, which often acts as a showstopper as it is very dramatic. He then shifted his gaze towards me. I smiled as welcomingly as I could, and he approached the desk. As he walked towards me, I noticed he was wearing a lanyard with one of those ID badges swinging from it, but I couldn't make out what it said and he looked far too young to be from the gas, electricity or other services.

He caught the swinging ID badge, holding it up in front of me and said, 'I'm from the Edinburgh Fringe and we're looking for locations to station our display boxes to distribute copies of our brochure and I was wondering if you would take one? Your vestibule looks ideal and we're signing people up. It doesn't cost anything, and we'll come and deliver the display unit and the brochures. You just have to keep it topped up; we'll give you all the materials.' It all came blurting out as if it had been rehearsed.

'Yes', I said in an instant. I couldn't believe my luck. Here I was sitting, wondering how to get people into the building and now we were getting a display stand that would be prominently positioned in our vestibule, which would at least attract people into that part of the building. It might only be to pick up a brochure but from there they would see all the other things we were running; a perfect opportunity! This scenario of thoughts being answered was something that would become a recurring theme. I would come to realise that I would get answers to questions I wasn't aware I had asked. But more was to come.

When the display stand and the brochures were delivered, Iain set up the display in a prominent position in the vestibule so it could be easily spotted by the public walking past our open door from the pavement. It looked good. Very attractive, I thought, as I picked up one of the brochures and leafed through it. The Edinburgh International Festival Fringe to give it its proper name is the biggest arts festival in the world. It is renowned as the place where young, up-and-coming new artists are to be found and many established and famous artists of various genres first came to fame at the Fringe, as it is commonly known. Understandably it also attracts talent scouts, producers and theatre and film directors looking for the next big thing. This adds to the cycle of what seems to be an ever-increasing demand from those performers wanting to put on a show and those who want to attend shows, be they talent scouts or the general public. It also serves as a huge tourist attraction for the city, drawing crowds from around the world who want to participate in the festival atmosphere of this world heritage site of Edinburgh over these three weeks in August. It is augmented by the Edinburgh International Festival. Once the main event, the International Festival has now been outgrown by the Fringe, which had begun as a grass-roots movement by those artists and performers who were literally on the fringe of the main event, and who started their own festival by running their own shows in a variety of different locations around the city. These locations tended to be small more casual affairs, some shows often being given free and nothing at all like the grand auditoriums being used by Scottish Ballet, Scottish Opera and the Scottish Symphony Orchestra in the main festival. There was always an accusation too that the main festival was not inclusive and very elitist; so the tables have been turned, with popular opinion swinging decidedly towards the Fringe.

Statistics show that the number of shows at the Fringe each year equates to over 50,000 performances over just a three-week period in August, with ticket sales of over 2.5million and that year in 2012 was no different. I flicked through the brochure as I stood in our vestibule. It was akin to a telephone directory or the pages of the classified ads in a newspaper with pages and pages of listings; some just small lineage ads, some little square boxes, half page, or even full-page ads trying to attract more attention. Where to start, I wondered. It was sectioned into categories. There were children's shows, cabaret, dance, theatre, comedy, circus acts, events, exhibitions, music, opera, musicals and the spoken word to name but a few. Phew! This has got to attract a wide section of the public. I was pleased.

Everything was going according to plan with people regularly popping in to pick up a brochure whilst Edinburgh's population quickly doubled over this time with tourists arriving from all corners of the globe to be in this small space of Scotland's capital city during August. As I watched this seemingly accidental plan fall into place, I also noted the contrast between the busy streets outside, where it was often impossible to walk along some of the pavements due to the crowds, and me, sitting at the reception desk at the Centre in a beautiful building – but an empty one. By August all our normal activities had ceased ironically because of the festival and the Fringe. It was far too difficult to get to Edinburgh if you were a medium, a tutor or even a student travelling in from any distance at all. And, it was far too expensive. Accommodation was at a premium both in terms of availability and price. And as for our regular, local audience, they were avoiding Edinburgh at this time because of these factors. There was no point in us trying to put on events then. We would be starting again in September, after the tourists had gone home.

And just then the voice that spoke to me in my head said, 'why not become a Fringe venue?' Why didn't I think of that? Suddenly everything just clicked into place. We would make an excellent Fringe venue. Our building was far nicer than some of the venues being used around Edinburgh. What's more, our building was usually empty at this time of year. We desperately needed the money and we could make a healthy income from hiring rooms to performers. But best of all we would get free advertising – in the Fringe brochure. The Fringe brochure is free and is distributed throughout Edinburgh and on-line and gets picked up by over 2 million people. We could never usually have afforded advertising such as this; what's not to like. I picked up the brochure once again and this time looked at it with fresh eyes; this time, I was looking at the venues. Yes, there was a separate listing of all the venues, and not too many of them. There were over 3000 shows but less than 300 venues. Not only that, but there was a map of Edinburgh to help find the venues. Talk about putting your name on the map – this was it! I skipped home that night with renewed vigour. We were going to become a Fringe venue.

'How do we do that?' Iain said.

'I don't know but I'll find out – it can't be that difficult'. I was on the case. I called the Fringe office the next day and they told me that I could make an application for the building to be considered as a Fringe venue – once they had considered all the documentation, insurances, fire and safety regulations and carried out an inspection of the premises they would issue an acceptance (or otherwise) of our application. Applications open in September, I was told, after this year's Fringe had finished. Once accepted as a suitable venue, this would then allow us to register the building as a participating venue in the next year's Fringe. Registrations for that opened in February 2013.

Sheesh, admin was never my strong point. Nevertheless, Iain and I – but mainly Iain – set about gathering all the necessary paperwork together. We got through the initial application stage and were ready for the inspection. We were visited by two very nice people from edFringe, as they called themselves, and they were delighted with the building and were pleased to have a venue in the West End of Edinburgh; something that was lacking, they said. Further, they said it was good for them to actually see the building because now they could discuss it with possible future performers who might be looking for venues to hire. That all sounded very positive and so we passed with flying colours. They reminded us that we needed to register as a venue for the 2013 Fringe but also advised that they would be running a series of roadshows on various subjects for performers and venues to assist with marketing and other such subjects to help participants prepare for the Fringe. These roadshows would run nearer the time that registration opens in February but as a new venue they recommended it might be useful for us to attend. And so we did. Now that the hard part was done, we thought it would be easy to register the Centre as a venue for the next Fringe – how wrong we were.

We attended the roadshows as advised, to gain as much information as possible before registration opened. We heard all about the various options that we could offer as a venue such as, providing front of house, providing ticket collection and ticket sales, providing refreshments and of course handling all the safety measures. The next subject matter was marketing. I was most interested in getting our name into the list of venues in the Fringe brochure, after all that was what had prompted all of this. I had already decided that to get ourselves near to the top of the alphabetical listings of venues we would register as 'Arthur Conan Doyle Centre' dropping the 'Sir' from our title, which would have put us at the bottom of the list. I listened intently to all the statistics being presented about how many brochures were printed each year, about their distribution and their display bins. And then the clanger, 'Of course we don't list you as a venue unless you've got a show booked at that venue.'

What – I couldn't believe it! This was a catch 22 situation if ever I saw one. We wanted to be listed as a venue in order to attract performers to hire the space for their show. But we wouldn't be listed as a venue unless we had a show. How were performers to find us, I asked the organisers?

'There's no point listing a venue in the programme if there's nothing on there,' he said.

'But how will there ever be anything on, if no-one knows we exist?' I retorted.

'We only list venues that already have a booked show.'

This was beginning to sound a bit like a closed shop with only existing venues getting the benefit of show bookings, as they had forward bookings of shows from the previous year when they had appeared on the listings. New venues were clearly at a disadvantage. I was angry and frustrated. We had gone through all this prior preparation only to be stumped at the last hurdle.

'What a waste of time,' Iain said. I couldn't put it better myself. It was so disappointing.

'I know what to do – I'll register a show.' I don't know where that inspiration came from, whether it was psychic, the voice in my head or a result of my sheer frustration but what I do remember is the look on Iain's face.

'You – you'll register a show – what are you going to do?' he said, with a tone that couldn't hide how ridiculous he thought this idea was.

'It doesn't really matter. No-one will ever see it. We already know there's over 3000 shows all vying for attention and competing for advertising space – they're unlikely to find mine. Look at the number of shows in that brochure. If we just use the standard small lineage ad, we'll be able to register a show and that will mean we can register the venue. And this will mean we will appear on the list of venues and attract real shows that are actually going to run.'

Iain looked dubious. 'What do we put in the lineage ad?'

'Just put The Arthur Conan Doyle Experience – nothing else.'

'And what are you going to do?' Iain asked, still puzzled.

'Nothing – I'm not going to be running a show because no-one will come because no-one will know it's on. They'll not find it in amongst all the other shows in that brochure.' Iain nodded in recognition of how difficult it was to decide what you wanted to see at the Fringe. He knew from experience that you couldn't walk along the streets of Edinburgh without being accosted by someone stuffing flyers into your hand or street performers trying to entice you to their show, let alone the advertising and marketing that some performers spent in trying to get their name across. I was confident my show wouldn't be found in amongst this lot. He agreed and we registered a show. It was then promptly forgotten about, but it had served its purpose in allowing us to register the Centre as a venue. Bookings were coming in nicely from performers booking their shows with us and there was a nice selection of performers. This included *The Tea Diaries,* which was a play about a tearoom, so they booked our tearoom for their show; we also had a mentalist called Ian Harvey Stone; Allister Savage from the BBC Symphony Orchestra, who was running his own show, so it was good to have him back with us; and we had Nikki Sinclair, previously UKIP MEP and colleague of Nigel Farage. Her show was called *The EU – It's not funny.* It was a political satire and a one woman show.

All tickets for the Fringe went on sale from May and these were handled electronically by the edFringe office, so there was nothing else for us to do but wait until it all kicked off in August. This was shaping up to be a good plan. I was secretly congratulating myself on a job well done when one day towards the end of June, Iain came home from the Centre and said, 'Well, you'll be pleased to know you've sold 28 tickets.'

'28 tickets – for what?' I said.

'For your show – the Arthur Conan Doyle Experience.'

'Oh no! Don't tell me people have found it – and actually booked?' I could feel the panic rising in my chest.

'Yes, they have – so what are you going to do now?'

'I've no idea.'

'Well, it's too late to give them their money back – I've already looked at that option and it's not possible. So, what are you going to do?'

'I really don't know.' I was feeling quite shell-shocked at the prospect. This was not supposed to happen. My mind whirred. I didn't really know anything about Arthur Conan Doyle. I was just using that title because we were trying to get the Centre accepted as a venue. What was I going to do now and how could I possibly live up to the title, The Arthur Conan Doyle Experience? What sort of experience could I possibly offer them?

'Well, you're going to have to come up with something as tickets are continuing to sell. There were another four sold today.'

If he was trying to reassure me – he wasn't. The increasing number of sales just served to pile on the pressure. This seemed like a good idea at the time, I heard myself saying silently. Now it didn't seem such a smart move. It was only 6 weeks before the start of the Fringe – I was going to have to come up with something fast. Thankfully it had been booked under the category of 'the spoken word.' I was certainly accustomed to public speaking, but I was not an Arthur Conan Doyle aficionado. I knew virtually nothing about him; Arthur was just the man who turned up to speak to me and direct me towards the Centre. How was I ever going to speak about him? I then remembered that a book had been donated to us by Muriel Finlayson, a visiting Spiritualist from Aberdeen. She had been with us the year before, running healing classes for the church and she gifted us a book which she dedicated, *to The Arthur Conan Doyle Centre with love and light, Muriel Finlayson, 3/2/12*. I remember her saying something like this book is meant for you or words to that effect. It was gratefully received and placed in our library but suddenly it took on much more significance. I went to retrieve it and take it home to read. Time was short. I spent most of my time working at the Centre during the day then mugging up on ACD in the evenings – taking me well into the wee small hours. I started putting together a power-point presentation of some of the snippets of his life, in the hope that I could string together a story. Although it had been Arthur who had led us to the building, I knew I couldn't reveal that as I had previously been instructed by Spirit that my Group and what happened within it had to remain confidential. So, what could I tell them? I'd tell them that he was an Edinburgh man and a Spiritualist; and that Edinburgh does not celebrate one of their most famous sons very well, so when we got a grand building such as this we thought it a fitting tribute to name it after such a great man. All of this was true of course, but it didn't reveal the real reason – that Arthur had led us here himself. But this had given me an idea. Since this show was for the Edinburgh Fringe Festival, I would focus on those aspects of his life when he was here in Edinburgh, before he was famous. After all, he was born here. It was also a convenient way to reduce the amount of reading and research I had to do since this was in fact the shortest period of his life, as he left Edinburgh in 1881 shortly after graduating aged just 18. He spent some time on the Arctic whaling ship known as The Hope of Peterhead and then left Edinburgh for Portsmouth to make his way as a doctor. I was hopeful that I could come up with an hour-long presentation of his life in Edinburgh for the Fringe, although how I was to make it an 'experience,' as advertised, was another question.

And then some strange synchronicities started to take place. I started reading the book that Muriel had donated to us. It was called *Arthur Conan Doyle A Life in Letters by Jon Lellenberg, Daniel Stashower and Charles Foley.* Charles Foley is the great-nephew of Arthur Conan Doyle and great-grandson of Mary Foley Doyle and is the present executor of the Conan Doyle estate. Jon Lellenberg is the editor of *The Quest for Sir Arthur Conan Doyle* and is the Conan Doyle estate's U.S. representative. Daniel Stashower is the author of the Edgar Award-winning *Teller of Tales: The Life of Arthur Conan Doyle* and many more titles. All three are members of the Baker Street Irregulars, a club of Sherlock Holmes enthusiasts founded in 1934.

Through some divine intervention, I seemed to have in my possession an authoritative biography of Arthur Conan Doyle by those in the know – just when I needed it most. I was later to find that Arthur's life is well documented by many biographers but there are also many contradictions between them. Through good-fortune, synchronicity or just coincidence I happened to have been given the book that put the record straight, not least from the writings of the great man himself since the book was based on the letters he sent to his mother over a 54-year period. This would do nicely.

As I read through the book, I was already aware that his father had been an alcoholic and had been institutionalised but what I didn't know was that his father was an artist; indeed, he came from a family of very successful artists. I must admit to some skimming of the book as I grabbed some facts that could add to my story without having to read through all the detail. Now I needed to know what had happened to his father's art. Was it still in existence? What did he paint? Where was it? And could we get a copy or photo of it to add to my presentation? Coincidentally, at that time we had an art exhibition going on in the Centre with an external gallery who had hired the space. They had an intern working with them and this girl looked like she was bored stiff. I asked if I could utilise her time to do some research for me into Conan Doyle's father's art. 'Sure', came the response. So, I said to this girl, 'just try to search the internet and find out what it is, where it is, and if you can download a picture or copy of it for my presentation at the Fringe.' She looked pleased to have something to do.

The next day, when I walked into the Centre for my after-noon/evening shift, she was waiting for me. 'I've tracked down his father's art,' she said, 'He painted fairies.'

'Fairies.' I said, 'that's interesting. Did you find a picture of this painting of fairies?'

'Oh yes,' and she handed me a printout of a download from the internet showing a small thumbnail picture of a painting of fairies and some background information on Charles Altamont Doyle – Arthur's father.

'Okay, that's great,' I said. 'Do we know where this painting is now? Does it still exist?'

'Yes, and it is just one of a whole collection of his art which consists of drawings, sketches and watercolours. And they were all bought by a private collector in London.'

'Ah, so they're not on display then' I was thinking this was a shame but I wasn't quite ready for what she said next.

'I've traced the owner of the collection and he told me no, they're not on display. They're actually stored in a filing cabinet. But when I told him what I was doing for you and that you were going to be talking about this artwork at the Fringe and that you wanted to show an example, he offered to send them up to you to be included in your show.'

'You're kidding.' I could not quite believe what I was hearing and still staggered that this young student had taken it upon herself to contact the owner and tell them about my show – the one that I was having to cobble together because it was not supposed to happen in the first place. And now apparently some artwork was coming up from London. 'Tell me exactly what's happened,' I asked.

'I found out that the whole collection was bought by a private gallery in London. It's called Chris Beetles Gallery and it's in St James, London. When I spoke to them and told them what you were doing, they offered to send the artworks up to you. All you have to do is make sure they're insured whilst they're here.'

'Wow. Well, I can certainly do that. What is it that they are sending me?'

'The whole collection.'

'The whole collection. How many is that?'

'He thinks there are over 30 pieces? They've been in the filing cabinet since he bought them. He's going to have them all framed and then courier them up here for the duration of the Fringe.'

'And who is paying for the framing and the courier?'

'He is – you just need to insure them.'

I couldn't quite compute what had just happened. I expected her just to print off some information from the internet that I could speak about and perhaps an image that I could use but now Arthur Conan Doyle's father's art was coming to Edinburgh and would be seen and displayed as a collection for the very first time. And the synchronicity continued.

Just a few days afterwards, a rather frail, elderly lady walked in with a polythene bag in her hands; she had been involved in spiritual circles in the past and used to pop in for a chat when she was passing the Centre. 'I'm clearing out my flat because I'm going to sell it – I'm going into a home – and I wanted you to have this.'

'I'm sorry to hear that, Adeline. What is this?'

'It's a book about Arthur Conan Doyle's father. I've had it for years and came across it when I was packing things up and I just thought I know who I'm going to give that to. I thought you'd like it, Ann.'

I loved it. Here was the book detailing the artwork of Arthur Conan Doyle's father, the very same artwork that was shortly going to be winging its way up from London. The book is called *The Doyle*

Diary – The last great Conan Doyle Mystery, by Michael Baker. It is the diary and sketch book of Charles Altamont Doyle from 1889 reproduced in its entirety. He used and kept this journal when he was confined – imprisoned he said – in Sunnyside, part of the Royal Montrose Lunatic Asylum in Scotland. Interestingly, the diary disappeared after Charles died (in another asylum in Dumfries) and it was bought in a job-lot of books at a house-sale in the New Forest in 1955 – probably when Conan Doyle moved from Bignell House, Minstead – and it lay undiscovered until 1977 when an artist friend of the owner suggested it be taken to a gallery in London to have them look at it. They soon realised the value of the find and helped establish and recognise Charles Altamont Doyle as a talented and successful artist and regain his place alongside his brothers and father.

Meanwhile back at the ranch I was keeping my head down as much as I could, trying to pull something together for The Arthur Conan Doyle Experience – my show. I now had an experience to offer – seeing Arthur Conan Doyle's father's art on show for the first time. What else could I offer? The Violins. I would ask Steve Burnett the instrument-maker if he would allow us to display the Conan Doyle Quartet as part of my Fringe show. When I contacted him, he said 'No' because the quartet had already been promised to a group of musicians performing at the Fringe from Japan. So, this option looked doomed. However, two days before the date of the first show one of the performers took ill and their show was cancelled. This meant that the violins came to the Sir Arthur Conan Doyle Centre and were put on display ready for my show.

But the most interesting fact was yet to come. The day before my first performance, Steve brought the Conan Doyle Quartet of instruments to the Centre and was setting them up in a display for people to see. I was next to him on the platform, just running through my slides to familiarise myself with them as much as possible before the actual performance the following day. I had a slide of Oscar Wilde because I was going to refer to the fact that Arthur Conan Doyle and he had dinner together with the editor of Lippincott's magazine in 1889. This had resulted in Arthur being commissioned to write a second Sherlock Holmes story – *The Sign of the Four* – and Oscar Wilde was commission to write *A Picture of Dorian Gray*. I was flicking through my slides as Steve set up the violins next to me and when I got to the Oscar Wilde slide Steve said, 'I know that man's grandson.'

'Oscar Wilde's grandson?'

'Yes, he commissioned me to do a painting for him.'

As it turned out, Steve was an artist before he was an instrument-maker and incredibly 100 years after that famous meeting between Arthur Conan Doyle and Oscar Wilde Steve was commissioned by Oscar Wilde's grandson to paint a picture – and that was *A Picture of Dorian Gray*. And now here he was in the Sir Arthur Conan Doyle Centre setting up his violins, the ones he had made from the tree that Arthur used to play in so they could be seen as part of a show called, The Arthur Conan Doyle Experience. The synchronicity was astonishing. That painting was presented to Oscar Wilde's grandson by the Curator of The Scottish National Gallery of Art just down the road from us at the Centre. It is now in the Oscar Wilde Archives in London.

Is all of this just coincidence? You make up your own mind – I would tell my audience. I was ready. I now had an experience to present as part of the show as well as my talk; it was going to be a walk and talk experience to reflect Arthur Conan Doyle's main interests outside writing: music (in particular violins), art (his father's family were all successful artists) and Spiritualism. We could emulate those interests here at The Sir Arthur Conan Doyle Centre. Indeed, since being a home for the arts, music and a Spiritualist Church was listed in our charitable aims, now we could demonstrate it. I walked my audience into the library, where they saw the History of Spiritualism, the book Arthur wanted to complete before he died.

They could also view the painting *The Dawn of Peace by Jane Smith Stewart*, a piece of art which has been in the possession of the Spiritualist Church for over 100 years. It signifies good triumphing over evil and has symbolism from almost every mainstream religion. From here, I took them upstairs to see the display of the Conan Doyle Quartet of instruments crafted from the tree he used to play in and all bearing a gold insignia specially designed by the artist to show the initials ACD; and then on to our main function room where for the first time ever an exhibition of Arthur Conan Doyle's father's art is on display. I finished the tour by taking my audience back downstairs under the mighty cupola to show them a plaque on the wall intimating that this building was once a music school and was opened by Sir Yehudi Menuhin – coincidentally another famous violinist.

On the night before my first show, I sat at my kitchen table in the wee small hours reading *Arthur Conan Doyle A Life in letters* trying to retain as much information as possible in case there was some Conan Doyle aficionado who might be in the audience the following day who might ask me a question I didn't know the answer to. I already knew from my Spiritualism studies that Conan Doyle had had a sort of epiphany in his later years and that he had devoted the rest of his life to promoting Spiritualism throughout the UK and the world in his quest to get the message over to people that there was life after death. Now I read this:

> 'In the days of universal sorrow and loss," he said in Memories and Adventures, "when the voice of Rachel was heard throughout the land, it was borne upon me that the knowledge which had come to me thus was not for my own consolation alone, but that God had placed me in a very special position for conveying it to that world which needed it so badly."
>
> Believing himself to be the harbinger of the New Revelation, he lectured tirelessly across the country, telling his agent that his fees

*were to be donated to the cause: "I do not make money in sacred
things."*

*The "Psychic question," gathering force since his earliest days
in Southsea, had emerged as the most important thing in his life,
and he was to become its most prominent and eloquent spokesman.
"It is the thing," he would write, "for which every preceding phase,
my gradual religious development, my books, which gave me an
introduction to the public, my modest fortune, which enables me to
devote myself to unlucrative work, my platform work, which helps
me to convey the message, and my physical strength, which is still
sufficient to stand arduous tours and to fill the largest halls for an
hour and a half with my voice, have each and all been an unconscious preparation.'* [1]

I read that and I had an epiphany too. I could identify with this
wholly. My experience and skills learned in business, banking, property management and marketing had all been utilised in the
purchase process, the refurbishment and the managing of the
Centre. I didn't have a modest fortune, but I could afford to work for
free at the Centre. The communication from Arthur Conan Doyle
had led me to find the Centre with an aim to get the message over to
the public. I was accustomed to public-speaking and could hold an
audience's attention; my Thursday Group had been selected for
they too had this ability. Now I found myself delivering a talk on
Arthur Conan Doyle and his belief in Spiritualism at the Edinburgh
International Festival Fringe, the biggest arts festival in the world. I
didn't need to travel the world to do that; the world was coming to
Edinburgh. Was all of this 'unconscious preparation?'

It was at that moment that I realised that all the work I had
undertaken on leaving my job, setting up the Group, finding the
Centre and setting it up and now filling a room with my voice was
not my initiative. It was not of my doing. I was just following the

signs, the clues, doing what I had been told – I was being used. This was someone else's agenda, and I was just following the plan.

The show ran for 5 performances over the three-week period of the Fringe and each show sold out. I was awarded the laurel wreath by the Fringe organisation to signify this. And this scenario continued over the next 5 years, selling out each year. The show was never advertised, other than in the Centre and the small lineage ad that comes as standard with each show that is registered, yet somehow the message got out to the people, and they came.

Notes:

It was amazing how all the elements came together to make up that show – the books all arrived when needed and indeed the pictures – which rightfully gained some publicity as above. Having the sketchbook about the artwork enabled me to speak about them in a little more detail and it was clear from reading it that Charles Doyle was indeed imprisoned; they had got rid of him, perhaps he was an embarrassment. Much later in life, as if Arthur Conan Doyle recognised what an isolated and miserable life his father must have had, he would recall, *"'My Father was in truth a great unrecognised genius...'"* And George Bernard Shaw declared that the paintings deserved a room to themselves in any national gallery. I'm glad we were able to do that. We are not a national gallery but we gave them pride of place in our main function room where they could be displayed in their splendour to the public, for free.

See Appendix 5 for copy of press coverage with photo of art work.

Chapter 10

The White Hart Inn

T here was another interesting coincidence that happened in November 2013. This had nothing to do with the energy in the Centre but with another building in Edinburgh, the White Hart Inn, the oldest hostelry in the city and a previous psychical investigation that had taken place there a few years earlier.

It was a Monday morning and I was conscientiously working away at my desk at the Centre that morning when the phone rang. It was Frances Ryan asking me if I had seen Friday's Edinburgh Evening News. It not being a newspaper I was accustomed to reading, I said, 'No, I haven't seen it – what does it say?'

'It's about the White Hart Inn,' she said, 'and they've photographed the lady in red – remember the lady in red that I talked about when we did that TV investigation with Kaye Adams back in 2003?'

Frances Ryan was a friend and a well-known and respected medium in Edinburgh. I had known her for many years and she, Archie and I had undertaken a number of psychic investigations, mainly back in my early years of joining the SSPR. Archie (Lawrie) whom I've referred to in my previous book, was my first paranormal investigator partner. He was at that time vice president of the SSPR and when I joined I was partnered up with him to handle and investigate the paranormal cases reported in the East of Scotland. As I became more involved in my own psychic and mediumistic development, my time was dominated by attending classes and workshops and so Frances was invited to join us and she and Archie carried out the bulk of the on-going investigations; although they always kept me updated with their cases and I would attend when I could. And so I was aware of the case to which she referred. I remembered her telling me at the time, 'There's a lady of the night who walks through this bar and she wears a red dress.' She went on to tell me that this woman was murdered (strangled, I think) in the basement. However during the investigation Frances subsequently went on to discover much more famous names, so this 'lady' was disregarded. Except now Frances posited they had a photo of her. So, I remembered the case well but not least because it was tele-vised by the BBC. Kaye Adams the Scottish Television journalist and presenter narrated the programme called, The Psychic Detec-tives and it featured two haunted locations – The White Hart Inn and The Britannia Theatre in Glasgow. I said to Frances, 'Yes, I remember.'

'We have to get back in there Ann; you'll need to phone them.' She was very excited and enthusiastic on the phone but strident too. She clearly wanted this to happen and urgently.

'Why have I to phone them, Frances? I wasn't really part of that investigation. I was just on the side-lines. You should phone them yourself?'

'No, no' she said, 'they're not going to listen to the likes of me. You're the Chair of the Sir Arthur Conan Doyle Centre and you've got your own psychic investigation unit – they'll listen to you.'

Frances was always very self-effacing – unnecessarily so as she was an accomplished and well-respected medium – but she was not the most confident of people. I realised that if she had felt confident about phoning about the case she would have done so already.

'Okay, I'll phone them and see what they say.'

'We need to get in there as soon as possible – you and I – we'll go and see what we can pick up?' She was clearly eager as she followed up by saying that she could meet me the following day and we could go to the pub together.

The following day Tuesday (12th November 2013) Frances and I walked into The White Hart Inn. I had been in it many times before – usually for a drink – but was also aware of its colourful past. It is in the Grassmarket, a very picturesque area of Edinburgh with lots of pavement cafes, pubs and small independent shops. It is situated almost directly under the world-famous Edinburgh Castle with the castle rock and ramparts towering above. The oldest part of the pub dates back to the 1500s and takes its name from the White Hart – a stag – which was being hunted by King David the first of Scotland. For when the stag turned upon him and he was thrown from his horse facing certain death from the charge of the stag, a fiery cross appeared between the antlers of the stag before both the stag and the cross disappeared. King David built a shrine to this miracle and Holyrood Abbey ruins can still be seen in the grounds of Holyrood Palace. (Holyrood being the old Scottish word for Holy Cross.) Moving forward a few hundred years to 1791, it is said that Robert Burns spent a week here when visiting his lover and penned the romantic love song *Ae Fond Kiss*. Just a few years later, the romanticism had changed to the murky and murderous activities of 1828 when the pub was host to the notorious body-snatchers Burke and Hare. These are just a few of its many famous faces and as Frances proved on the BBC documentary, some have never left. However, in 2013 we were interested in much more recent activities and in particular in the photo which had appeared in the newspaper.

The Bar Manager Michael Johnson was busy behind the bar when we arrived, so we ordered our food and just waited until he had finished his chores and could come over and sit with us. He was a big affable New Zealander and although by this time he must have been asked the same questions over and over again he very kindly and patiently recounted his experience. 'You're actually sitting at the table where the picture was taken. They were just a couple and their daughter and they were sitting here. I was giving them some jip about the rugby – me being a Kiwi. They were tourists and had been taking snaps. I had gone back behind the bar when suddenly I heard a lot of commotion and when I looked across they were looking into the view-finder of their camera to see what had just been taken and there was a lot of excitement. They called me over to have a look at it. Now if I had seen that shot printed off as a photo, I would have sworn it was faked – photoshopped. But the fact that I was here when it was taken means it is absolutely genuine. I don't believe in this stuff and that's why I would normally have said it was a fake but this has convinced me that there's something going on here. There's a lot of stories here about staff and former staff seeing or hearing things but I've not taken any notice of that – I've always thought it was nonsense – but now I'm beginning to wonder.'

It was interesting to watch – by his own admission the sworn sceptic – changing before us from a solid, determined, rationalist to the now not-so-sure surrealism of the recent experiencer.

I made notes of his comments for our records and then asked if we could come and carry out another investigation in the pub. He told us that because of the level of interest the newspaper article had generated they were being bombarded with questions and requests to come and do ghost-busting and such-like in the pub, so much so that his head office had expressed concern over the impact this was having on their clientele and ultimately their business. Because of this they had taken control of this issue and decreed that any such requests had to be authorised by head office.

I explained that we were not an amateur outfit and that we had a pedigree behind us and that we intended to undertake a serious investigation. He advised me that I should say all of this to his head office as it would be they who would make the decision; he gave me their contact details.

It took several months of emails and phone calls until I eventually got permission from their head office to hold an investigation in the White Hart Inn after hours. It was planned for Saturday 19th April, 2014. Archie Lawrie who was now head of our own Psychic Investigation Unit at the Sir Arthur Conan Doyle Centre was unable to attend that night, so we joined forces with another group whom we had connections with, the Edinburgh Ghost Hunting Society (EGHS). David Deighan of that organisation and Ewan Irvine, from our own unit, stepped in to take charge and conducted a joint investigation.

The permission given by their head office was very much Centred around not disturbing the clientele and I had given assurances that we would set up our equipment and do all our filming after everyone had left the pub, and that we would be away very early the following morning before opening time. This was also agreed with Michael the bar manager. Our team had agreed to meet in the pub at 10.30pm, so that I could buy everyone a drink – a soft drink – and in this way it got us all in place beforehand and also gave some little revenue to the pub. The pub was due to close at 11pm and the EGHS team walked in and joined us just before then. But the pub was jumping – it was full of folk all in high spirits drinking, laughing and generally having fun. It was a rugby weekend in Edinburgh. So, as it approached closing time, I walked up to the bar as if I was any other customer about to order some drinks, but I really wanted to speak to the manager. Michael saw me approaching and moved to the end of the bar to speak to me. 'We're not closing at eleven,' he said, 'there's far too many people in here to close now. This is when we make most of our takings.'

'Well, when then?' I asked.

'We'll just have to see – once it's quietened down a bit.'

I walked back from the bar to our team who were distributed throughout the bar area and told them that we were having to wait. They were a bit frustrated by this piece of news but given the length of time it had taken to get this arrangement in place everyone just accepted it and settled down to wait for the revellers to settle down too, and go home. 11pm turned to 11.30pm and there was little change in the numbers in the pub. I glanced over at Michael behind the bar and he just shook his head as if to say, 'No – not yet.' As the time approached 12 midnight our team were becoming restless. The numbers in the bar had reduced considerably by this time but there was still no sign of the bar being closed. I walked about between each of our team members trying to keep them motivated, as some of *them* wanted to go home too as we watched our time in the pub slipping away. I returned to stand beside David and Ewan, the team leaders. We were standing at the wall – just next to the table where the infamous photo was taken – with our backs to the window looking at the bar and the now dwindling customers who showed no sign of wanting to leave. In frustration, David picked up his camera that was dangling round his neck and began taking pictures randomly. 'He can't stop us taking pictures,' he said, as he snapped away not looking through the viewfinder but just pointing and shooting at various areas of the bar. He then turned the camera lens to face the floor so the viewfinder was facing upwards as he casually flicked through the images he had just taken. 'Look at that', he said excitedly, and as I was standing next to him I glanced into the viewfinder. And there it was, the image of the woman in red! I only saw a glimpse but knew instantly he had captured something anomalous.

'Take another one – quickly – take some more.'

He quickly followed my train of thought and swung the camera back into action again and I heard the rapid electronic clicking of the camera taking repeated shots in the direction of that last shot. These were carefully reviewed again by the three of us – Ewan also looking in on the viewfinder – but there was only the one shot that captured that image. But that one shot was enough. It substantiated the earlier photo taken by the tourists. Both images show the same shape of a figure in red appearing to walk through the bar. By taking the subsequent photos – which were taken within seconds of the first one – it helps demonstrate that the phenomenon is not something that is ubiquitous to the pub like a reflection from a mirror or a shadow from a light or a reflection from a passing car as these would easily be recaptured in quick succession but this was not. You'll notice I'm not claiming that we've captured a ghost on camera because I'm aware that there could still be some material explanation for these images. But as David Deighan says, I know of no other instance where the investigators have been able to produce a photo of the same anomaly from two different cases, taken five months apart. Here is David's statement from 2014:

'The Edinburgh Evening News featured an article in November 2013 on the White Hart Inn in Edinburgh 's historic Grassmarket, and under the headline 'Has ghost of White Hart Inn been caught on camera?'. During its history this pub has played host to the likes of Burke and Hare.

A few weeks ago, the Psychical Research & Investigation Unit, part of the Sir Arthur Conan Doyle Centre, along with members of the Edinburgh Ghost Hunting Society undertook a private investigation at the Inn.

The Psychical Research & Investigation Unit is headed up by Archie Lawrie, currently President of The Edinburgh Society for Psychical Research and the Vice-President of The Scottish Society for Psychical Research.

The investigation included two mediums, along with investigators who look at the scientific side of paranormal activity. All have significant experience in investigating the paranormal.

Interest in the Inn peaked last year when a photo taken by a tourist appeared in the Evening News. It appeared to show a ghostly apparition and we never could have imagined that on taking camera shots at our investigation we would have captured a near identical image in exactly the same spot.

Although at the time the bar was still occupied and staff moving around, CCTV footage showed no one walked past the camera as the shot was taken.

The photo taken by a member of the Edinburgh Ghost Hunting Society is attached and we do not know of any cases where there has been a similar scenario in two completely different investigations.'

— David Deighan,
Edinburgh Ghost Hunting Society

The photos are reproduced at Appendix 6 – so you can make up your own mind:

Chapter 11

McEwan's is the best buy

After the buzz and excitement in August of our first Fringe, both as a venue and for me as a performer had passed, the Centre resumed normal operations. The classes all re-started for the autumn term and there were workshops and demonstrations of mediumship booked in for September too. It was a bit of a relief that it was all over but it was great to have the Centre full of new visitors all coming to attend different Fringe shows and it was great to hear the Edinburgh residents' surprise at finding the venue for the first time because they didn't know we were here. So, the plan was working. But I knew I'd have to follow it up with something else if we were going to build on this momentum and have other mainstream activities for the public.

Towards the end of September my mother asked me if I would like to accompany her to the Signet Library.

'Why are you going there?'

'Because I want to see it,' she said. 'I've always wanted to see it – so now's my chance.'

'What do you mean – now's your chance?'

'I'm going as part of Edinburgh Doors Open Day – it's open to the public and its free,' as she handed me the brochure.

Eureka! Here was another Fringe-type opportunity for free publicity and in a brochure that once again would be distributed freely around Edinburgh to encourage the public to access buildings of historical or architectural significance. That was exactly what we wanted; the Edinburgh public to access our building. We can do that I thought. Our building is architecturally beautiful, and it sits in a world heritage site. I didn't know anything about its history (other than it being a dilapidated back-packers hostel) but that didn't matter; I was sure the architectural value would be attractive to the public. I had found my next mission – apply for inclusion in Doors Open Day. I knew it wouldn't happen until the following year, 2014, but that gave me time to find out what was required in the application.

The application asked what we would be providing in terms of a customer experience – there's that word again – an 'experience.' It then listed a multiple-choice response: Guided tours, lectures, display board, info on history of the building, info on architecture of the building, leaflets, handouts, audio visual displays, café/refreshments, etc. I ticked all of them. I didn't have any of that information but I guessed it would give us the best chance of being accepted if I said we would be providing everything. I wasn't really holding out much hope of being accepted as I was aware that anything to do with Spiritualism generally gets bad press but I wanted to give us the best possible chance. I would think about how we would produce it all at a later date, if and when we received an acceptance, which was several months away.

It was with great surprise then when the acceptance finally came through and we were included in the Edinburgh Doors Open programme for 2014. The programme of course listed all these interactive experiences we were going to offer; I needed to get my skates on! I had no knowledge at all about the architecture or the history of the building. I couldn't produce any 'experience' without this base-line knowledge from which to work. I started with the architecture, believing this would be of the greatest interest to the visitors. I searched Historic Scotland's website:

The property is a magnificent Category B Listed Victorian town-house. It was built in 1881 by The Walker Trustees of The Coates Estate, who employed builders John Watherston & Sons to carry out the construction. The Architect was George Gilroy.

This large mansion house has a curved bay window to the front elevation, integrated with a Roman Doric porch, sidelights and rectangular fanlight.

There are 5 bays to the Chester Street elevation and consoled balconies at 1st floor level (although the ironwork no longer exists).

The balustraded French-style roof was raised in 1886, creating a fourth floor to provide additional servants' quarters.

It was designed by George Gilroy, who had previously created the spectacular glass dome, which can be seen from the entrance hall.

Source: Historic Environment Scotland. http://portal.histori cenvironment.scot/designation/LB51340

That was enough to get me started. I'd incorporate this information into some sort of leaflet but now I headed off to see the Register of Sasines. This is similar to the Land Registry in England and holds the details of the title deeds of all properties in Scotland. It is kept within the Registers of Scotland at their office Register House at the east end of Princes Street and is situated directly behind the large bronze statue of the Duke of Wellington on his horse, which looks southwards towards the north and south bridges. Register House is a palatial building adorned internally with beautiful Italian marble and it occupies an elevated position high above the pavements and

busy streets of the East End. I asked the keeper of the records for a
search of the title deeds of 25 Palmerston Place. I wanted to know
who it belonged to, from when it was built right up until the present
day. When I told her I wanted the information for Doors Open Day
because we had been selected as a venue and I wanted to be able to
talk about the building's history she launched into a lecture about
Palmerston Place telling me that it was named after the British
prime minister Lord Palmerston and proceeded to print out a lot of
background information about him which was interesting but not
what I wanted. She searched the records I had asked for and printed
out a copy of all the changes in the title as it had changed hands over
the years. She glanced briefly at what she had printed off and simply
handed me the copy – clearly she was not as interested in this as she
was in Palmerston Place and the then prime minister. I thanked her
and took the three or four pages to one of the study desks just to
check that I had indeed got what I had asked for. The records were
in date-order with the most recent dates on top. I quickly flicked to
the back page where the records began. I wanted to know who was
the first owner and I saw that it was built for a William McEwan,
Brewer, Fountainbridge. Now that *was* interesting and it would
certainly give me something to tell the visitors on Doors Open Day,
i.e. that it was built for the famous brewer – his beer best known
today as McEwan's Export and for *the best buy in beer* [a strapline
from their advertising campaign of the 1970's]. I grabbed the papers
and rushed home to search the internet and find out what I could
about a certain brewer from Edinburgh. I sat down at my computer
desk armed with this sheaf of papers and typed into the search bar
'William McEwan' and up popped Wikipedia in its usual format.
What I wasn't ready for was the image showing in the top corner of
his profile page; it was a sketch from Vanity Fair magazine from
1902, showing an elderly man with a long beard wearing a dress-
coat, waistcoat and top hat. I could not believe it. I pushed myself
away from the computer in an automatic reaction to what I was

seeing as I exclaimed out loud, 'I know you – you're the man on the stairs.'

I was dumb-founded – pleasantly dumbfounded – it all made sense now. This was *his* house. It was built for him. I was later to find out that it was the first house he had ever owned and he was instrumental in its design and finishing and this is why it was so grand. No wonder he turned up when Iain and I decided to build an IKEA kitchen in his bedroom!

Another remarkable revelation was yet to be experienced but for now I was researching the life of William McEwan in Edinburgh and finding remarkable similarities to Arthur Conan Doyle.

McEwan was a self-made man and became incredibly wealthy after founding the Fountain Brewery in Edinburgh and creating McEwan's Export, which was exported throughout the world. He was also a notable philanthropist presenting paintings to the National Gallery of Scotland and donating the funds for the building of the McEwan Hall for the University of Edinburgh's Graduation Ceremonies. In 1897 when the Hall opened, McEwan was granted an Honorary Doctorate and was presented with The Freedom of the City of Edinburgh. He was also Deputy Lieutenant of Edinburgh for 30 years and was appointed as Privy Councillor to Edward VII in 1907. He declined a peerage from the King, stating 'I would rather be first in my own order, than be at the tail end of another.' He was a Gladstonian Liberal serving as MP for the Central Edinburgh Constituency from 1886. He retired in 1900, due to ill-health.

Conan Doyle was also a wealthy, self-made man and proud of it. Interestingly, he too wanted to turn down his title but was eventually persuaded by his mother to accept the honour. She told him it would be an insult to the King if he didn't accept. [*King Edward VIIth Knighted ACD, June 1902*]. Coincidentally, Joseph Bell the inspiration for Sherlock Holmes was also a Deputy Lieutenant of Edinburgh at the same time as William McEwan and he lived just round the corner at 2 Melville Crescent (now the Japanese Embassy) so it is not unreasonable to consider that the two men would have known each other as indeed they served together in this capacity.

Coincidentally, Arthur Conan Doyle was also made a Deputy Lord Lieutenant but of Surrey, where he was living by this time. [*At Undershaw, his home in Hindhead, Surrey*].

Armed with this information, I started to assemble some notes to help me guide the people whom I hoped would soon be visiting the Centre on Doors Open Day. It was as I was doing so that the wee niggle in my head that I was used to by now was drawing my attention to something in the research. I had decided (or perhaps someone else had put the thought in my head) to make my theme *There's no such thing as coincidence*, partly inspired by the similarities between Arthur Conan Doyle and William McEwan. And I was drawn towards another similarity; that they had both run for seats in Parliament. I knew this from the very brief research I had undertaken the year before for the Fringe but I hadn't put much store by it as I had also remembered that Conan Doyle was unsuccessful, whilst I was now reading that William McEwan seemed to be a very successful MP, being re-elected unopposed for a second term in office. He also won favour from the Temperance Society – not bad for a brewer. So where was the connection? Where was the coincidence that the niggle in my head was now directing me towards with even greater fervour? I leafed back through the notes and re-read the bit about McEwan as an MP for Central Edinburgh and knew instantly this was it – Central Edinburgh – the words seemed to be jumping out at me as if highlighted with psychedelic colours. My mind was racing through its memory banks to try to recall what I knew of Conan Doyle's run for Parliament. All I could remember from my Fringe talk was that I had told my audience he had run twice for Parliament, once in the Scottish Borders – Hawick – and the other time in Edinburgh. Edinburgh – could it possibly be the Central Edinburgh

Constituency? Could it possibly be at the same time as McEwan? Could it be that they both ran for the same seat? These were my questions but at the same time my logic was telling me – unlikely and probably not – but I was up and running. Most of the websites gave the same brief information I had already given at the Fringe. Where was I to find the detail of exactly which of the Edinburgh constituencies he had run for? Then I remembered, 'His Life in Letters' the book where I had found most of my research for the Fringe, which was based on the letters written to his mother. Surely he had written to his mother about running for Parliament, but did he mention which constituency it was? I quickly leafed through the book trying to find the appropriate timeframe and here it was, a letter to his mother written from the Edinburgh hotel where he was staying during his campaign; strangely enough, the hotel was called the Old Waverley Temperance Hotel, which I immediately noted nods back to the support McEwan had amongst the Temperance Movement. And the letter confirmed it was indeed the Central Edinburgh Constituency that he was running for. It had become vacant when William McEwan decided to retire from politics in 1900, and so my notes for Edinburgh Doors Open had a nice summary to all the coincidences. Arthur Conan Doyle had tried to run for the vacated seat of William McEwan in politics and now the vacated home of William McEwan (in the Central Edinburgh Constituency) has become The Sir Arthur Conan Doyle Centre, and we knew nothing of this when we bought the building.

I was ready now for the Doors Open weekend in September 2014, but would anyone come? Would anyone be interested in the home of William McEwan? It wasn't the brewery, after all; it was just his house.

We had over 1000 visitors over the two days of the weekend. I was the only one giving tours but I had helpers running the Sherlock Holmes Tearoom and Iain and Jim, who were corralling the people into the Sanctuary to wait for the next tour. I was taking about 20 people at a time on a tour of the building, pointing out all the notable features and the coincidences as we walked and talked. And I left them with a question to ponder. I told them that with the picture of Conan Doyle on the wall outside our building people – especially tourists – would run in and ask 'Is this Conan Doyle's house?' And that I could see the disappointment in their faces when I have to say, 'No.' In desperation they'll say, 'Well was he ever here?' And again I'd have to say, 'No.' But given that both Conan Doyle and McEwan were both Liberals (although at that point, the party had split and become the Liberal Unionists and the Gladstonian Liberals, after their earlier Prime Minister William Gladstone had supported home rule for Ireland; Conan Doyle supported the Union and McEwan did not. And since one was running for the other's seat and we know that McEwan, like Conan Doyle, was involved in great political and literary circles of that time and that Joe Bell, the inspiration for Sherlock Holmes, served as Deputy Lord Lieutenant together with McEwan, the chances are that they did meet. And, I am looking for the evidence to support this. What I do know, I told our Doors Open Day visitors, is if Arthur was not here in person, he is most definitely here in Spirit.

Our Doors Open event was one of the most successful events ever held at the Centre in terms of numbers through the door; it didn't make us any money but it did help with name-awareness and especially with local Edinburgh residents. And just as I had been handed a business card by someone who had attended my Fringe show, which revealed he was from the University of Arizona, a Sherlock Holmes Aficionado and a lecturer on Harry Houdini, whom I've yet to introduce you to, during one of the Doors Open tours a gentleman handed me his card and said 'perhaps we can speak later.' I looked at the card it read, John Martin, Chairman, Scottish Brewing Archive Association – Promoting the History of Brewing in Scotland. My immediate thought was that I had got my facts wrong somewhere along the lines and he was going to correct me or that I had misrepresented William McEwan in some way. But when I plucked up the courage to phone John he was most complimentary about what had taken place, so much so that he wanted to hold the next meeting of his members at The Sir Arthur Conan Doyle Centre so that he could present the talk to them. This was duly achieved, thereby extending our reach and name-awareness to yet another group of potential new customers.

Just a week or two after the event, we got a call from the Cockburn Association – the organisation which runs Doors Open Days – telling us that we were one of the most popular destinations on the Edinburgh Doors Open Days map and encouraging us to re-apply for next year. During this conversation, they told me that the next year's theme would be food and drink. This was a no-brainer, as they say, and with John's help I approached McEwan's Beer Company, now part of the Wells and Young group and I asked if they would like to participate in Edinburgh Doors Open Day in 2015 and perhaps promote their beer from the home of their founding father. So, how do you top the most successful event ever – by giving away free beer.

Wells and Young kindly gave us permission to use all their McEwan's logos in our promotional material and they supplied the graphics of these, together with videos of all the TV adverts for McEwan's Beer over the years, so it was great to be able to show these on a continuous loop in the Centre and bring back some happy memories for many of our visitors. The following year, John, who was by now a regular visitor to the Centre as he helped me search for information on William McEwan in the Scottish Brewing Archives which were housed in Glasgow University, informed me that 2016 marked 160 years since William McEwan built the Fountain Brewery in 1856 and the McEwan Beer Co would be celebrating this anniversary. Part of those celebrations took place at the Centre with a new beer also being launched there. So, some very fruitful associations were achieved from the Doors Open event and the research on McEwan was handed over to one of our volunteers, Eleanor Docherty, who followed up together with John Martin and this information was later used in the production of our Guidebook – thanks Eleanor. But what I continue to search for is the illusive evidence that McEwan and Conan Doyle had met – and hopefully at 25 Palmerston Place – The Sir Arthur Conan Doyle Centre. I'm still searching.

Notes

These possible connections between McEwan, ACD and Joseph Bell may give further credence to the hypothesis forwarded by Barry Fitzgerald that they could have been involved in The Hermetic Order of the Golden Dawn and its Edinburgh Temple whose location remains a mystery. But I have no evidence to support this conjecture – yet.

Further info at Appendix 7

Chapter 12

The Vortex

I have outlined over the earlier chapters how the energy in the building was experienced by me, Iain and many others, starting from the workmen helping us with the refurbishment to various visitors to the building over a number of years. This has caused me to question: Why this building? Why now? Why were we being directed to find the building over the previous 5 years? The building had been derelict for years – why could we not have been here sooner? Was the energy developing during that time? I was aware that when buildings are dormant or quiet for a length of time, followed by some DIY or in our case major refurbishment works, these are the conditions that can make it more conducive to psychical phenomena taking place. Was someone making sure that the conditions were right so that we could experience more physical phenomena? The Thursday Group had been promised such by Arthur Conan Doyle, once we found our new building. We certainly had an active building. Or was it something to do with the geography? The topography? The architecture? I was aware of ley lines and had some experience in the past of dowsing and using a pendulum to find such energy sources but it was Gordon who was the master of this discipline. He, like the others in the Group, had been aware of the energy in the building whenever we had first walked through that front door. And it was Gordon who had got his pendulum out and had chosen our room – and his own room – so I knew the building was sitting on powerful ley lines. Indeed, after having taken up occupancy of the property I was aware of the different energies in the building and how the energy differed in the various parts of the building – the basement, the stairs and the bedrooms on the upper floors being obvious examples. But I was also aware of something else, something quite different.

When I would be sitting at the reception desk at the bottom of the main staircase and under the giant domed ceiling of the entrance hall I would feel this strange energy. It didn't feel like a spiritual being but just an energetic swirling. It felt like a spiral of energy reaching up towards the dome. Somehow it seemed to mimic the formation of the staircase or was contained within it. Sometimes it was spinning faster and it was quite defined; you could step into it and out of it. It didn't reach wider than the opening of the stairwell. I also felt that it was diluted when there were a lot of people in the building, especially on the staircase. It seemed stronger and possibly faster when the building was quiet. It gave me the impression that this energy was spiralling up from the bottom of the stairs – or maybe even from below the stair, from the earth – up towards the dome but on through it up skywards and beyond. I wondered if this had something to do with Iain's legionnaires and others that he had seen going up and down the stairs. Was this some sort of portal? I wasn't aware of anyone else who had felt this energy; certainly no-one had ever mentioned it to me. And it wasn't anything to be concerned about. It was just there and in actual fact I quite enjoyed sitting in it when I was at the reception desk.

Very occasionally someone would approach the reception desk, perhaps with a question, and when they were standing next to the desk they would comment about suddenly feeling dizzy or something similar. On those occasions I would suggest that they take a seat, knowing that the seat was placed beyond the edges of the spiralling energy. But by 2015 two things happened to confirm this for me. Firstly, I was asked by a friend to meet a German couple who were visiting Edinburgh for the first time and wanted to see the castle and other tourist destinations. I picked them up at their hotel and brought them to the Centre for a coffee so they could see our building before heading up to Edinburgh Castle. As they walked towards the reception and stood under the dome, the only word I could understand from the woman, who spoke no English but in her strong German accent said, '... vortex...' I knew instantly that she was picking up the energy I was accustomed to and her partner translated and confirmed this.

Also in that year Nick Kyle, president of the Scottish Society for Psychical Research (SSPR) called me to tell me that the speaker for their next meeting had suddenly had to cancel and asked if I'd be willing to help out by giving a talk in his stead. So, I agreed. (Coincidentally, the cancelled speaker was Roger Straughan.)

It was very easy by this time for me to speak about Arthur Conan Doyle, as I had done at the Fringe, but this wasn't a general interest group. This was a specialist group who studied and investigated the paranormal; they had already undertaken an investigation and vigil in the Centre by this time, although I didn't have the results - it was an on-going investigation. I wondered what else I could tell them about the building that would be within their sphere of interest but without giving away any of the information about the happenings that had already taken Iain and me by surprise.

[It was important to adhere to SSPR protocol to ensure that those undertaking any investigation had no prior knowledge of what had taken place in the premises beforehand. For this reason I had been asked not to be present in the building when the SSPR investigation and vigil took place, so it was important not to undermine that protocol now by divulging anything that could otherwise have been established independently by their investigations.]

So, what could I tell them? I know – I'd tell them about the vortex – that wouldn't hamper their investigations.

Back home I sat down at my computer desk and began to put together a PowerPoint slide show for the talk I was going to give at the SSPR. I had slides about Arthur Conan Doyle and I would give some general information about him and his spiritual beliefs but what would I tell them about the vortex and how would I substantiate that claim? I knew if I couldn't produce empirical evidence then it wasn't worth mentioning at all, as it would be disregarded as anecdotal information. Then the little voice that spoke to me in my head said, 'you've got a photograph of that.' I automatically disregarded it as nonsense. Then I heard it again, 'you've got a photograph of that.' I pondered for a moment but disregarded it again. I didn't have any photographs of a vortex; that was impossible. I carried on putting together my PowerPoint presentation, trying to disregard the voice from Spirit. But again it repeated, 'you've got a photograph of that.' I stopped what I was doing, beginning to get a bit frustrated by these constant interruptions because I knew what was being said was just not credible. I didn't have any photos and knew of no-one else who had or even knew of such a thing. But I had heard it for a third time, so I stopped what I was doing and thought for a moment. If it was I who supposedly had such a photograph where could it possibly be? I had taken many photos of the Centre over the years, mostly for promotional purposes in which case I would've pondered over them in great detail to make sure I had captured the Centre in all its glory. If it was one of those that was being referred to surely I would've seen something before now. I looked again just to be sure but was correct in my assumption; there was nothing there. I thought again – where else could I possibly have photos of the stair, let alone the vortex? I had already trawled all the photos on my laptop. Where else could there be photos? Not on my phone; these had already been downloaded. Then I remembered my old phone and my old laptop. When we first purchased the building and Iain and I were commissioned to handle the refurbishment work I had gone around taking photos of all the various rooms in the building with a view to reminding myself what needed to be done in each so I could make a plan. And, with the best laid plans of mice and men, I had never looked at them.

I got the old laptop out and saw the file that I had downloaded before handing in my old phone for replacement. The file had never been opened; it was dated 2nd March 2011. So, four years later I opened it. There amongst various pictures of how the building looked back then was a photo of the vortex, spinning like a top. I couldn't believe it!

I have printed it here together with a photograph of the stair when it is not spinning so you can make the comparison.

After giving the presentation to the SSPR I sent the photo to a professional photographer just to see what he made of it. His response, 'how did you do that?' I told him I didn't do anything. I just took a random photo of the stair and this is what turned out. He told me that he would have difficulty producing an image like that using conventional means.

The first photo (over) is of our grand staircase (taken after the refurbishment) looking down from the second floor to the ground floor, while the next photo (over) is again of our grand staircase looking up to the dome from the ground floor. The final, largest image is the original unadulterated photo taken directly from my phone and downloaded to my laptop and now reproduced here.

The grand staircase looking down from second floor

The grand staircase looking up to the dome

The Vortex

As a psychical investigator, I am aware that there are many fake photos of so-called psychical phenomena and with photoshop and other modern electronic photographic programs it is relatively easy to do. To explain, if someone wanted to fake a photo such as this (without using computer graphics) the plan would be to put the camera on a slow shutter speed and spin the camera on a central spindle of some sort thus creating the spinning image. However, if this was to be done the resulting image would show the outside edge of the photo more blurred than the centre of the image, simply because the outside of the spin (the circumference) would be spinning faster than the centre point. In the image above I hope you can see that it is the centre of the picture that is spinning faster than the circumference of the spin and this is borne out by looking at the carved wooden architrave which can be seen on the top left of the picture and right/centre, which are both in focus, showing that the camera was held steady whilst the centre of the vortex spun.

I have always been of the opinion that the energy either originated or was accentuated by the geographical location as well as the architecture of the building and that this natural energy can be utilised by external forces – be they human, spiritual or unidentified – and for either positive or negative purposes. I feel another indicator of this is that St Mary's Cathedral, our neighbour and one of the grandest religious buildings with the highest spire in Edinburgh, sits on the same land as our building, which once formed part of the Coates Estate. (It is common for churches, chapels and other spiritual buildings of the traditional religions to be situated where two ley lines cross and therefore a point of increased earth energies). Also, as pointed out on a recent visit by David Lorimer, Programme Director of the Scientific and Medical Network, these large buildings have lightning conductors and they are struck more regularly than we realise and these high voltage electrical charges are discharged into the ground – the same ground on which our building sits – so they act almost like a battery.

In more recent times, I have been liaising with Barry Fitzgerald and Steve Mera in a paranormal investigators group in which we are all members. Steve Mera is an investigative researcher, author, lecturer, spokesperson, executive producer, and radio and TV host. Like Barry (whom we heard from in Chapter 7), he has spent over 30 years actively investigating, researching and analysing numerous subjects of phenomena that include earth mysteries, parapsychological studies, the paranormal, cryptids, ancient sites and Unexplained Atmospheric Phenomena such as UFOs. Unfortunately Steve has not yet been able to visit the building personally but from his desk-based research here's what Steve says about the strange forces at 25 Palmerston Place, Edinburgh:

'What I can say for now is that the ACDC lies in an area of green gravitational waves which is a standard norm, nothing odd there. However the ACDC does lie in a positive magnetic region of around 100nT.

When it comes to unusual disturbances throughout buildings, I have noted a couple of interesting discoveries over the years. Firstly, some buildings have the capability of generating their own electromagnetic fields which are often said to have an association with paranormal encounters. This can be through the process of construction and/or design. Some buildings have an imbalance, produced by design. Such design would be as an example, large structural metal of the building frame entering into the ground in the vicinity of underground water ways, natural or man-made. Running water against metal can cause a small electrical charge over time which can build up and produce acute EMF in given locations of the building.

This is usually identifiable via building plans and that certain disturbances not only seem to take place in certain areas of the building, but go hand in hand with what is referred to as 'directly proportional phenomena'. DPP can be identified in two ways, one being the vexation cycle of those in the building witnessing phenomena having a direct association with the frequency and severity of phenomena witnessed. As an example, high vexation and high frequency/severity incidents can have a direct link, just as DPP can also be identified with high EMF signatures. The diagram below demonstrates this action.

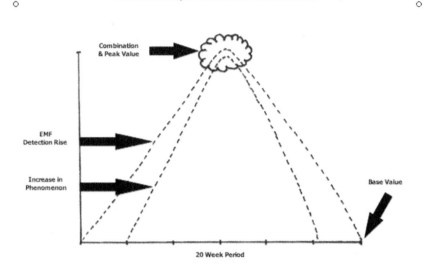

Please note: This also applies through increased vexation cycles.

I am unaware of the buildings structure and design at this time, however this may not be the case. There is also EMF fluctuations in buildings which have some construction using granite stone which over periods of time can have micro-vibrations from traffic etc causing micro crystalline structure within the granite stone to rub together and generate a micro-electric charge, which again over longer periods of time can build up and dissipate in locations where reported phenomena has been witnessed.

After eliminating the generated EMF hypothesis, then we are left with some form of possible intelligent type haunting that can interact with those in the environment from time to time. It is theorized that such phenomena does require some kind of energy input which is then collected and utilized by the phenomena.

Identifying what energy this could be can be difficult and a longer study of the environment may be necessary. Especially those interactions considered high severity and abrupt. In most incidents of such paranormal behaviour, the phenomena is theorized to be old, even dating back into ancient times within some buildings. Such phenomena can become dormant for long spells of time, occasionally gathering its energetic momentum from natural geomagnetic fields (GMF), such as underground rivers and of course Ley Lines.

It's true to state that, not only is the building in question in close proximity to Ley's but also a nearby Cathedral which are often built with large spires and heavy conducting rods into the ground below so to disperse huge amounts of electrical energy from redirected lightning strikes. At this time, any phenomena reported and experienced in the building could be the product of a number of things working together. Last but not least, there is the invocation theory. This usually comprises of actions of invocation through magical practices and other similar anti-religious acts. If such things have previously taken place, they are often below the ground level of the building, clearly away from ultra-violet contamination. This would of course require further research pertaining to the buildings ground floor or any cellars.

Please note, carrying out building alterations can cause a sudden and abrupt change in the environment causing on occasion what is referred to as the 'kick-back phenomena'. Thus giving previous phenomena a new lease of life. Caution should always be applied when carrying out significant changes in old buildings that have a long history of EMF changes.'

— Steve Mera, Paranormal Specialist

In answer to the questions posed at the beginning of this chapter; were we directed to this building because of its EMF? Or because of its proximity to the cathedral, which acts as a battery charging the earth? Is it because of the GMF and Ley Lines? Or the strong magnetic discrepancy in the basement felt by Barry Fitzgerald, which caused a 10-degree shift in the compass and made him feel disorientated? Or is it Steve's 'invocation theory' because William McEwan and others possibly dabbled in the occult in the basement, which itself might indeed hide a secret tunnel possibly to the location of Amen-Ra Temple of The Golden Dawn? Or did Iain and I stir up a 'kick-back phenomena,' when we started the refurbishment of the building?

As both Steve and Barry agree, further investigation is required. My own sense is that there are strong natural energies prevalent in this location and these energies originate underground. These earth energies seem to cross or amalgamate under this corner building which is adjacent to the cathedral (and they may well be continually charged by its proximity as a lightening conductor). The architecture of the building and in particular the grand staircase (which takes up almost half the volume of the property) seems to act as a sort of funnel for this power, concentrating it within the spiral of the stair and conducting it upwards towards the dome and outwards into the atmosphere and beyond. I can sense that this 'vortex' is sometimes spinning stronger than at other times and also that this may indeed be a portal through which Iain's Roman Soldiers and other entities could travel.

I also have a sense that this energy can be utilised by us as well as those non-physical entities and that we and they can use it for either positive or negative effect. This may well be why we were guided here – either to demonstrate the power of the non-physical and allow us to learn from it and/or to help change it into a positive force. It may also be the reason why previous occupiers of the building were guided here to this particular location and to design a building of this type because they too could use it for their purposes and they might possibly have been members of the Golden Dawn or simply experimenting with the Ouija board or magical practises where the actions of invocation have resulted in raising something from ancient times, which as Steve says has lain dormant until sufficient energy is collected and we come along as the catalyst that triggers that power.

I agree that further investigation is required.

Notes:

See further investigations in Appendix 8

Chapter 13

Where there is evil

By 2015 the Centre was well established as a Centre of excellence in the provision of mediumship training and psychic development. We had some of the best mediums in the business both from the UK and abroad working from the Centre, together with a professional and impressive line-up of speakers from the scientific and academic fields. Our reputation was known and respected internationally, and this was represented in our students who would often travel from far flung countries to attend courses at the Centre.

A regular visiting medium and tutor was the popular Tony Stockwell. Tony had previously been on TV with his own shows in both the UK and America. He was a major part of the original 'The Best of British Mediumship' tour (2005, 2006 & 2007), demonstrating in such venues as The London Palladium, The Manchester Apollo and St David's Hall Cardiff. Tony regularly worked in the USA, Spain, Holland, Germany and Australia as well as Italy, France, Denmark and Sweden, and ever since we opened, he was with us too at The Sir Arthur Conan Doyle Centre.

Tony used to come to the Centre each July – he would do a demonstration of mediumship (a psychic show) on the Friday evening and a weekend workshop of mediumship development on the Saturday and Sunday. He had been following this pattern of regular visits with us since 2012 and indeed in 2013 and 2014 he was joined by the famous American Medium, James Van Praagh, when they did a joint tour. But in 2015, he was back on his own. He arrived as usual on the Friday around lunchtime, and I picked him up from the airport. We travelled to the Centre and got him settled into the apartment. By the evening we were getting ready for his show and people were arriving early to get the best seats.

I would be the compere of the show. It was my job to welcome the audience, deliver the safety instructions and then just warm them up a little with a joke or a story before introducing the medium and explaining what he was about to do. I would normally tell the audience that if the medium wanted to speak to them i.e. give them a message from someone in the Spirit Realm then they just had to respond with a 'yes' or a 'no' or a 'don't know,' as this helped the others in the audience know if the medium was right or wrong, since they would not be able to see a nod of the head. They should not give the medium any more information than this; it was his job to give them the information. The mantra being – don't feed the medium. After doing this, I would start the applause to welcome the medium to the platform and I'd go and sit quietly to stage-left but still in sight of the audience and vice versa, just so I could step back in to wrap things up at the end or to sometimes draw the medium's attention to anyone in the audience who perhaps had their hand up to accept a message but hadn't been seen by the medium.

So, after the audience gave Tony a rousing welcome, I took my position at the corner of the stage and sat quietly watching him perform. Everything was going really well, and the audience were very responsive to his messages from Spirit and to his friendly stories and personality. Then I saw him take a step towards the audience as if just to give his next message, when he stopped stalk-still and his head slowly bowed until he was looking straight down towards his shoes. He stood like this for what seemed like an eternity but in actual fact was probably about 30 seconds. But it was a long time to stand silent with an audience out front wondering what was going on. I saw the audience staring at him and then looking towards me and then back to Tony again, as he continued to stand silent and I wondered what on earth was going on. And just at that moment, as I sat staring at him, I became aware of what seemed like a heavy, dark energy which somehow seemed to be rolling towards me across the floor from where Tony stood. As it rolled right up to me and enveloped me, it was horrible, beastly and repulsive. As I was sensing this energy, I thought no wonder this has stopped him in his tracks and just at that, he slowly raised his head and started speaking again.

'I've got a man with me and he has murdered someone – in fact he might have murdered more than one person.' He paused for a moment and then said, 'someone here has gone to a police station to report a death in a tower block in one of those industrial cities like Bradford.....' As I listened to what he was saying, I wondered if that was what I was picking up too. But I wasn't sure; it felt more sinister than that to me. Tony continued, 'He has also sexually abused children – he's a paedophile.' There was a collective gasp from the audience as he issued that last statement and he quickly followed it up by saying, 'and he *has* been reported to the police for some of these offences, but nothing happened, it didn't go any further so he's never paid the price for his crimes.'

After that you could have heard a pin drop; not a sound was heard from the audience as they waited in anticipation of what was coming next. And what should have happened next when giving out messages from those in the Spirit Realm is that someone will raise their hand to indicate that they recognise the communicator, usually as a member of their deceased family.

You're on a hiding to hell here Tony, I thought to myself as I envisioned the unlikely scenario of someone waving their hand and saying 'oh yes he's mine that paedophile chap.' It wasn't going to happen. I knew Tony was right as I too could feel the energy and it was vile, but no-one was about to claim a paedophile in a public meeting. And just as I was thinking he's talked himself into a corner, Tony pointed directly at a woman sitting in the Centre of the hall and said, 'And I want to come to that lady sitting on the aisle seat – this man connects with you.' There was another gasp from the audience as they turned in unison to follow the line of his out-stretched arm to see what the woman was going to say.

'Yes, that man is my father, and it was me who reported him to the police.'

That was not at all what anyone was expecting to hear; the audience was gripped by this most recent revelation and in their voyeurism they wanted more. Ever the professional Tony gave a few more details of a barn that connected somehow and a woman who may have fallen – or been pushed – out of a window of a high-rise flat and this may well have been one of his victims. But he quickly followed up by saying, 'this is a public meeting and so I won't go into any more detail here but you can speak to me afterwards if you want.' And then he moved on with his demonstration. It was an excellent show but of course the highlight of the evening was that enigmatic introduction to the alleged paedophile communicating from the Spirit Realm.

I asked the audience for one last round of applause to thank Tony for his demonstration and then he and I both left the stage and headed downstairs to our reception area where Tony stood to sign autographs and allow some members of the audience to take selfies with him. I watched as the recipient of his message slowly walked down the stairs. She was a very smartly dressed woman, probably in her 60's. I could see her move towards Tony and a few words were exchanged and then she left as he continued to be mobbed with fans. Our reception area was very congested but in the melee I thought I recognised her. Just then Jim and George made their way through the crowd to speak to me. 'Do you know who that is?' said Jim.

'I do recognise her. I think she comes into the Centre for something but I'm not sure what.'

'That's the woman who wrote about the Moira Anderson case. I don't know what the book is called but it's about her father.' Jim said. I was familiar with the Moira Anderson case. It concerned an 11-year-old girl who had disappeared whilst simply going to the shops for her grandmother in Coatbridge – a town on the outskirts of Glasgow – in 1957. No trace of her had ever been found. Although she disappeared before I was born, the old black and white grainy picture would often appear in the newspapers over subsequent years; each time someone disappeared, Moira's face would appear alongside the most recent disappearance. The case was also easily remembered too because she shared a name with a popular Scottish singer back in the day – no relation.

'That was supposedly her father who was communicating,' I said, 'the murderer and paedophile.'

'I can't imagine she'd want to speak to him.' Jim said.

There was further discussion between the three of us about how evidential the information coming through that evening had been and then they too left to go home as did I. When I got home, I told Iain all about what had happened and the dramatic revelation of the evening. I told him that I recognised the woman but didn't know who she was or why she came into the Centre. But I knew she did. Iain as usual had helped me manage the show earlier that evening by taking tickets at the door and making sure everyone was seated before handing over to me to be on stage with the medium; he would then go home as he had an early start back at the Centre the following morning. So, when I described the woman, he said 'I know who that is. I don't know her name, but she comes in to see Liz Hay. She's one of her clients.'

Liz was one of the therapists who worked from The Sir Arthur Conan Doyle Centre and hired one of our therapy rooms to see her clients. 'Liz was there,' I said, 'but they weren't sitting together.'

'That's who it is,' Iain said, 'I spoke to them when they arrived. They were late – they probably couldn't get seats together by that time.'

I wasn't sure if Iain had the right person or not; as we both worked different shift patterns, Iain tended to know the people who came into the Centre during the day whilst I was more familiar with those who attended in the evening. But it didn't really matter. It was what had happened during the evening that I was trying to convey to him, so I told him that Jim seemed to know who she was and that was the end of the conversation until about a week later. I came home from the Centre, and it must have been a Friday because we were off that evening and weekend (having worked through the previous weekend during the Tony Stockwell events) and there waiting for me on my kitchen table was a book, *Where There is Evil* by Sandra Brown. Clearly during the week Iain had found out – probably from Jim – about the book, it's author and had sourced it from Amazon and here it was as a present for me. I looked at it and took an instant aversion to it. I couldn't even touch it let alone pick it up.

'I got that book for you.' Iain said.

'I know Iain, but I don't want to read it.' I could feel his disappointment, especially since he had tracked it down for me. 'I just can't even contemplate reading that Iain. I'm really sorry, but I don't want it.'

I don't know why I had such a strong reaction to it; perhaps it was because I had been enveloped in the energy of the communicator on the evening of the show or perhaps it was its title. But whatever it was, I didn't want anything to do with it. The other factor at play here was that I was channelling healing each week to my aunt who was suffering from pancreatic cancer; her condition was terminal so we both knew there would be no cure. But it appeared that the healing was helping and she told me before she died that she had suffered none of the expected side-effects and this she attributed to the healing and for this she was grateful. Her name coincidently was Sandra Brown.

Iain must have put the book away because I didn't see it again until we went on holiday several months later to Mexico as usual. I was lying on a sun-lounger at the side of the pool with Iain enjoying the sunshine and the relaxation when he said, 'I've brought this book for you,' and he handed me *Where there is Evil.*

'I don't want to read that, Iain – especially on holiday when I'm trying to relax.' I didn't have the strong aversion I had felt before, probably because it had been such a long time since that evening with Tony Stockwell when I had felt that horrible energy. Also my aunt had passed several months ago too. But I just didn't feel like reading about such a subject when on my precious holiday.

'Just read the first chapter,' he said, 'and if you don't like it then don't read any more.' Clearly Iain knew exactly what he was doing as after reading the first chapter I was hooked and just couldn't put this book down. It was utterly captivating and although I'm not a mother myself I found myself feeling strongly that this should be a must-read for any parent or guardian of children. Apart from it being an incredible true story of one woman's quest for the truth, it is also very well researched and is peppered with facts about paedophilia. As I lay there on the sun lounger musing on the information I had just discovered of the percentage of the population (usually men) who will have paedophilic tendencies, I was vaguely aware of someone shouting at their child just a few feet away. As I put the book down to look to see what was going on, I saw a small child a girl of about 3 or 4 years old who had removed her swimsuit and was casually swinging it around her head whilst happily dancing around at the side of the pool completely naked. Her father was urging her to put it back on again. I found myself doing a quick calculation, that there must have been around 750 rooms in this large hotel complex, and assuming those statistics I had just read applied here too, some of those could be housing paedophiles, possibly lying around this pool. I nearly got up and put the little girl's swimsuit back on her myself.

The author Sandra Brown won the accolade of Scotswoman of the Year in 2005 and she was awarded the OBE in 2006, and she entirely deserves both. She is a remarkable woman, and I can thoroughly commend her book. But what intrigued me even more was that she used mediums in her search for answers. She details in the book her encounter with one but in early 2016 she approached me and asked about another.

'Do you think Tony Stockwell might help look for Moira's body?' referring to the girl she suspected her father had abused and murdered.

'Do you want me to ask him?' I said.

'Would you?' asked Sandra, 'what do you think he'll say?'

'Yes, I'll ask him. I know him well and if we can arrange it for when he's up here anyway then that'll make it easier and if I drive him through, he'll probably feel a bit more comfortable than going into a situation with people he doesn't know. I'm sure he'll help. Leave it with me.'

I emailed Tony outlining Sandra's request. He was working in the USA at the time but phoned me when he returned home and I remember him saying, 'Oh course I'll help. It's a mercy mission, Ann.' But Tony also asked me to check that the police had no objections to him getting involved. So, here's an excerpt from the email Sandra sent me in March 2016 in response to that question:

Hi Ann

Spoke to the DCI in charge of the Moira case and he has no problems at all re a visit to the locations near Coatbridge when Tony S is up for the Edinburgh trip. You are also more than welcome to come too, with the other person mentioned by yourself.

I have said it will be July and that should ensure a quiet spell and not interfere with any of the work being done by the forensic experts re: soil changes and digital photographs they are comparing with Ministry of Defence aerial photos from 1957.

He is keen to meet with Tony since he knows that he met with Janet Hart in Sydney recently- sister of Moira. Also because of the things that Tony commented on last July in the Centre re the Barn which was located in September and which has associations with the paedophile ring...

Thanks so much for your interest and offer to help arrange what could be a major helpful step to progress everything...!

In appreciation
Sandra

There were some interesting revelations from Sandra's email. Firstly, that Tony had met Moira's sister whilst he was in Sydney, which I didn't know. But I presumed that Sandra must have told her of the message from Tony the year before and she had followed this up when he was in Australia. Secondly, and perhaps more importantly the mention of the barn in July 2015, which Sandra tells us was actually located in the September – just a couple of months later – and has associations with the paedophile ring. It sounded like real progress was being made and I looked forward to being included in some small way with the investigation, if only as the driver.

When I confirmed to Sandra that all was confirmed for when Tony returned to us in July, she told me she too was looking forward to it as she was looking forward to meeting Tony Stockwell. She said that she had been due to meet him once before but that it hadn't actually happened.

'When was that?' I enquired.

'It was in 2006 and he was filming for his TV show, I think it was called Psychic Detective or something like that, when people were encouraged to send items in to the show which were connected with a crime so he could see what could be picked up from them. The producer kept the items and gave them to Tony, so he never knew anything about them before the cameras started rolling, and he was filming in Glasgow. I had sent him in a wee glass bottle – or what was left of it because it was a bit smashed up – and he got some really good information. I've still got a video tape of the show and I sent a transcript of it to the police because Tony said that he was sure that a dentist was involved and that was where the chloroform had come from which was used to overcome their victim. That's what was in the bottle I sent in. I was supposed to meet him afterwards, but they just ran out of time on the show and he was getting married I remember and so he had to rush for a flight, I think. So, I never got to meet him.'

'And what did the police make of what was in the video?' I asked.

'Well that's just it; they dismissed it. None of it tied up with their intel, so they ignored it for all those years. But they know now that there was a dentist involved and that's why DCI Pat Cameron is keen to meet Tony too. He is in charge of the investigation now and heads up their cold case unit and the case is part of that.'

'That's amazing. I didn't know that. I don't think Tony will know that either, that this is the continuation of something he psychome-trised[1] ten years ago.' I was just processing this new disclosure when I suddenly thought, where did the bottle come from? If the police didn't think there was a dentist involved and dismissed the information as irrelevant where did Sandra get the bottle that held the chloroform? The answer to my question is quite literally unbelievable.

There were many times in Sandra's quest for the truth and to find Moira's body when she reached a dead-end in the investigation; her fortitude is quite remarkable. But on one such occasion she decided to go and see a medium. Amongst other things the medium actually drew out a sketch of a location and told Sandra that she was aware of a scene where there was an odd-shaped little bridge over a burn and that connected to Moira. Armed with this information, Sandra returns to see the medium and this time brings her to Coatbridge. In the car en route the medium tells Sandra, 'We'll see something significant where we're going: a large, sunshine-yellow coloured card. A marker. It's a clue we'll spot ...'. From the drive around the area the medium was able to pinpoint the location of the bridge but it was behind closed gates on private land; they would have to seek permission to gain access. Once permission was granted, the medium returned once again but this time she was able to walk the site with Sandra and the landowner. And as they were looking over this strange-shaped tiny little bridge, there below them was a bright yellow plastic poster; so they had found their 'marker'. But the medium was confused. Something was not as it was in her vision. 'Where's the ditch?' the Medium asked. The landowner confirmed that there had indeed been a ditch there, but it had been filled in many years before as the land had been built up to help widen the adjacent track. She felt that they needed to look in that ditch for links to Moira's body and now it was four metres down. Remember that this incident – if indeed it was connected to the crime – would have taken place some 50 years beforehand, before the medium was born.

Never daunted Sandra managed to gain permission to be allowed to dig in that area (where the yellow 'marker' had been found) and eventually she got it. With the help of a JCB digger and driver she and her husband, Ronnie and another couple of friends watched as the digger pulled out shovel after shovel of earth from the burn bank and tipped it on to a large tarpaulin where it could be sifted through by the two friends with their spades, so they didn't miss anything. It was helpful that Ronnie was a civil engineer as the digger got so deep that the burn almost burst its banks into the newly created hole at one point.

The medium was not present at the dig but back home in Edinburgh but she phoned somehow knowing that they were near to finding something. Suddenly one of the men sifting with the spades shouted that they had found something.

'Ask him if it's a bottle,' the medium told Sandra on the other end of the phone.

Sandra shouted and the man with the spade straightened up, holding a black object, and called back. 'Yeah, he's just yelled it is a bottle.'

'Ask him if it looks like a small whisky miniature,' the medium said excitedly. 'A bottle made of green glass with a broken neck?'

The man cleaned the find with a rag, as Sandra repeated her queries and she nearly dropped the phone when he yelled, 'Yes!', then described what he had found.

'It's tiny, like a whisky miniature and it's definitely green-coloured glass.'

'You've found it! It's connected to Moira. It had chloroform in it,' the medium was relieved. 'Those men chucked it away when they first dumped her.'

Sandra carefully collected all the glass pieces that had been broken by the spade and put them in a jiffy bag and it was this that was subsequently sent to the TV Producer of Psychic Detective for Tony to psychometrise.

I thought this was an utterly incredible story when I heard it. I was accustomed to following the signs and signals from Spirit even when I didn't know why or where it would lead me – The Sir

Arthur Conan Doyle Centre is testament to this – but I'm not sure I would've had the guts to arrange for a JCB digger to dig a big hole at the side of a burn on private land in the hope of finding something from 50 years ago. Sandra Brown is a truly remarkable woman and this is just one example of her tenacity, grit and fortitude to keep going in the face of adversity to find the body of Moira Anderson and to seek some peace and justice for her remaining family. I salute her resolve unreservedly.

Tony was due back with us in Edinburgh from Friday 8th – Sunday 10th July 2016. Since the demonstration (show) was to be held as usual on the Friday night, the Saturday evening was the date agreed for us to go to Coatbridge with Sandra to help with the investigation. When Tony arrived at the Centre on the Friday lunchtime, I got him settled into the apartment and then went over the agenda for the weekend activities with him and particularly the trip to Coatbridge.

He said, 'I was with my class at the studio last night and I was telling them that we were on this mercy mission Ann, and one of the girls said, 'you'll know you're in the right place when you see the deer.'

I had to hide my smile when I heard this. Tony's London studio was where he would run his own classes and clearly here were some southerners thinking that as Tony was coming to Scotland he was going to be surrounded by whisky, tartan, heather and deer – not to mention the odd haggis. This was Coatbridge we were going to, on the outskirts of Glasgow, the major conurbation in Scotland and just a mile or so from the M8 motorway that links the central belt. It was not the Highlands. If they were hoping to see a deer, they would be sadly disappointed I thought, but decided discretion was the better part of valour and said nothing.

I had told Sandra that we would probably just leave the Centre immediately after the workshop ended for the day at 5pm and although I was intending to drive, she volunteered to come and pick us up and she also kindly offered to take us for supper afterwards.

When we got to Coatbridge, we went directly to the police station and picked up DCI Pat Cameron [pseudonym], a very fit-looking man in his 40's who was very chatty and amenable. He sat in the front passenger seat whilst Tony and I sat in the back of the car with one of his students, Carl Seaver, who had joined us. Pat had a clipboard and a file in a blue folder and said that he would not divulge any information to us but he told us that there were five locations of interest in his files and he would instruct Sandra to drive to each one so we could see what we could pick up from each. Even if we were able to prioritise these locations for him, that would help, he told us.

It was about 6.30pm by this time but it was a glorious summer evening, and the sun was splitting the bright blue skies as we headed off to the first location. At Pat's direction Sandra pulled up outside a house in what would have originally been a council-run housing estate in Coatbridge. He turned to us and pointing out a house he said, 'that's her grandmother's house,' and looked at each of us expectantly. Tony and I looked at each other and I shrugged my shoulders, as Tony shook his head. There was nothing of interest here.

'Okay,' he said, 'let's move on,' as he continued to give Sandra directions to the next location. As we drove through the town, Sandra and Pat chatted incessantly in the front of the car. They were both in good spirits and she was back in familiar territory. As we drove away from the town and out towards the countryside, he instructed Sandra to turn off the main road and down a dirt track between the fields of wheat that were swaying in the gentle breeze and were so ripe their yellow colour was almost reflecting the light of the bright sunshine. It was such a glorious setting. I wondered what on earth we were doing in the middle of a wheat field, as Sandra and Pat continued their animated conversation in the front. Tony gestured to me that he would have liked less noise but for me I quite liked the fact that they were distracted, as it meant there was no pressure from their expectations and I was happy just to ignore the chattering. As the car continued to bounce along this dirt track between the fields on this glorious summer evening, I had already decided that there was no point being in this location. But it was pleasant enough. It just seemed unlikely that there would be a body here. So, I decided just to sit back and enjoy the scenery and wait till we got to the next location. As the chatting continued in the front, the car turned the corner at the end of the fields and started down a slight slope and into a copse of trees. As we approached the bottom of the slope, I was suddenly hit by an overwhelming feeling of utter helplessness, fear that was so tangible I thought I might be sick and I was so gripped by this energy I couldn't speak because I couldn't find my voice through the emotion that was building in my throat. I looked wide-eyed with shock across at Tony and all he could do was slowly nod his head and then lower his head into his hands in his lap, equally overcome with this energy. When I eventually managed to find my voice and splutter to Sandra to stop the car, I realised we had actually driven right through this energy and out the other side. I felt fine again. Pat and Sandra turned to look back at me and Tony wondering what had just happened and why I had suddenly inter-rupted their lively conversation.

I looked at Tony to see if he too was okay and he said, 'it was back there.'

'Yes,' I said, 'back at that corner.' We both jumped out the car and started walking back along the track that we had just driven along. Since it was just a single track there was no space for the car to turn so it had to drive further on to be able to find a turning space and then drive back along the track to join us. Tony and I were already back at the corner and sensing again the energy which had gripped us so unexpectedly in the car, but we were ready for it now and I was able to verbalise this time what I was feeling. It was abject fear so strong that I knew I was going to die but was utterly power-less to do anything about it. The hopelessness was tangible.

As I relayed all these feelings to Tony, he nodded in agreement, then added, 'but she didn't die here – her body is not here.'

This surprised me as it certainly felt to me as if she was expecting to die and Tony caught my quizzical look and said, 'she was abused here, but not killed.'

I accepted this explanation – his knowledge and experience in this subject being far greater than mine - but I felt drawn further into the copse of trees. I just followed my instinct until I was standing by a river with a distinct feeling that something had been thrown into the river at that spot. But of course there was nothing to see.

We got back into the car and once again drove through this energy and out the other side. I had never experienced anything like it before: to be inside a moving vehicle that drives into energy that is so powerful it almost chokes you, until you drive out the other side. Just think how powerful those emotions must have been if that residual energy is still in place in an open-air environment more than 50 years after it happened.

We drove on to the next location and the chattering in the front had become a bit more subdued as I think subconsciously Pat and Sandra had decided they'd better keep an eye on us. But the next three locations where I think Pat had hoped he might get a result proved less interesting. Even the barn – indeed he took us to two – did not attract our attention. By now it was around 9pm and the sun was beginning to go down, so Pat directed Sandra to start to drive us back to Coatbridge for we were still out in the countryside. For my part I was still thinking about the energy we had encountered at the second location and wondering if I could perhaps find my way back there at a later date to try to sense again what had gone on there. Meanwhile, we were driving along a main road with hedges at both sides of the road and we were driving at a fair speed when suddenly Tony and I both looked at each other in the back seat of the car and I once again shouted to stop the car. The brakes were quickly applied, which forced us forward in our seats until the car came to an abrupt stop. 'I want to see over there, don't you?' Tony said to me.

'Yes, and there's a gap in the hedge back there that we just passed.'

Then we were out the car again and walking back along the road we had just driven, much as before. Pat and Sandra remained in the car and as Tony and I marched along the road I heard the car being put into reverse gear, as Sandra backed up to where we were. We got to the gap in the hedge and stepped up on to the grass verge for a closer look. There beyond the field that was adjacent to the hedge was a slight hillock and sitting on this wee hill was a farm with a barn and as we both stood silently looking at it for a moment I quietly said, 'We've got to get over there.' And I started looking for the access road to the farm, which wasn't immediately noticeable. I turned to Pat Cameron who had now got out of the car with Sandra to join us, 'We've got to get over there – how do we access that farm?' I asked him.

'You don't – well not tonight anyway.'

'It's not too late – I think the access road must be at the end of this road and up to the left.'

'I can't just turn up unannounced with a couple of civilians and walk into someone's farm. We'd have to write and ask for permission in advance.' He told me.

'But surely if we drove up there and explained the situation and just asked them, they'd be happy to help?' I suggested.

'Yes – unless they're involved.' He brought me down to earth with a bang. I hadn't thought about that. I was so focused on the energy and trying to find out what was going on the analytical part of my brain had seemingly shut down. Which is of course what you would want it to do when you're doing energy work but, in this case, I needed my wits about me.

Suddenly, Tony points and shouts out at the same time. 'Look at the deer.' And a single, solitary deer rose up from the corn field in front of us and sprang across the field and down into the copse at the far side of the field. 'You know you're in the right place when you see the deer.'

Notes

The overwhelming feeling that I had felt in the car when we drove into the energy at the bottom of the field that night has never left me; it was so overpowering that I felt compelled to go back there in the hope of finding something more to help Sandra in her quest. I was in regular contact with Tony, so asked him if he would be happy to go back again the following year as I was keen to re-visit that particular spot. He agreed that we could do this when he returned to the Sir Arthur Conan Doyle Centre, and so I asked Sandra if she would like to do this too; she was only too happy to oblige and drive us through once again.

This time there were only the three of us in the car and Sandra drove us round some other locations that she was keen to have us visit. But I waited patiently until she drove to the point of interest for me. Tony and I were ready for it this time and we did feel it in the same place. Sandra again drove through it, turned the car and then we drove back through it for a second time waiting at that location for a few moments but nothing further was gleaned whilst the car sat there in the energy. On leaving that spot, the car pulled away up the hill and as we moved off, I was suddenly aware of a strange smell. I had to think for a moment whether that was coming into the car from outside or whether it was inside the car. It was then that I realised that it was a psychic smell. 'I can smell a strange smell,' I said, 'I can taste it in my mouth – it's a sort of chemical smell.'

Sandra stopped the car on the brow of the hill. 'It's chloroform.' I suddenly realised what I was experiencing and to my surprise it was Sandra who exclaimed, 'I can smell it too.'

I remember her saying that the smell had almost filled the car.

This is just a further example of how powerful that energy was and the level of fear that was inflicted on that little girl all those years ago. In my quest to ensure that the facts given here are accurate and to provide further corroboration, I have spoken again to Sandra Brown (in 2023) and she has checked and amended this account for accuracy. Sandra is currently working on the sequel to *Where there is Evil*, which is called, *No Secret Better Kept*, and I know it will be another 'must read' for all of us involved in the case and for anyone interested in the care of a child.

Unfortunately, the body of Moira Anderson has never been found but if I know one thing about Sandra Brown she will never give up.

Testimony of Tony Stockwell

'Of the many cases I've worked on, the Moira Anderson case got under my skin – I think about her a lot. Right from the early psychometry on the pieces of glass I was handed during the filming of the TV series, I was picking things up about her that intrigued me, even although I had never heard of Moira Anderson.

Then in 2015, when making my usual visit to The Sir Arthur Conan Doyle Centre, when Ann was hosting the Dem, I became aware of a man – a murderer and paedophile from the Spirit World who wanted to communicate with a woman in the audience – this, I was later to find, was Sandra Brown, his daughter.

Ann phoned me just a few weeks afterwards and asked if I would be willing to try to help find the body of this little girl. I was glad to accept. The experience I encountered together with Ann was profound. We were both in the back of the car being driven by Sandra and with the police detective in the front. It was like driving into energetic barbed wire! It is always confirmational when someone else responds at the same moment and in the same way; it was affirming my own experience when I could see Ann reacting to the same traumatic experience.

I am still striving and hoping to be of help in this case and want it to be solved, however, this pales into insignificance compared to the work that Sandra Brown has undertaken – I have the utmost respect for her. I have made a commitment to Moira Anderson and one day, God-willing, we will find her.'

— Tony Stockwell, Medium

Chapter 14

The Group

By November 2015 my Thursday Group were heading for Malta. We had been sitting together in our own room on the top floor of The Sir Arthur Conan Doyle Centre since just before it opened in 2011. We felt at home in our own wee room, knowing that no-one else would walk in unannounced as had been the case in the Theosophical Society building; for it was quiet being at the very top of the building. We had our own keys, so we knew that the energy in the room would not be disturbed even in our absence. Evelyn, Jim's wife, had joined the Group as well as the previously mentioned George, so together with Tricia, Gill and I, we were still a group of six, despite Gordon's sad death.

Gordon was a sad loss both as a friend and as a valuable member of the Group, but he still made his presence felt from time to time, especially if healing was required as this was always his speciality. Indeed, he sometimes made his presence felt more publicly too.

Gordon had been on a long and painful journey of treatments for mouth cancer. When it was found in 2010, it was so advanced that despite some interventions allowing him some respite the prognosis was terminal. Gordon died on 25th March, 2013. Latterly, when he was moved to a hospice where I would visit him regularly, he was confined to bed and each time when I arrived I would ask him if there was anything he wanted or anything I could bring for him. His standard answer would always be, 'just bring yourself'. One day on arrival I asked again if there was anything I could get for him. 'Slippers....,' as he lifted a weak hand and pointed aimlessly. I sprang to my feet looking around the floor near his bed for his slippers. This was a lovely large room with a bay window to the back of the property with long drapes. I lifted each of the curtains individually looking underneath for these slippers – none there. I found one of his shoes – huge shoes, I thought – but strange there was only one. I continued and scanned the floor in this large room wondering where else his slippers could be. Perhaps in the bathroom. I opened the door to the en-suite but there was nothing in there. I came back out and wondered if perhaps someone had tidied them away into the wardrobe or cupboard but a search of both revealed nothing. Then Gordon's weak and wavering voice said, 'what are you doing?'

'I'm looking for your slippers,' I said.

This weary wavering hand pointed again as he said, 'They're on my feet.'

We both burst out laughing, as I realised I hadn't waited on the rest of the sentence before I had sprung into action. Gordon had wanted me to take his slippers off, as he had wanted to put his feet back under the covers. And here was I doing a sweep of the room looking for slippers that were in plain sight. We also laughed about the fact that I had found one shoe but only one. I made a joke that it was so big that a mast could be erected on it, and it could be sailed down the Clyde if the other couldn't be found. This seemingly trivial encounter would be repeated back to me a few years later when a medium doing a demonstration on the platform told me, 'I've got a man here who is your friend. His name is Gordon'.

The medium continued to say that Gordon was missing me and sending me lots of love and that he was keeping up with what I was

doing. Whilst all of that may well have been true it is always important to analyse the information coming from mediums and I was
thinking to myself that it was very well known that I had had a
friend called Gordon who had died. I was also thinking if this really
was Gordon, he would know the way I thought, and he would give
me something to confirm that it was really him.

At that moment, the medium shouted out, 'and he's holding up a
shoe – just one shoe – and it's enormous!'

Strangely enough, the first signs of Gordon's illness were discovered just before the Group was due to go to Spain together. This was
going to be our first sojourn as a group to sit together in a more
focused and intensive way by having a week-long spiritual retreat.
Now in 2015 we were headed to Malta. These trips were always
prompted by information received in the Group – usually by myself
– and it is always a source of great pride to me and appreciation of
the way the Group would have no hesitation in just following the
information received and go to wherever we were directed. We
would usually be told that we were to find something or receive
some information in a specific location, and we would just go as a
group. This time around I had been receiving information from and
about the Knights Templar and been shown Malta as somewhere we
should go to sit together. Jim had also been shown a white horse and
told we would know we were in the right place when we saw this
white horse. This type of information was usually given in advance
of our visit, as a sort of signpost to help confirm when we got there
that we were in the right place.

We flew off to Malta and checked into our hotel. We were
simply using the biggest bedroom as the room where we would sit,
and we sat together twice a day. The energy was not ideal in a
modern tourist hotel, but we made it work. Very late one evening
Tricia and I decided to sit again together as we were sharing a room
together. During the sitting I became quite overshadowed by the
presence of a Grand Master of the Templars who imparted some

important and relevant information for the Group. He then showed me some locations we were to visit in Malta, which we did and one in particular was Valetta the capital. We hired a car to access the further flung locations, but it was quite easy to travel to Valetta by bus. When we got off the bus, we found we were facing a huge line of horse-drawn carriages all waiting to take tourists on trips around this capital city. I was so focused on finding a location which had been foretold the night before that I had forgotten about Jim's prior vision until he said, 'Look at all these horses, and there's not a white one amongst the lot.'

He was clearly disappointed, but we decided to walk into the old capital city and just as we were walking towards the gates that would take us through the city walls a carriage drew up and dropped off the tourist who had obviously decided to complete their journey here rather than return to the terminus. Jim exclaimed, 'Here's the white horse – it has come to us!'

'Then we should get in it, Jim,' I said. For I realised he had received his 'sign,' as the carriage had drawn up right beside us and was drawn by the only white horse we could see. We jumped in and the driver seemed pleased that he had picked up a new fare without the need to go back to the terminus and wait his turn. Just as I was thinking that this was not a particularly evidential sign, the carriage started to make its way back towards the terminus, so I asked the driver just to stop and let us off in the city rather than go back to the city limits. When he brought the horse to a stop, we stepped out of the carriage and found that we were standing immediately outside the door to the Templar Museum, where we found the information we were looking for.

On returning home and buoyed by our success in Malta and despite it now being December, I persuaded the Group to meet up in Roslin, just in the Glen in what I called my 'natural cathedral' – in a clearing the in the trees. From childhood I had always felt this to be a magical place and I wanted the Group to feel that too. I have always been convinced that the power of Roslin originates in the Glen. As we stood in a circle in silence and tuned into the energy around us I became aware of ACD coming close to me and as he made his presence felt he let me know that he agreed with that sentiment as he too was aware of the energy in the Glen because he had visited when he was alive. I was pleased to hear his message and felt the comfort of his support which I told the Group of. Later, as usual I looked for the confirmation of this latest message – had ACD ever visited Roslin? I searched but could find no mention of it. I have a book by Brian W. Pugh, *A Chronology of the life of Sir Arthur Conan Doyle*, which is an excellent reference book, but when consulted, there was no mention of Roslin whatsoever. It is strange but I'm now quite familiar with the confirmation that I seek coming from the most unusual sources and this instance was no different. Just a few weeks later an article appeared in the Edinburgh Evening News. It was a piece about The Royal Botanic Garden in Edinburgh who had discovered in their records 'that as part of his medical degree, Conan Doyle took a summer course on Vegetable Histology and Practical Biology at the gardens.' The article finishes by stating, 'We've been able to find out that students at the time were taken on excursions to areas such as Roslin and Penicuik to collect samples.' I was so pleased to see this I phoned the Group to tell them that I had received my confirmation of his latest message. That article is reproduced in Appendix 10.

The following year in March 2016 we visited Portugal. This was due to information received in the Group by Gill, who then proceeded to source and organise our trip to Albufeira where we hired a villa by the harbour for a week. This was much better suited to sitting as a group as it was a private villa all to ourselves, so we were not disturbed by anyone. We didn't know why we were told to go there we just knew if we did that we would find out and we trusted that we would 'get something.' Again, we sat twice a day which still allowed us time for some sight-seeing in between.

One day we had sat in the morning and then decided to walk into the town just for a browse around. We walked past the harbour walls and along the promenade that seemed to be skirting old, fortified walls to the landward side and we headed for the old town. The Group walked along jovially; we had bought ice-cream cones, which we were enjoying as we strolled along the old city walls in the sunshine. Later that day we sat in circle again in the villa, when I became aware of someone from Spirit who let me know that he had been walking with us earlier in the day. This was a monk. He wore a simple brown cassock with a rope tied around his middle and he was wearing old leather sandals. I could tell that the route we had been walking was part of a path that he would have taken regularly but many years beforehand. I could see him walking down to the sea and he seemed to be talking to the sea. He held his arms up in a gesture towards the sea as if he was blessing the fish – something which I thought was most odd. I could tell that he was Portuguese, but it seemed he had travelled to other countries, particularly Italy and possibly France on some sort of pilgrimage or mission and I felt that he had come home, spiritu-ally. This was a deeply religious man. When the Group were doing their de-brief of the session, I outlined my vision to them and told them that I knew that this man was going to prayers and that part of the path that we had walked earlier in the day was a regular route he and the other monks would take to go to the chapel or some sort of place of worship. Gill sprang to her feet and picked up her iPad saying, 'Well let's look and see where he was going?'

She was looking at Google Maps and tracing the steps that we had taken that morning into town. 'Ah, there's a church marked on the map just up the hill from where we walked this morning.'

'Let me see,' I said, as I moved towards her to see the electronic map. 'No that's not it. He walked along here.' I said it with absolute certainty, as somehow I was able to point to the route he would have taken. As I did that, I was able to say, 'the church or temple he was going to would have been here,' and pointed to the location.

'That's not a church, Ann. That's a museum' Gill was looking at the graphic icons on the map.

'Well. that's where he was going, that building there.' I was aware of the monk's presence at that moment guiding my senses as I pointed to the location on the map.

'Well then, let's go and check that out tomorrow,' said Gill.

And that's what we did. The next morning Gill used her iPad to guide our walk towards the spot I had identified until we came to the museum that had been pinpointed on the map. It was Museu de Arte Sacra – The Museum of Sacred Art. I was disappointed. I felt sure I was going to find a monastery of some sort or a church or chapel where the monk would have gone to pray, not a museum. I walked around the building to the back to investigate further, as I was sure I was in the right place. It was scruffier to the back and there was some spray-painted graffiti on the walls but high up on the wall there was a painted tiled icon of St Anthony. This seemed significant, so we took a picture and as the museum was closed we headed on and into town. It was only when we got back to the villa and Gill got linked up to the internet that she read out:

The Museum of Sacred Art in the old town of Albufeira is a lovely space in the restored 18th century Chapel of San Sebastian. This hermitage was originally built in the 16th century and went through an important architectural renewal in the first half of the 18th century.

'Ah, so it was a place of worship then, after all?' I was pleased at least some of the information I had received seemed to be correct.

'And there's more.' Gill was now switching between websites and paraphrasing. 'Saint Anthony of Padua was a Portuguese Catholic priest born in Lisbon and a friar of the Franciscan Order. He was known as St Anthony who preached to the fishes.'

'You're kidding?'

'No, there's a picture of him here in his brown cassock, standing by the sea with his arms outstretched just as you said, speaking to the fish. Wikipedia says, *'The story of Anthony "preaching to the fish" originated in Rimini, where he had gone to preach. When heretics there treated him with contempt, Anthony was said to have gone to the shoreline, where he began to preach at the water's edge until a great crowd of fish was seen gathered before him. The people of the town flocked to see this marvel, after which Anthony charged them with the fact that the fish were more receptive to his message than the heretics of the church, at which point the people were moved to listen to his message.'*

'Okay,' I said gingerly, 'so the information we've been given is accurate, but it feels more like we're getting clues again to follow rather than connecting to St Anthony himself. I think the monk that I sensed was local to this area and he showed me that *he* would've taken that path to prayer but was directing me to the icon of St Anthony as a message or signpost to us. So, on that basis what's the significance of this for us?'

'It says here, there's a tradition of praying for St. Anthony's help in finding lost things and it is traced to an incident during his lifetime in Bologna. According to the story, Anthony had a book of psalms that was important to him, as it contained his notes and comments for use in teaching his students. Basically, one of the students took it either by mistake or stole it but St Anthony prayed, and it was returned. So, maybe it's about *your* book, Ann, or about finding something, maybe about where or what the Group does next?' Gill postulated.

'Or it could be about *your* students, Ann?' Tricia too was speculating.

'Do you mean to tell me that we've come all the way to Portugal to be directed towards the energy of St Anthony to help us find something – and we don't know what that is?'

'It certainly looks that way,' Tricia said.

'At least they've chosen a nice place for us to do it – nicer than Malta,' George said with tongue in cheek, as he smiled at the inspiration shown by Spirit.

Six months later, in November 2016, Gill and her husband David decided to return to the area for a holiday and during that holiday Gill too seemed to be directed by a monk from the Spirit World who was again able to influence her to follow his direction along a certain footpath. This path eventually led to a Knights Templar house and a statue of Saint Vicente known as the 'forgotten saint,' which is quite an apt title since no-one seems to know much about him. Was this our local monk who first made contact six months before and led us to the icon of St Anthony? He certainly was local; he was born in Albufeira, so that is a possibility.

The monk would remain with the Group and make his presence felt from time to time. I got the feeling that because he was local and would know this area well, he could quite easily direct us to the hermitage where he used to pray knowing that the icon of St Anthony was there and that this could be used to convey a message to us that we were to look for something or find something. As I reflected on that thought, I realised that for the five years running up to us finding the building that now was The Sir Arthur Conan Doyle Centre my Group had been totally focused on that aim – finding the building. After we had found it and got our wee room at the top of the house we had been focusing on our own work with Spirit - were we now to find something else I wondered? And if so, what could that be? It would be the end of the year before I was to get an answer to that question.

Chapter 15

People Drawn in – Arthur drawn out

2016 marked the fifth anniversary of the opening of The Sir Arthur Conan Doyle Centre, established in October 2011. It had been Arthur Conan Doyle who had directed me and my Thursday Group to find this building, warning that he could take our development no further until we had found it. We were told that we needed a room to ourselves where the Group would not be disturbed, and it was only when we had found this place that we would be able to experience further physical phenomena. As I reflected on that and thought about all the strange spontaneous phenomena that had been experienced here over these last five years, I realised that this was not what anyone in the Group had expected. The phenomena had generally taken place throughout the building rather than in the confines of our wee room and it had been experienced by others too – many unsuspecting – visitors to the building who would have had no knowledge whatsoever of this type of phenomena. I wondered whether that had been carefully orchestrated to provide independent witness to some of these happenings. Iain and I had probably experienced the most dramatic happenings, with Iain being actually bodily thrown not once but twice. Was the purpose of that just to demonstrate how powerful this energy was? And were others involved just to provide corroboration? What I was certainly sure of by now was that someone or something was in control and directing operations. There was a higher authority – a supreme intelligence that always seemed to have a master plan – and we were just catching up. All I had been doing was following the signs, the symbols or indications that I should follow a particular path. I knew that if I did that, it would bring me to the next signpost. All seemed to fall into place when I did this, whether that be the Fringe show or the Edinburgh Doors Open talk. I knew if I just followed the lead, things would work out fine. I also knew that if I deviated from the masterplan, I would end up just going round the long way to eventually end up where I should have been in the first place. This phenomenon also manifested itself in the realisation that others too were being manipulated by this higher intelligence. Indeed, I began to realise that people were being put in front of me, either just to prove this point or to provide them with something that they needed, or more often than not to provide a particular skill or service that I needed. An early example of the former was one evening when Mairi had come to visit me, after she had finished work. I was on reception duties at the Centre and most of the classes were in session in the various rooms, so the reception area was quiet as Mairi arrived. She had come to tell me that she was having to pull back from the Thursday Group as work was getting in the way. Her work place had relocated and now her journey to work was far longer, making for longer hours away from home, so she felt reluctantly she would have to withdraw from the Group. I had been driving her home from the Group meetings when I could to try to help with this dilemma but notwithstanding she had come to this painful decision. Just then, as we sat together at the reception desk, a young woman walked in and said, 'this is a lovely building.' As she raised her eyes skyward to look at the massive dome above our grand staircase, she said, 'I just want to sing for you, would that be alright?'

Not waiting for an answer – which was just as well as both Mairi and I were non-plussed by this stranger – she started singing with the most angelic voice you could imagine. As she held her head upwards looking towards the tiny stars adorning the dome, her voice seemed to echo and somehow reverberate around the staircase as if there were more than one small voice singing. It was incredible. When she finished, she just said, 'there you are – that was for you,' and walked back out the door again.

I remember Mairi saying, 'Does this happen often?'

'All the time,' I answered. Although it was the first time anyone had actually sung, I had had many experiences of people just being drawn into the building and often they didn't quite know why. There was something quite different about that girl though. She seemed to know exactly why she was here and seemed to deliver her message or achieve her mission and then simply disappeared back out the door again. At the time I just chalked it up to yet another example of this strange phenomenon that seemed to attract people into the building but when I reflected upon it, I think the messenger was for Mairi and she was getting her thanks from the Spirit Realm for all she had contributed to the Group, and much more meaning-fully than anything I could have said.

On another occasion, back in the early days when I had been thinking about how we could get our name across to the public and recognising how much we needed a P.R. campaign but couldn't afford one, a woman walked in. This time it was in the evening, when I was once again sitting at the reception desk contemplating these thoughts. She looked every inch the businesswoman, very professional and confident as she asked in a most confrontational manner what precisely we did here. As I explained to her that we were a spiritual Centre and offered a holistic approach to the mind, body, spirt, she interrupted and said, 'the problem with spiritual places is that their image is all wrong.' The woman then picked up one of our brochures and pointed to a picture of one of the mediums and said, 'look at that – that picture just sums up what the public think of Spiritualists – that they're all staring into space and away with the fairies. If you want to attract the general population, you need to appeal to them by showing pictures where it presents the mediums as normal people that people can relate to.'

I was intrigued as to how she seemed to know that my aim was to attract the general public. It was almost as if she had read my mind as I responded to her statement, 'It sounds like you have some knowledge in this field?'

'I'm a P.R. Consultant and I'm working with a firm around the corner, and I was just walking past on my way to the train station when something made me feel that I had to come in here.' As she talked I was getting the prompt from Spirit – if ever it was needed – that she had been put in front of me just when I needed it.

I challenged her. 'You obviously feel quite strongly about it – perhaps you could help us if you're just working around the corner?' She went on to explain that she was self-employed and needed to earn money for her time. She was travelling through from Glasgow each day to work with a firm around the corner but whilst she was there, she would help by reviewing some of our material and giving us some pointers on where things could be improved, which she did. And each time something like this would happen I would just say a silent thank you to the Spirit Realm.

The man with the wee dog

Another example was during our first Christmas in the Centre, after the grand opening when all the frenetic activity had settled down and everything was quiet on the run up to Christmas. I believe I might also have been put to the test – the first of many.

It was just a few days before Christmas; and so most activities around the Centre had already closed. The yoga classes were closed, the church had stopped meeting until the new year and even the resident artists seemed to be too busy with Christmas preparation to come into the Centre. But I kept the door open for as long as possible hoping to encourage people in and late one morning a large burly man walked in. He had a wee dog with him on a lead, a terrier of some sort. He carried a holdall with him, and I thought he might have been looking for the West End Hotel just a couple of doors further along the street. He approached the desk and asked, 'Are you the woman who runs this place?'

'Yes, I am – how can I help you?'

'Then you're the woman I'm looking for,' he said, which made me feel a bit apprehensive since I was in the building on my own.

He said, 'I was told that you could help explain things to me.'

'Okay,' I said hesitantly, 'what is it that I've to explain?'

'Can I show you something on my phone?' he asked, and then proceeded to show me a number of pictures and videos of orbs. The footage was very impressive and most unusual as they seemed to start outside and be shot against the night sky, but the trajectory of the orbs flew into what seemed to be a barn where they circled around inside. I gave him a brief and balanced explanation of the two differing trains of thought as far as orbs are concerned stating that some believe they are Spirit entities, and some believe they are specs of dust that the digital camera picks up. I also suggested that if he had a genuine interest in such things then he could attend our lecture programme or indeed that of the SSPR in Glasgow, and I gave him their contact details.

'I call them Spirit lights and they're real because they speak to me, and I speak back. It was they who told me to come here and find you – that's why I'm here.'

Getting worried now I enquired, 'and why are you here?'

What he told me amazed me and disturbed me in equal measure. He said that he was a farm labourer in Angus, in the north-east of Scotland. He was actually a welder by trade and did some welding on the farm but generally helped with the livestock. He told me that there were horses on the farm and that the farmer ill-treated them so much that several had died, and the farmer had ordered him to dig a hole using the tractor shovel and bury the horses so the neglect would not be discovered. He told me that this had disturbed him greatly as he was very fond of the horses as he worked with them. He also told me that prior to this he had become more and more aware of something in the night sky. He lived in a converted stable on the farm and so he could open the half-door of the stable and look up at the sky. He then found that the Spirit lights he was seeing would come down from the sky and come towards him, eventually they came right into the stable, which he had shown me on his video. He had been scared initially but then found they could communicate with him – in his head he told me – and that he could speak back.

'What did they say?' I asked.

He told me that he was very unhappy about being on this farm because the farmer was so cruel to the animals, and he really felt close to the animals; he felt he could speak to them too. But he didn't know what to do to get out of the situation as this was his job, his only income and his home, since he had nowhere else to go. 'So, I asked the Spirit lights what to do and they told me that I needed to leave and go to Edinburgh and find the woman who runs the big building that they showed me in my head – and that's you,' he said. 'They showed me where it was, and I knew I had to get off the train at the first station in Edinburgh [Haymarket Station] to be able to find it and not the main station [Waverley Station].'

'Do you mean to tell me that you've packed up everything left your job and your home to come here?'

'Well, there wasn't much to pack up,' he said, 'just what I've got in my bag and Archie,' as he indicated the wee dog that was sitting patiently, as if listening to his every word – as I was.

I was shocked and concerned at what he had just told me and whilst I could happily discuss the orbs he had been seeing, I could not think how I could possibly be of any help to him in finding a home and a job. 'I'm not sure what I can do to help you,' I said.

'I need to find a job,' he said, 'and I want to work with horses. I love horses.'

I explained to him that this was Edinburgh's West End and there were neither farms nor horses around here but what he did need was somewhere to stay the night and this should be his first priority. I suggested that he go to one of the hostels to secure accommodation for tonight before he did anything else. I gave him directions to places to try and to social services since he was now homeless. I said we could chat further once we knew he had somewhere to stay. He said he would come back and let me know how he got on. And with that he strode back out the door.

I felt somehow responsible for this man who had packed up his worldly possessions and got on a train to Edinburgh to a place he'd never been to before. I knew he was seeing Spirit and like me was following their lead but I could not think why he was here when what he really needed was a place to stay and a job on a farm with horses. So, why send him here? I pacified myself with the notion that social services would find him somewhere to stay and if not, there were a number of hostels in Edinburgh that were cheap where he could find a bed. He'd be fine.

Later that evening, he strode back in through the door.

'Did you find somewhere to stay?'

'No. I went to all the places you said and there were a few that offered me a bed but none that would take Archie – they have a policy of no dogs - and I'm not leaving him. I can't take a bed and leave him out in the cold. One place said I could hand him in to the cat and dog home but I'm not doing that.'

'What will you do? I asked.

'I'll find somewhere.'

He sat at the reception desk and spoke to me for the rest of the evening whilst I brought him cups of tea and something to eat from our tearoom, as well as something for wee Archie. As the evening wore on, I knew I'd have to ask him to leave and this worried me. I contemplated letting him stay in the Centre and then realised it was not my building to offer this option to, and to someone I didn't know. I knew our insurance would be null and void if anything happened and it was later discovered that I had willingly handed over possession of the building to a stranger.

Iain arrived to pick me up that night and the man I now knew as Bill [pseudonym] and his wee dog Archie walked out into the darkness. After I locked up the building and got into the car, we drove along Palmerston Place and there I saw Bill preparing to lie on a park bench on the pavement outside the Cathedral. As we drove past, I asked Iain to stop so we could pick them up.

'What are you going to do with him?' Iain asked.

'I was going to let him stay in the Centre but I thought I'd better not, but we could take him home with us.'

'So, you thought you'd better not let him stay in the Centre but it's okay for him to come and stay in our house?' Iain said with surprise. 'We don't know who he is. He could be conning you. He could be a criminal – you don't know. There's plenty of places for him to stay in Edinburgh; he came here of his own accord. It was his choice.'

By the time Iain had finished speaking, we had driven past the man and his dog and through the traffic lights and were en route home. I felt guilty and worried for Bill. It was December, the temperature was already dropping and could well be below freezing that night. I was beginning to wonder if I was being tested – this had all the hallmarks of *there's no room at the inn* – and it was almost Christmas. What could I do? I silently asked for help.

When I had reluctantly asked Bill to leave the building that night, I had also stressed to him that he should come back the following morning, telling him I'd be opening up at 9am. So, I was pleased and more than slightly relieved when he walked back through the door. I got him some hot coffee and something to eat and we sat in the tearoom to chat again. He started to show me more pictures on his phone but this time they were of his art. Not only did he sketch horses, but he made sculptures in metal using his welding skills – a bit like the Kelpies in Falkirk - they were amazing. But I stressed again that he really needed to find somewhere to stay and that sleeping rough on Edinburgh's Streets in December was not the best plan. He told me that he had found a shop doorway the previous night as the bench outside the Cathedral was too cold and that Archie had kept him warm. We searched out a number of options using the internet, made a few phone calls to check that they had availability and would accept dogs and Bill was off again this time hopefully to check in. Although I hadn't told him, I had decided if he came back again not having found somewhere to stay that I would call my fellow trustees and tell them that someone was going to be staying in the building. As it turned out, this was not necessary.

Later that same day I took a phone call from a young woman who said that she and her friend wanted to buy each other a private sitting with a medium as a Christmas present and she wondered if we could fit them both in that day as they were finishing work early for the Christmas break and wanted a sitting if possible before Christmas, as they thought it would be too difficult for them both to find time to attend together afterwards. As it was really quiet at the Centre, I said I would see them that afternoon.

I did not normally speak to my sitters before they arrived for their sitting. I had set up procedures in the Centre to ensure that none of our mediums would get information on their sitters before-hand but because I was on my own, I had answered the phone. And from the brief telephone conversation it sounded like a couple of work colleagues who had decided to have some fun before the Christmas break, in the same way you would go to the pub or a karaoke. I generally don't like sittings such as these. I felt that communication with the Spirit World deserved more respect than this. However, when the women arrived, they were very respectful and I got the initial impression that they were both in need of something from their sittings. So, I took the first lady into the library whilst asking the other to have a seat in the reception area. I cannot remember anything of this sitting but when they swapped over, and the second lady entered the library and sat in front of me, I immediately saw horses and what appeared to be a ring, a trotting ring with fences and riders on horse-back.

'Do you have something to do with horses and teaching people to ride?'

'Yes,' she said, 'I have a small-holding where we keep horses and I offer riding lessons to disabled children – that's right,' she said.

'Okay, then I'm going to give you your sitting and afterwards I'm going to speak to you about that, as I feel you're here for a reason and if I'm right then everything will fall into place and check out. And if not, you can just ignore me,' I said.

'You know, I knew something like this would happen. I didn't really want a sitting, but my friend wanted one – needed one – so I said I'd come along too just to keep her company. But I knew there was a reason behind me being here too.'

At the end of the session, I asked if by any chance she was looking for a chargehand – someone to work for her. Amazingly, she told me that someone had just left her employ to travel abroad and she had been left in the lurch with the horses to look after.

'It is difficult to find people who will do this work – it's hard work – and it's only basic pay, so you really need to love horses to be able to do it,' she said, almost repeating what Bill had said earlier.

Okay, here goes I thought. 'I know someone who is looking for this type of work, who loves horses. He is also a welder, and he does these amazing sculptures of horses too but at the moment he needs to find somewhere to stay. So, I've sent him to try to find a hostel for the night in Edinburgh – where is your place?' I asked.

'I'm in West Lothian,' she said, 'and I've got an old static caravan on site – he can stay there – and I've got a workshop he can use for his sculpting, that would be interesting to see.'

There was one more element to put to her, 'he's got a wee dog?'

'That's okay – the kids would love that.'

'Here's my contact details – get him to give me a ring,' and I could feel the sense of accomplishment rising in her as she reunited with her friend and they both strode out the building, looking and feeling as if they had both achieved something. Maybe they had. I, on the other hand, was left once again with a sense of wonderment at how these things happen and then just seem to fall into place and with little intervention on my part. I'm just the conduit who joins the dots.

I texted Bill with the details and left it with him. During the Christmas break I wondered about him, about where he was and what he was doing and then a few weeks into the New Year he strode back into the building with wee Archie by his side as usual. Bill was sporting a new jacket and he looked like he had a new sense of pride and purpose in his demeanour. He had got the job, moved into the caravan with Archie and was now back enjoying his artwork in the workshop. He even told me that they were planning on displaying and hopefully selling some of his works there. Later, when he returned to see me again, he told me that he had been commissioned by the Royal Highland Show to do a piece of sculpture for their showpiece. Amazing.

Prof. Gary Schwartz

I was already very well aware since opening The Centre of how things would just fall into place. I didn't have to try too hard; I just had to be alert to the signals and follow the signs. I had watched as John Martin, Chairman of the Scottish Brewing Archive had been in the audience during our first Doors Open event, which resulted in him bringing his organisation into the Centre but also an introduction to McEwan's Beer Company, which in turn meant that the next Doors Open Day was held as a joint event at which they offered free beer. They also launched a new beer and did a beer-tasting evening with us; all of which just helped our name-awareness, our credibility and in being more accepted in the mainstream.

Bob Stek, Research Associate from University of Arizona, appeared in the audience of my first Fringe show and I knew when he mentioned that he had worked alongside Prof. Gary Schwartz that Bob had been put in front of me for a reason and that sooner or later I'd be connecting in some capacity with Gary. Bob returned to the Centre the following year to run his show alongside mine. His talk was about Harry Houdini and his relationship with Arthur Conan Doyle. Bob has continued to visit the Centre over subsequent years and to attend our talks on-line from the U.S. He has introduced me to Gary Schwartz, Professor of Psychology, Medicine, Neurology, Psychiatry, and Surgery, and Director of the Laboratory for Advances in Consciousness also at University of Arizona. Gary has published more than 500 scientific papers, including six papers in the journal Science, co-edited 16 academic books, and is the author of 12 books, but he is most famous for the Soul Phone[1] – following Thomas Edison's attempt to invent a phone to call those in the Spirit Realm. And I'm pleased to say he too is now a speaker at The Sir Arthur Conan Doyle Centre, and has generously written the foreword to this book.

There were other examples of people being drawn into the building to help, which were none the less surprising and there seemed to be a theme materialising to do with books. This started in 2015 when I was contacted by various newspapers asking for comment because a new Sherlock Holmes story had been discovered which no-one had known existed until now. It was a short story of Arthur Conan Doyle's and it had been found in someone's attic in Selkirk in the Scottish borders. It had been written in 1904 and lain undiscovered until now. It was found by a retired gentleman who said it had probably been in his attic for the last 50 years. The story was called, *Sherlock Holmes: Discovering the Border Burghs and, by deduction, the Brig Bazaar*. The bridge in Selkirk had been swept away in the floods of 1902 and two years later the town held a bazaar to raise funds to replace the bridge. Arthur Conan Doyle opened the bazaar and contributed this short story. I was able to tell the newspapers that he enjoyed being in the Borders and that in 1906 he ran for a seat in Parliament in nearby Hawick, the market town, but just like his campaign in Edinburgh he was unsuccessful there too. For photos of the press coverages see Appendix 10.

Rev. Stewart Lamont

Just a couple of months afterwards, one afternoon in mid-summer, a man walked into the Centre. He was a big man, tall, very well spoken with a refined west of Scotland accent. He told me that he was re-locating from Broughty Ferry in Angus to Edinburgh and as he was down-sizing he wondered if we would like his books for our library. He told me he was retiring as a Church of Scotland minister. I couldn't imagine why a Church of Scotland minister would choose to walk into our building. I was well aware of the hostility Spiritualism seemed to engender in the mainstream religions but nonetheless here he was. When I enquired why he should not choose to donate his books to the Church of Scotland he told me, 'They'll not want them – these are books on the paranormal'.

Now that *was* interesting, and I had to find out more. It turned out that this man had been interested in the paranormal all of his adult life. He had been a broadcaster and journalist specialising in religious affairs. He had worked for the BBC as a radio producer and as a freelancer producing both radio and TV programmes and as a correspondent for the Glasgow Herald newspaper and for the Sunday Times. He was an author of several books including an exposé of Scientology but best of all he had written the book and was the producer of the TV programme based on the Enfield Poltergeist called 'Is Anybody there?'

I couldn't believe it. The Enfield Poltergeist is one of the best documented and evidential reporting of poltergeist activity anywhere in the world and here in front of me was the man who had reported on it – and filmed it – whilst it was happening. It is at these moments that you recognise instantly that it is by no accident that he was standing here before me.

Rev Stewart Lamont not only donated his books to us, but the following year he took over from Archie Lawrie as Head of our Psychical Investigation Unit. (Archie was finding it increasingly difficult to travel to the Centre from Fife where he lived and was caring for his wife.) I quickly recruited Stewart, firstly to give a talk about the famed Enfield Poltergeist – from someone who was there – and then as a Trustee of The Sir Arthur Conan Doyle Centre.

See Appendix 11 for press coverage of Stewart's appointment.

My own religious background is also Church of Scotland, so I was familiar with Stewart's religion. One afternoon I had a casual conversation with Stewart when I told him about our first Christmas at the Centre in 2011. I had handed in Christmas Cards to our near neighbours and fellow churches in the same street – St Mary's Cathedral and the Church of Scotland. I told him how badly I had been treated by one whilst the other just ignored me completely when I extended a hand of friendship towards them both and intro-duced myself as the new neighbour on the street. I told him my naive thought that we might at some future stage collaborate, perhaps even attending each other's services, a bit like interfaith meetings but on a smaller scale. –My hope was that we would explore the similarities that exist across the three different faiths.

'I can do that,' Stewart said immediately.

'Oh, I don't' think so – and even if you can, I don't think you should. They'll just turn against us even more.' I pleaded.

'You just leave it with me,' he said.

I was concerned. I had long since given up hope of any mutual respect from our near neighbours and fellow churches and was happy just to let them be. But I was concerned that Stewart would damage his own reputation with the church if he tried to intervene on my behalf since he was still getting locum work from the Church of Scotland. I stressed to him that I had given up on this vague notion and it didn't really matter but he seemed undeterred. The following year (2016) he came to tell me that he was planning to put together an evening event, similar to Question Time on the TV. He said he had lined up representatives from the Church of Scotland, the Episcopal Church and the Catholic Church. He was going to be taking on the role of Robin Day, bow tie and all – although that was a dated reference I knew exactly what he meant.

'I've got the top man from the Church of Scotland,' he said, 'the moderator of the General Assembly, the Rt Rev Dr Derek Browning; the Vice Provost of St Mary's Episcopal Cathedral, Rev Canon John McLuckie and the Very Rev Monsignor Philip Kerr, Parish Priest of St Patrick's Parish in the Cowgate in Edinburgh.'

'Wow, what I line up,' I said, 'I'll have to get one of our heavy weights to represent Spiritualism.' I was thinking perhaps of David Bruton the President of the SNU or perhaps one of the other Minister/Mediums from Scotland, maybe Janet Parker.

But Stewart said, 'No, it has to be you.'

'Me, oh no I don't think so, Stewart. I can't be on a panel with those guys, we need someone who has more of the religious credentials behind them and I don't.'

'It was your idea,' he said, 'and what's more I've told them it'll be you on the panel.' I could tell there was no arguing with Stewart. He had done all this work in following up one of my earlier suggestions and now he had pulled it together, he wasn't in the mood to consider any shrinking violets.

I've never considered myself a shrinking violet and I don't think anyone else who knows me would attribute that description to me either, but I've never been so nervous of an event ever. I felt that they all had their scriptures to rely on and to provide answers from; I was simply speaking from experience. But it went down a storm. We were sold out almost instantly and had a waiting list for tickets. There was standing room only in our ante-room adjacent to the main function room and it had only been opened to aid the flow of air since we were so busy. It was now populated by our volunteers, therapists and others who were working in the Centre who wanted to see and hear this event. It was great to see that the paying audience was mainly new to the Centre, so they had clearly come from these other religions and were interested to hear this debate; thus addressing the main aim of my initiative from the very start.

I was most grateful to all my fellow panel members for attending this event and would again extend my appreciation to them, for I know that some ran the gauntlet of their own religions in doing so. I am a firm believer that the tenet of most mainstream religions shares the same philosophy; they all believe in life after death, in some form or another, and so it is important to explore our similarities rather than what divides us.

Although as it turned out the most searching questions were put to my panel members – and clearly by some of their own members – it was an excellent evening. It was peppered with some laughter and some anecdotes, which all led to making the evening light-hearted although with a deeper meaning and mission. Stewart made an excellent Robin Day, so he too deserves much praise for pulling the whole thing together. I do hope we can do it again sometime, although Stewart resigned as a Trustee in 2018 to go and live in France. I wish him well.

See Appendix 12 for more details of Question Time.

Statement from Stewart Lamont:

'Reflecting on my experience as a Trustee, I regret that there continues to be such a divide between conventional religions and what is roughly called 'New Age'. Much of what goes on at ACD could come under the latter heading.

The 'Old Age' has proved itself unable to cater for some of the new spiritualities that appeal to people who in past generations would have been loyal church members. One response is to see New Age stuff as 'of the devil' and another that most of the people who embrace it are a bit kookie. Certainly, many aspects are not my cup of tea (or tea leaves!), such as crystals, but those who practise clairvoyance or mediumship are dealing with issues which all of us will face when we die, as we all will. It seems to me that facing our mortality is THE most important issue, and many simply never get round to it. Yet if death snuffs out our brief candle, and there is nothing beyond, not much is left that gives meaning to the lives of many people.

I was frustrated at our Question Time that the churchmen guests were rather waffly when it came to survival of death. For me, it is a mystery. We will not have arms and legs and look the same as humanoids, or even have the same personality traits but we should be open to evidence when we can acquire it, which will settle the question.

Sadly, many of the 'cases' the Investigations team looked at belonged more to the realm of mental illness than psychic research. The bit of Trustee work I enjoyed best was organising the Tuesday Talks at ACD, which brought a wide variety of thinking and evidence to the wide variety of normal people who frequent the place. That is one of its strengths, bringing together honest enquirers rather than a society of odd balls. ACD alas does not own the property in which the Centre is housed and hopefully the Spiritualist church body which does, will continue to promote that inclusive attitude.'

— Rev. Stewart Lamont, Retired Trustee of The Sir
Arthur Conan Doyle Centre, Edinburgh

In a strange coincidence, David Lorimer, Programme Director of the Scientific and Medical Network and former President of the Wrekin Trust and the Swedenborg Society, had previously spoken at the Centre a couple of times over the previous years. And as he too was moving to France, he contacted me and asked if we would like his books as a donation to the Centre's library. Amongst a varied collection of authors on related subjects, he also donated a comprehensive collection of SPR journals which we were grateful to receive and which are now safely in our library. Thank you, David. And it was Stewart who collected the books from David on our behalf – thank you again Stewart.

2015/16 certainly was the year for books. Another such example is taken from the testimony of Hong Kong Solicitor, Hector McLeod (referred to in Chapter 8). What it does not say is that when he and his wife came to see me concerned for their son Ruairidh is that Hector's wife Rongrong spontaneously offered to translate my first book, Arthur and me into Chinese, even though I hadn't written it yet. [That book was published in 2021].

A Lady

Yet another strange synchronicity happened that year when an elderly lady walked in one Sunday afternoon. I was on my own. The church service had taken place that morning followed by the healing service, and everyone had left the building. I must have been catching up on paperwork whilst it was quiet and as always keeping our door open as often and as long as possible to encourage people in. This woman looked to be in her late 70's or early 80's but was very sprightly and very well-dressed with her handbag and pearls. In a very cultured accent, she asked if our café was open. She said she had just come from the cathedral and wondered if she could have a cup of tea. My immediate thought was that this lady had no idea where she had just stepped into – especially since she had just left the cathedral – but she just wanted a cup of tea. I had been about to close the door and go home but I told myself this is why you kept the door open, so people can just walk in. So, I showed her into the tearoom, gave her a seat next to the window and went behind the counter to get her tea and since there was some cake left from the church teas earlier I brought her a little portion on a side plate. We served our tea in bone-china cups and saucers together with little individual teapots and side plates; she seemed genuinely delighted with this and asked how much she owed me. 'Nothing,' I said, I was just about to close, so she was welcome to a free cup of tea and cake. She seemed keen to talk and surprising to me, she actually knew that we were a spiritual Centre and felt perfectly comfortable and unfazed by the fact she had walked in here on her own. She was talking about the service she had just attended at the Episcopalian cathedral and went on to start reminiscing about earlier times and referred to her friend, Patty Burgess and to Father Roland. I immediately knew who she was talking about and said so, 'That's Canon Roland Walls,' I said, 'of Roslin Chapel?'

'Yes,' she said, wondering how on earth I could possibly know who she was speaking about.

'He became a monk and lived rough – she lived with him – she was a nun and there was someone else, but I can't remember his name,' I added.

'John Halsey,' she said, 'how do you know them?'

'That's where I'm from. I went to school in Roslin, and I remember they used to live in this tin hut on Manse Road. I used to walk past it when I went to play badminton at the East Church Hall, which was also the Boys Brigade Hall. When I was just a girl, I remember he used to attend the bible study class that my Mum and Dad attended in Bilston– I used to think he was a tramp. He used to cycle around on an old bicycle and latterly he wore a canvas cassock tied at the waist with a piece of old rope.'

'Yes, she said, that sounds like him – and her.'

We hit it off, she and I, as we both recognised that we had a shared – if somewhat peculiar – connection. It prompted me to cast my mind back to this time and I particularly remembered his bare feet and open sandals. Roslin is about 700 feet above sea level, so in other words it's cold. I remember as a child we always had snow when no-one else had, so it was not the place for bare feet. She brought me back from my trip down memory lane.

'What's your name,' she asked, 'I'll pop in again and see you.'

'Ann Treherne,' I said.

'Ann...?' as she struggled with my last name, as most people do.

'Just Ann will do – they know who I am here, if you just ask for Ann.'

'I'll remember that,' she said, 'because I'm Ann too.'

'Well, so will I,' I said.

'Are you Ann with an 'e'?' she asked.

'No, just plain Jane,' which was my normal response to this question.

She smiled at this and said, 'me too.'

What I was later to find out was there was nothing plain about this lady at all – and she was a lady. She popped back in a couple of times and on one occasion said that she was reluctantly having to sell her house in Edinburgh and move to be nearer her sons who were both in England, and asked if I would like some of her collection of books for our library as she couldn't take them all with her as there were far too many.

'Would you not prefer to offer them to the cathedral?' I asked 'You see we only take spiritual books here.'

'And that's exactly what they are,' she said almost indignantly, 'they're not the sort of books the cathedral would have.'

I was truly surprised by this. I was still under the impression that she wasn't fully aware of what we did here – how wrong was I –but I thanked her, nonetheless. She said I should phone her to arrange to come and collect the books from her house in Dublin Street and she gave me her phone number and her last name – Ann Clyde.

When I called the number later in the week and asked to speak to Ann Clyde the person on the phone said, 'Lady Clyde is not available just now, may I take a message?' Lady Clyde – this was the first time I realised that this lovely lady was indeed just that – a lady.

I was later to find out that she was married to Lord Clyde, a judge in the Scottish law courts. He was made a life peer in 1996 with the title Baron Clyde of Briglands. He served in many positions during his career – Director of Edinburgh Academy, Governor of Napier University and Vice-President of the Royal Blind Asylum, until his death in 2009. But he is probably best known for chairing the Orkney child abuse enquiry in 1992.

When I phoned back later, a familiar voice answered the phone. 'Hi, Ann, so Lady Clyde wants you have her books, she tells me?'

'Loretta?'

'Yes, it's me.'

I knew Loretta as someone who would attend various events and workshops at the Centre. She was a qualified nurse and midwife.

'What are you doing there?'

'I met Lord Clyde when he was going into hospital for an operation a few years ago and I was to provide the aftercare at home as a private nurse. And I've just kept up with Lady Clyde, Ann, since then and she's very into the spiritual stuff, so we talk quite a lot about it.' Loretta told me.

'Yes, I'm now finding that out. I thought they would be religious books that she might want to donate to the cathedral, but she says no.'

'No, they're definitely for you, Ann. But there's lots of them, so when you come to collect them you'll need to bring your car. At the moment, we're going through them one by one because she's reluctant to part with any of them but knows they can't all go with her to England – where her son is.'

'Okay, well you just tell me when I've to come and I'll come. I don't want to put any pressure on her. It'll be a sensitive time for her leaving her home and her possessions to go somewhere new. Just you phone me, if and when you have any books you want me to collect. And if not, that's okay too. I understand. She's a lovely lady.'

Loretta agreed. She was indeed a lovely lady and Loretta was helping her make up her mind which books she would take with her and which would go to The Sir Arthur Conan Doyle Centre for our library. I got a call a couple of weeks later from Loretta who was clearly back at Dublin Street, and she told me the books had been boxed up and were ready to collect but that when I did so I was to park the car and plan to spend some time here as Lady Clyde wanted to speak to me. I agreed. I was happy to do that. I suspected she probably wanted some reassurance that her books would be properly cared for, documented and stored in our library. Again, I was wrong.

I parked up in Dublin Street and rang the doorbell. I was invited in by the housekeeper, Alison. This was a very impressive town house over about three floors but clearly a cosy family home. I was shown into the drawing-room where Lady Clyde and Loretta sat amongst piles of books some in boxes and some just in various piles on the floor.

'These are for you Ann,' Loretta said, as she pointed out the boxes that had been placed along one side of the room near the window. 'But come and sit down for a moment. Lady Clyde wants to speak to you.'

I thanked Lady Clyde for the books, telling her that I'd send an official acknowledgement from the Sir Arthur Conan Doyle Centre once I got back to the Centre. I sat down and Lady Clyde asked Alison to get us all some tea and we had some general chit chat about what a lovely house and garden it was and how sorry she was to be leaving it. But what she said next was totally unexpected.

'I'm 82 now and I want to leave a legacy, something lasting, something spiritual. I want to give you Shiel to use for spiritual work and as a healing sanctuary.'

'What is Shiel?' I asked.

Ann Clyde turned to Loretta and said, 'Oh we must take Ann there – she must visit and see it for herself.' She went on, 'it is the most wonderful place, wonderful energy, the flowers, the trees – it's just so perfect.' Her face seemed to light up as she spoke. She continued to tell me it was the family home in Kinross-shire which had been built on the land of Briglands, the original family seat which had had to be sold to pay death duties when the previous Lord Clyde had died. And so they had built a new house in the grounds. This was Shiel. I was quite overcome; I had just gone along to collect books.

Lady Clyde continued, 'Loretta tells me that you used to be in finance and so you know how to manage money and that you refurbished the building that is now the Arthur Conan Doyle Centre so you know how to manage property and you've created a successful spiritual Centre in Edinburgh from scratch and that you are Chairman of the charity that runs it – so you're the right person to bequeath Shiel to.'

She had obviously done her homework. This was no spur of the moment decision; it had clearly been considered long before I had been brought into the equation. I was impressed with her thoroughness.

Strange, but although this was excellent news, I didn't have the inclination to celebrate this most generous of donations. I was already aware from the earlier conversation that she had two sons, one whom she was relocating to live beside and another that worked in London. What would they make of their mother's desire to give away the family home? I said nothing of my concern but instead looked forward to seeing this special place in Kinross-shire. And it really was a special place. A date was set for the visit, and I was to pick up both Loretta and Ann at Dublin Street. But when I arrived, Ann had been having trouble with her back and decided it was too far for her to sit in the car. She handed the keys to Loretta with directions and access instructions and then stood on her doorstep happily waving us off.

In a little secluded part of Glen Devon, I found Shiel. I drove into the drive and Loretta opened the front door and we stepped into the house. It was a fairly modern house, with a nice hallway and stair. But when we walked into the lounge it was the view of the garden which drew my attention and the land that seemed to stretch outwards into fields, where sheep were quietly grazing. It had an amazing feel. And whenever I stepped into the place, I just seemed even more eager to be outside in the garden. We walked through the large kitchen/diner and out through a conservatory to the garden. It was just magical, full of little nooks and niches, with a Japanese garden complete with bridge over a fishpond. There were rhododendron and azalea bushes in full bloom, which added to the beauty of the garden. But what surprised me most as I walked around the grounds was finding a sweat lodge[2] and then a labyrinth.

'How are these here?' I asked Loretta. I wondered if Lady Clyde had perhaps offered this place to someone else who previously tried to create a spiritual Centre and perhaps given up as they both looked a little overgrown.

'Ann's friend, Rosy is allowed to use the land for Shamanic Retreats, and it was she who built the sweat lodge. She still uses it from time to time.'

'That's good news,' I said, 'it means that her wishes have already been established in some small way. It means her family will already be aware of her intentions, perhaps also her desire to leave her legacy in this way. So, it might not be so much of a shock to them?'

'Yes, I think that's right, and Ann's been into this esoteric stuff long before anyone else. She qualified as a bereavement counsellor years ago and was right into alternative therapies and different healing modalities, so they'll be well aware of her views,' said Loretta.

'And the Labyrinth? Did the Shamanic people create that too?' I asked.

'No, it was James who built that.'

'Really? The judge? Lord Clyde – he built this?' I wasn't expecting that answer.

'And in one weekend, I'm led to believe,' stated Loretta.

'So, he must have been into the spiritual stuff too?' I asked.

'Yes, if you just take a look at their books upstairs in their book-shelves, you'll see what they were into. This place was their 'get away from it all' place, so this is where they would both read those books on healing, homeopathic remedies and other esoteric stuff – and yes James would too.'

I confided in Loretta that my only knowledge of Lord Clyde was that he was the judge who handled the Orkney child abuse inquiry into the scandal, and I was very familiar with it as I had worked in Orkney. I was a regional manager at the time and one of the branches I was responsible for was in Kirkwall, Orkney and I would visit three or four times a year. I remembered the TV crews being there as they covered this most unfortunate and traumatic of cases. It was most incongruous to think of the same man who could sit in judgement over these gruesome details to be sensitive enough to be aware of the subtle energies that govern our wellbeing, healing and spiritual connectedness. As if picking up on my quandary Loretta said, 'Why don't we sit while we're here?'

What she meant was for us to sit in this energy and just extend our sense to see what happens and what we might pick up. We moved back into the conservatory and set up a couple of comfy chairs facing each other, and just sat there in the quiet of this beautiful place. What I remember of that session was first becoming aware of Arthur Conan Doyle, but this was a regular occurrence for me by then and he would just make a brief appearance to let me know that he was around. I then saw a man and he just came close enough to allow me to feel his spirit, his character, his true self, and I realised this must have been James just letting me know what he was really like, a bit different to the persona that was presented to the world. He was nice. I liked him. Then there was another I became aware of; in my vision, this man was much more formal and more distant but he showed me that he was a judge too. I was shown a scene of what appeared to be the old Queen Mary and King George who appeared to be in Edinburgh and were standing outside on a pavement with a lot of people around them. I wasn't sure what significance that had to us being here at Shiel, but it didn't matter. It was clear the place was most conducive to sitting for Spirit.

When we returned from our meditative state it seemed Loretta had experienced some clairvoyance and she had seen Arthur Conan Doyle and Lord James Avon Clyde together too, but in her vision they were shaking hands. I described to Loretta the first man I had seen in my vision, and she said I had described Lord James John Clyde, Ann's husband. But when I told her of the other man and this scene of the King and Queen in old black and white or maybe even sepia footage she said, 'I've seen a picture in Dublin Street of the King and Queen when they visited Edinburgh in the 1930's, as it was Lord Clyde (James' father – the earlier Lord Clyde) who welcomed them.'

I always find that Spirit has a way of bringing confirmation that you're in the right place or on the right track and I accepted this picture and the appearance of both Lords Clyde to be just that. Loretta was keen that I should tell Ann Clyde what I had seen. But I left that to Loretta, when I took her back home. I said I would wait to hear from Lady Clyde if she wanted to proceed further with her plan as I did not want to force the issue; If she wanted to proceed, then *she* would have to instigate it and she would have to discuss it with her sons before she brought me back into the scenario.

Here's Loretta's testimony to those events:

'I first met Lord and Lady Clyde in 2009, the day before he was admitted to The Murrayfield Hospital for surgery. I was to be employed as a private nurse for James's rehabilitation on his discharge. He was a wonderfully elegant gentleman, very kind, with a certain serenity in his demeanour. I was not aware of who he was at this time.

Although he was quite unwell at the time, he insisted on standing up to shake my hand, when I was introduced to him. I was very much looking forward to working with them both. I received a phone call from Lady Clyde a week or so later telling me that James had died. I asked if I might visit her, and this was the start of our friendship.

We discovered that we had a shared interest in all things esoteric. Ann was incredibly sensitive to energy and would use her pendulum to guide her in just about everything. James was very much a presence in the house, and I could feel him around her. She was bereaved for so many years and missed him every day. Ann loved that I could sense his energy, and sometimes I was able to pass on a message for her.

Ann had the most amazing library in her home with a ladder to reach the higher shelves. Despite her advancing years, she was incredibly fit, (which I discovered after we returned from Shiel and we had to walk up from the bottom of Dublin Street to her house, near the top, she strode ahead while I was quite out of breath!)

The library consisted of books from mediumship to psychotherapy and everything in between. Ann had trained as a

Jungian Sand Play therapist and with the help of little Duplo figures could help children use play to identify and work through trauma. She was very much a woman before her time and would say to me that she wondered what she could do to be useful to people.

Ann loved to help anyone. Despite her title, she had the ability to speak to anyone and put them at ease. I remember when I went to Ethiopia in 2011, she bought me Australian Bush Remedies for travelling and emergency rescue remedies to support me on my travels.

Ann spoke of her home, Shiel, in the Crook of Devon. She took me and her friend, Rosy, a shamanic practitioner over to the house one summer afternoon. Ann loved the place. It was where she felt closest to James, and the energy both in the house and particularly the grounds, was palpable. Rosy often used the house and grounds to run sweat lodges with groups of women, and there was a permanent skeleton for the sweat lodge at the top end of the grounds.

James had built an iron framework over a paving slab with the directions on it (N, S, E, W). We three stood under this arched metal frame as Ann told us that the energy was strong here. She was not wrong. We had a shared spiritual experience, consisting of philosophy and words downloaded from Spirit. James did not communicate on this occasion. It was the most amazing experience, and we were all quite high afterwards.

Ann had always expressed a desire to use Shiel as a spiritual retreat, as the energy was very strong, and she felt that the space should be used for healing. I was privileged to be invited to Tim and Rebecca's wedding where I once again had the opportunity to enjoy this beautiful place.

Fast forward to 2015, when Ann was looking to move from Dublin Street to be closer to the family. She asked me what she could do about her books, as she wanted them to go to a good home. I suggested the Arthur Conan Doyle Centre.

When Ann Treherne came to collect the books, Ann Clyde had already decided that she wanted to leave a legacy in her will and that legacy was Shiel. She wanted to bequeath it to Ann Treherne to turn it into a spiritual Centre in the same way she had done with the building at Palmerston Place. She told Ann this when she arrived. I think Ann Treherne was in shock. I had previously told Ann Clyde about Ann Treherne and they had also met when Ann Clyde visited the Centre, so she was certain that this is what she wanted to do – she had dowsed to check that she was right in her choice.

The day arrived when Ann Clyde, Ann Treherne and myself were due to visit Shiel. On the day, Lady Clyde's back was playing up and she felt that she would not manage to cope with the drive. She gave me the keys for Shiel and Ann and I set off. Lady Clyde would often stand on her doorstep and look towards Fife saying "Dear Shiel, I do so miss it".

Ann and I arrived. We looked around the gardens admiring all the features as described, also the little bridge over the water in the Japanese garden with the iron heron looking on.

We went into the house for refreshments and a chat about the suitability of using Shiel as a spiritual retreat space in association with ACDC. We both felt that it would be good to meditate and connect with the energy in the place for guidance.

I am not usually clairvoyant. Almost immediately I had the vision of two Victorian gentlemen shaking hands with each other and looking at me and smiling. I recognised one as Arthur Conan Doyle, from his image at the Centre. I did not know the other gentleman. They said, "Welcome home".

They were standing in front of a stately home, which I later found out was Briglands, the Clyde residence close to Shiel. I also later discovered that the gentleman was Lord Clyde's grandfather, although I did seem to know this intuitively. It was confirmed by Lady Clyde when she showed me a photo of him after I shared the experience with her.

I was quite shocked initially as I am not used to receiving information in this way, but it was so clear. I opened my eyes, desperate to share what had just happened with Ann, only to discover that she had had a very similar experience to me.

On our return to Edinburgh, I told Ann Clyde all about the wonderful experience. She was fascinated and took it as a sign that Shiel was to be used for this purpose.'

— Loretta Dunn, Independent Life Celebrant

Another few weeks passed when I got a call from Lady Clyde telling me that she wanted me to meet her son Jamie. He was her eldest son, and he was coming up to Edinburgh for the rugby and she wanted me to meet him – she had discussed her plans with him.

As arranged, I visited the house in Dublin Street again to meet Jamie Clyde and he was lovely. I hoped to put him at ease as I felt sure he would be concerned as to my motives; I think I would have been. So, I told him I had been thinking of ways to achieve what everyone wanted and suggested that I didn't need to own the place to be able to turn it into a place of spiritual retreat; I didn't own the Sir Arthur Conan Doyle Centre, I paid a rent to the owners. I proposed that something similar could be achieved at Shiel thereby fulfilling his mother's wishes whilst he retained ownership. He seemed relaxed about this suggestion and asked if I could come up with a proposal to take forward this initiative. We ended the meeting with us both agreeing that this was a good first meeting to explore options and I was glad that he was open to the idea. Indeed, he was most positive and most gracious. I agreed I would start by thinking how best I could make use of the place and then think about the financials. We had a plan.

I put together a rough draft of how we might promote Shiel as a spiritual retreat. I came up with a strapline of *Shiel – the Clutha*. Clutha is the Gaelic name for the river Clyde or the Spirit of the Clyde (being a water Spirit or goddess) and I thought it was an interesting play on words since it was going to be a spiritual Centre whilst retaining and connecting the Clyde name as Ann's legacy.

Here's the flyer

Shiel

A Spiritual Retreat

In The Heart of Scotland

Less than 1 hour from Edinburgh Airport!

Set in 5 acres of gardens, forest, ponds and river.

- A country house retreat, built on ancient, Celtic land.
- A place of special magical energy.
- A powerful spiritual sanctuary .
- We welcome people of all religions, or of none at all to come and join us.
- Reconnect with nature, with your own spirit and with the energy of Shiel!

First draft brochure from 2015, page 1

Shiel at Briglands

Shiel sits on the land belonging to the magnificent country house of Briglands. Originally a small Georgian country house, Briglands was dramatically extended and enhanced in the late 19th and early 20th Century by that most celebrated architect of the Scottish Style - Sir Robert Lorimer. Briglands was commissioned by James Avon Clyde, the Edinburgh advocate and later judge, Lord Clyde, in 1897.

The original Georgian house, with date stones from 1743 and 1759 still in place today, was remodelled and extended to Lorimer's designs in two stages, firstly in 1897-8 and then in 1908. His free adaption of 17th century Scottish architecture enabled the use of the forms and details that came to typify his work. Steep roofs, crow step gables, carved animal heads, stone topped dormer windows, relief carving, turrets with ogee roofs, are all to be found in this example of his early work.

Robert Lorimer also designed the layout for the gardens, remodelling existing outbuildings and forming a walled garden, a sunken garden containing a well and a basin fountain. Around these well maintained gardens of today include rhododendron walks, a rose garden, many ornamental trees and shrubs, yew topiary and a host of spring bulbs. But today, Briglands is no longer held in The Clyde family, it having to be sold because of Death Duties, in XXXX?

However, when it was inherited by James John Clyde, grandson of James Avon Clyde (above), when forced to sell, he built for himself and Lady Clyde, a small, modern country hideaway in the extensive gardens of the estate - this is Shiel!

Lord James John Clyde, like his ancestors, was a Scottish Judge. He was also Vice-President of the Royal Blind Asylum and School from 1987 and assessor to the Chancellor of the Edinburgh University between 1989 and 1997. He chaired the 1992 Orkney child abuse inquiry.

On 1 October 1996, he was appointed Lord of Appeal in Ordinary and additionally was made a life peer with the title **Baron Clyde**, of Briglands in Perthshire. In the same year he was invested as a Privy Counsellor. He retired as a Lord Of Appeal in Ordinary in 2001 and sadly died in 2009.

First draft brochure from 2015, page 2

The Fairy Ring   The Sweat Lodge

Shiel - The Clutha

When Lord and Lady Clyde built Shiel in the grounds of their country house estate, they created a little hideaway in this land where descendants of the Clyde Family have resided over 3 generations.

This land is special, not least because of its ancient underground springs and historical interest—Briglands House dates back to the 18th Century. But when Lord and Lady Clyde chose this spot to build their little sanctuary, they were clearly guided as to just where to situate it in the extensive grounds of the estate. The earth energies that surround this site are powerful beyond belief and this coupled with the positivity that has been created inside the house means that this is a very special place, indeed.

Lord Clyde seems to have sensed this too, as not only did he build Shiel, but he also built an amazing Labyrinth, created out of local water reeds and rushes found on the estate. This Labyrinth is still in use today and what is more impressive is that this man -more accustomed to being surrounded by legal pomp and ceremony- built it himself, with his own hands (see pictures at the foot of the page). He also designed and created a beautiful metal Pergola which seems to act almost like a beacon for attracting positive energy—stand inside and see for yourself! A Fairy Ring, Sweat Lodge and beautiful Japanese Gardens with bridge and pond completes the magic of Shiel.

Clearly Lord Clyde was very much in touch with his spiritual side and lady Clyde most certainly is for she has donated the use of Shiel as a Spiritual Centre so that others too can come and feel the magic of this place and benefit from its powerful energy.

As a mark of appreciation and respect for Lord and Lady Clyde and to ensure their names live on in this sanctuary they have created, we are giving a fuller name to this place: Shiel –The Clutha.

The name Clutha is an ancient Gaelic word meaning 'The Clyde' or 'Spirit of the Clyde'. Since Shiel will now be used as a Spiritual Retreat where people of all faiths or none can come and attune themselves with nature, reconnect with their own spirit and develop their own intuitive skills in the silence and sanctity of this special place, we feel it only fitting that it should forever carry the Clyde name as part of its title so that Lord and Lady Clyde can be recognised for their spiritual foresight and the legacy they have created for future generations.

First draft brochure from 2015, page 3

I presented these draft pamphlets to Jamie Clyde in November of 2015, and I was planning on working up a proposal of income and expenditure when early in 2016 I heard the news that a new Centre was to be opening in central Scotland complete with twenty en suite bedrooms. I was aware of the limitations of Shiel in terms of the numbers it could accommodate and that at some stage we would have to look at how more accommodation could be found. Now it seemed there would be direct competition. When I fed this latest news back to Jamie he was most supportive and talked about quality rather than quantity but he also informed me that prior to him hearing of his mother's plans he had offered Shiel out as a long-term rental proposition to the Water Board who were working nearby to divert and pipe-in a burn. They had now responded to him as they needed somewhere for their workers to stay. Shiel would not now be available for the next few years, but this would allow us to see how this new Centre developed in the intervening time.

As I write this chapter now, I have to report that sadly Ann, Lady Clyde passed away on 25th November, 2020 at the age of 87. I feel honoured to have been invited to attend her memorial service which was held at St Mary's Cathedral on 4th June 2021, especially since the numbers of those who could attend were restricted due to the pandemic.

Jamie had contacted me to tell me of her passing and to extend an invite to the memorial service but also to ask if I would like her remaining books for the Centre. These were her precious books that she had so carefully selected to take with her to her new home; they are indeed most special, and I am again most privileged to have received them.

Notes

It was indeed her box of books that is referred in in Chapter 7 – Ann's Experience, where a book is calling to me to be read. It was,

Spiritual Pilgrims by *John Welch, O.Carm.* Was she trying to help me in my quest to find an explanation?

It was also the collection of Ann Clyde's books which Barry Fitzgerald referred to in Chapter 7, 'How to become Supernatural'.

Chapter 16

It's time

Apart from all the donations of books and potential use of a retreat space we were also very successful in attracting top quality mediums to our platform and it seemed that they would just connect with us, usually through someone else or having visited once would decide they wanted to come here. This was true of Gordon Smith who was originally invited by Janet Parker as a guest to one of her workshops (Janet had also invited Simon James and Brian Robertson from Canada too) but Gordon decided to base his School of Intuitive Studies at The Sir Arthur Conan Doyle Centre and by 2016 we had added retreats and were running these together in various locations, both in the UK and internationally. James van Praagh was another *coup*. He was accustomed to filling venues that were the size of football stadia in the US, yet he came to us. Invited by Tony Stockwell initially, they ran joint workshops, but James also returned on his own to run a workshop and indeed I organised for him to present a show at the Fringe in 2015. There were many others too but there was an interesting similarity I noticed. It was not me who had asked them to come; indeed, I hadn't made the approach at all. Instead, they had all ended up coming to the Centre usually through some other connection. You could just call that networking, but it struck me that there was something about the energy of the place that attracted people to it and made good things happen.

By 2016 the Centre was busy and buoyant with the top mediums, top speakers, sell-out shows in the Fringe and the Doors Open days, and we were definitely on the map, both in Edinburgh and internationally, as we attracted students from across the globe. We were also achieving that all important benchmark I had set myself to attract the general public into the building; even attracting a church of Scotland Elder as a regular visitor to our tearoom each day. My job was done. I could do no more. I was happy with what we had achieved but I was exhausted. We would be approaching our 5-year anniversary later that year and I had only intended to work in the position of Chair on a voluntary basis for one year, with the aim of recruiting further staff to replace me whenever we had the resources to do so. I was pleased to realise that this would be possible now and I could look forward to retirement. Iain had already decided that he was going to retire at the end of this year. This was never his initiative, but he made it so. He was simply supporting me in my quest, as he knew that Arthur Conan Doyle had directed us here. But after 5 years, Iain too was exhausted and ready to hand over to a new manager now that we had the funds to do so. In July the first steps were initiated. I attended the usual SNU Annual Conference and resigned my membership whilst I was there. I also resigned as Vice President of the Church and as Director and Trustee of the SNU Trust (the internal bank that owned the building). The only remaining tenure therefore was that of Chair of The Palmerston Trust (the body that runs the Sir Arthur Conan Doyle Centre) and I knew I had to find someone to replace me in this position before I left, but before doing so I also had to find a new manager. I placed the advert and sifted through the applications to come up with a short-list which eventually narrowed down to three candidates in the final interview. I employed the Andrew Carnegie philosophy, *'Give me a man of average intelligence but of burning desire and I'll give you a winner every time.'* Forgiving the sexism of the statement, it had always held me in good stead in my working career when I was recruiting – indeed I can identify with it myself in my own career – and here in the line-up for the final interviews was a young woman showing *burning desire.* Shereen Fazelli (now Shereen Elder) started with us in September 2016, and she has certainly fulfilled that philosophy. She's an excellent Manager of the Centre. However, my own position proved a little more difficult to fill, especially since it was an unpaid and a full-time role. I knew I would have to stay until someone was found as I did not want the Centre to fail after all that had been achieved. But I felt sure that someone would emerge soon and I could look forward to my retirement having done my bit and achieved what Spirit and Arthur wanted.

Remember too, at this time the fact that Arthur Conan Doyle was communicating with me had still not been revealed; our Group had been instructed to keep this confidential until it was time to communicate the message to the wider population. But just as I had noticed the number of incidents of books being donated, I was also noticing a trail of evidence of Arthur breaking this code of confidentiality he had set us. In various ways, Arthur was now making himself known. This had started in the regular Wednesday afternoon open circle that I tutored. An open circle just means that it is open to anyone to attend, whereas a closed circle is by invitation only, like my own Thursday Group. In the open circle some people would drop-in and attend just for one week or because they happen to be in Edinburgh for the day and some were regulars who would attend every week for their own development. It was in this circle that some of the regular students began to give me messages from someone they described as a big man with a big moustache. Initially the messages were just platitudes 'he's proud of you', 'you've done a good job.' There was no evidence given that could identify who he was. But I knew; I could feel his presence and I was puzzled as to why he had chosen to influence students in an open circle. My own Group had adhered strictly to his guidance to keep the Group, what happened within it and his presence confidential, and this they had maintained over several years. Now he was breaking the rules himself. I wondered why.

One afternoon as I was preparing to take the afternoon open circle, a man walked into the Centre. He looked to be in his 30's, casually dressed with a laptop bag over his shoulder. I was in the library setting up for the circle and one of our volunteer receptionists walked over to greet him and then showed him into the tearoom. She then came into the library to tell me that he was a freelance journalist and was doing a piece on contacting the dead and had seen our open circle advertised and had come to attend. I could see by her demeanour that she was as concerned as I was. Generally, Spiritualism and mediumship does not fare well when reported in the press or indeed on TV or film (although that situation has improved somewhat in more recent times because of its growing popularity).

'What do you want me to say to him?' she asked looking concerned.

'Welcome,' I said, 'it's an open circle and it means just that – it is open to anyone. We can't discriminate against him because he happens to be a journalist.' But in truth I was concerned too. Here we had a journalist who appeared to be using the fact that we were hosting an open invitation to anyone to come in and now he would use that opportunity to put his own slant on what happens in a circle. I could almost envision the exposé, and our reputation which had been hard won disappearing with his withering take on what he was about to experience. I would have to be careful.

When the open circle began, I could tell the regular members were also feeling wary of the new man in their midst, so I took the opportunity to have everyone introduce themselves. In this way the others would also be aware of who he was and what he was doing. I also outlined the fact that some of the information that may be presented from Spirit communication was personal and private to the individual concerned and lastly, I made sure that I explained what I was doing each step of the way so at least if he did not understand what we were doing he would hear the explanation as to why we were doing it. That was all I could do, I told myself, and just trusted that those in the Spirit Realm would not allow us to be harmed in this way. As it was, I need not have worried. At the end of the session and with fingers crossed I asked him if he had got what he wanted, and surprisingly he asked if he could come back each week as he wanted to learn more about psychic and spiritual communications. He wanted to learn to do it himself and he was planning on writing a book about his experience.

Mark Johnsburn [pseudonym] became one of our regulars and indeed developed his own awareness of the psychic and spiritual energies that surround us all. I remember him once remarking on how much fun it was to stand next to someone in a bar or café and sense just what they were like and what was going on in their life. I reprimanded him for this, telling him that was not what this was for and that he should always seek permission and not simply invade someone's space psychically. So, it was in one of the sessions whilst Mark was sitting in the circle that my apprehension was raised again. A new girl came along to join us, and her mediumship was progressing well when in one session she said, 'There's a man here and he's a big man, elderly, he's got a moustache.'

'Okay,' I said, whilst sensing the presence of Arthur Conan Doyle and wondering why he was once again back in this open circle, and with a journalist present.

'He's showing me books. I think he wrote books. I think he was an author.' At that statement, Mark the journalist became more interested in what she was saying. Perhaps he was thinking that an author from the Spirit Realm had come to offer him some advice. I could feel him prick up his ears.

'There's someone here who is writing a book,' she said.

Mark answered, 'Yes, I'm writing a book.'

She seemed to ignore his response and continued held in her connection with Spirit. 'He was a doctor too and I think he came from Edinburgh or went to Edinburgh University.'

At this, one of the others in the Group spoke up and said. 'I know a doctor who studied at Edinburgh University, and he wrote a book about medicine and the pharmaceutical industry.'

'The book is not about medicine, it's about here,' she said, as she looked skywards.

'My book will include my experience here,' Mark was keen to claim the message and clearly wanted to hear more. I was equally keen not to.

'I can see a pipe, one of those old-fashioned curly pipes,' she said 'And there's a tweed coat and a magnifying glass.'

'That's Sherlock Holmes,' Mark exclaimed, 'that's amazing – Arthur Conan Doyle is here.'

Undeterred, the girl continued, 'he says you've got to get the message out.'

'What message?' Mark asked, 'what is the message?'

'Ann knows,' she said, 'the message is for you.'

As everyone looked towards me, I simply said, 'thank you.'

As a final prompt, she said, 'he's pulled out his pocket watch and he's tapping it and saying – it's time.'

Mark was still reeling from the thought that Arthur Conan Doyle might be in our circle, and he was looking to me for further explanation of what that communication was all about. I did not enlighten him, for I was equally searching for answers. Did this mean that it was now time to tell everyone that it was Arthur Conan Doyle who had been communicating all this time and had led to the founding of the Centre? I wasn't sure, and when something that has remained secret for all those years was almost revealed in an open session and with a journalist present then there is some reflecting to do.

I received confirmation in my own Thursday Group that he was indeed telling us that it was time to get the message out there. And as if to confirm that message he appeared again, this time in Germany. I was attending a training session run by Paul Jacobs in his Centre in Hanover. I had chosen to go there as an opportunity to improve my own mediumship, since I felt it was being neglected as I focused on running The Sir Arthur Conan Doyle Centre. We were all sitting in a horseshoe shape with Paul at the head, telling us of a certain aspect of mediumship and in an attempt to demonstrate his point he turned to me and said, 'Let me just get a contact for you, Ann, and I can show everyone what I mean.'

He continued to describe a big man with a moustache. I could already sense the presence of Arthur Conan Doyle. I knew he was here and that he was influencing Paul, but I said nothing, allowing Paul to continue to make his point. This was going to be interesting.

'This man is showing me an old photograph and it looks like one of those funny postcards, the old-fashioned ones that you would see at the seaside. It shows a boxer but an old-fashioned boxer with handle-bar moustache, long baggy shorts or trousers and he's got his fists raised but no gloves, bare-knuckles.' Paul continued, 'actually I think it's a pamphlet for a boxing match and not a postcard at all. This man must have actually taken part in a boxing competition. You must have known someone who was a boxer, Ann?'

Paul looked at me for confirmation. At that point I had no idea that Arthur had been a boxer, but I knew he was present with us and if this was what he was saying then it must be true. I simply said, 'yes' and allowed Paul to continue.

'He's telling me that you're writing a book, Ann, and that he wrote a book too. Actually, he wrote many books?'

'Yes, that's right, Paul.'

'That's a strange combination, boxing and writing. And now he's telling me that he was into this too – Spiritualism.'

Just at that moment I could see that the realisation of who he was communicating with had been revealed, as Paul looked at me in astonishment, 'This is Arthur Conan Doyle?'

'Yes, it is.'

I could see Paul's surprise and wonder at who he was communicating with and as we discussed it later at the break I said to him, 'Paul I don't tell people that I work with Arthur Conan Doyle, as firstly it sounds like boasting and secondly, they wouldn't believe me anyway – it took me a long time before I believed it myself. So, I just let you find out for yourself.'

'And was he a boxer?' Paul asked.

'I honestly have no idea, but I know this, if he said he was then he will have been and there will be proof of that somewhere. He always gives me proof, as he knows that's the way I work. I'll search on the internet later and let you know.'

As promised, when I got back to my hotel room, I searched the internet for references of Arthur Conan Doyle and boxing only to find that he had actually written a book based around boxing – bare-knuckle boxing – called *Rodney Stone*.

And this from
http://www.westminsteronline.org/conandoyle/Sport.html:

Sir Arthur was not exaggerating when he wrote to the Editor of The Times that he had "sampled most British sports"; he certainly had. In his Memories and Adventures, first published in the Strand Magazine, he rightly, if harshly, describes himself as an all-rounder and a second-rater. Dismissing horse racing as not really a sport at all and shooting animals as barbarous (he excludes fishing, acknowledging the inconsistency), he extols the virtues of boxing. Doyle recalls some of his own experiences of boxing, including an end-of-night match which involved boxing in his formal evening clothes. While praising the benefits of boxing with gloves, Sir Arthur expressed his opinion that the old prize-fighting (that is, bare-knuckles boxing) was an excellent thing "from a national point of view.... Better that our sports should be a little too rough than that we should run a risk of effeminacy."

I emailed Paul to tell him this and sent the links to the references I had found. Paul was due to be interviewed by an American radio station that night and so he mentioned this encounter with Arthur Conan Doyle earlier that day. Another example of Arthur getting his message out there and this time to an American audience.

Another example but on a smaller scale came few weeks later, when I was back in Edinburgh and at the Sunday Spiritual Church Service. I was sitting in the back row as usual with one eye on the open door in case anyone walked into the Centre whilst the service was on. The medium was on the platform and was presenting evidence of survival of their deceased relatives to some of those present in the congregation. I had long since stopped looking for messages; I didn't need them any more. I was well aware of Spirit, and it was far better that the few messages that were given went to those who really needed them.

The medium then pointed to me in the back row and said, 'I've got a man here who says you are writing a book?'

I could feel everyone turn around to see what I was going to say, as no-one knew that I had been instructed to write a book. At that stage I hadn't had time to write anything further than the first chapter and even that had been written whilst lying on a sun-lounger when on holiday in Mexico. I was too busy running the Centre. But I nodded my head in acknowledgement.

'He is showing me that there have been lots of books coming here to the Centre – people have been giving *their* books to you?' she said.

'Yes, that's right, we've had a few donations of books to the Centre,' I said.

'He is saying that you've got to get *your* book out there. You've got to get it done,' she said, 'You've got to get the message out – it's time.'

It was confirmation of what had been said at the open circle; some of it was almost verbatim. And it seemed clear to me that Arthur was deliberately using public meetings to emphasise his message and making the point that I had to get that book written. Was this why I had been getting all those prompts about books, I wondered? Another prompt was yet to come and in a much more tangible way.

In December I had organised another retreat together with Gordon Smith. This was the advanced class and it was the final workshop in the series, so these students were in high spirits. It was a residential retreat, just before Christmas and they were about to receive their certificates recognising their achievement. They were now mediums in their own right.

It was at one of these sessions when we were working with trance that Sandy Campbell, one of the students, was asked to demonstrate his skills. He came forward to the front of the class and sat on a chair on the platform. There were approximately 20 students in this group, and they sat in chairs in a horseshoe shape facing the platform. Gordon and I took up positions at each end of the horseshoe opposite each other and nearest to the platform. I guided the whole group into an altered state and then closed my eyes myself and went into the silence. I could feel the energy building and with this group that was hardly surprising, but then I felt the distinct presence of Arthur Conan Doyle behind me in an almost physical way. It seemed like he had put his hand on my shoulder. I opened my eyes just to check that no-one else had and as I raised my head my eyes met Gordon's. He was looking straight back at me. I got the impression he had been looking over for a while and he just nodded his head as if in acknowledgement that he too was aware of what I was experiencing and perhaps who was there. I closed my eyes again, quite happy in this energy and the company of Arthur. I then heard footsteps as if someone was walking about in the group, but I didn't open my eyes again, presuming this was Gordon walking round the students as he often did. Just after that, Sandy started speaking and he was clearly over-shadowed speaking in the first person and that person was Arthur Conan Doyle. I'm not sure everyone in the room would have realised who he was, as we had a number of foreign students present but it was an uplifting message of support, encouragement again to get the book written and published.

As the group began to give individual feedback on what they had experienced, one of the students from Germany, Maria Teresa, said, 'I felt that there was a man walking around the room. I wondered if it was Gordon but when I looked, he was still sitting in his seat and I became aware that it was a man from the Spirit World and so I made a sketch of him and got the impression that I was to give it to Ann, as she would know who he was.'

Here is the sketch

This was a nice sketch by Maria Teresa Lassus and I was glad to receive it. It was a good likeness of Arthur Conan Doyle by someone who did not know who she was seeing or drawing. I took it as further confirmation that it was indeed he who was making his presence known and in a public setting, whilst giving me the message that I had to get on with the writing of the book and let everyone know that it was he who had directed me to the Sir Arthur Conan Doyle Centre.

I was to get his message across - I was ready to retire! I felt I had completed my mission. I had found the building, created the Sir

Arthur Conan Doyle Centre and it was now very successful with an international reputation. I was aware I still had to write the book and it seemed I now had been given permission to tell people about how it had come to be and thereby propagate the message of life after death. I started planning in my head how I would achieve that. I figured that now we had a new manager in place and a good group of volunteers if I could just find someone to take over from *me* then I could look forward to retiring and that would give me the time to get on with the writing of the book. As I contemplated how attractive it would be to have the luxury of doing so, I heard a distinctive voice from Spirit. That refined Scottish brogue saying:

'That was Phase One – this is Phase Two.'

Chapter 17

Phase Two

Phase Two, he had said. Phase Two! I was ready to retire. I knew that I couldn't possibly contemplate writing the book until I had retired from The Centre; I just wouldn't have had time to consider such a thing. I was much too focused on The Centre and ensuring its continued success. And what was Phase Two, anyway? There it was again, that automatic questioning that I seem to ask spontaneously and without thinking. And the answer came from Spirit just as quick as the question had – it was a second Centre. This current one is in the city, they explained, and the next one will be in the country; it will be a country retreat. My immediate thought was, then you'll have to do it; I'm bushed! And with that thought I had symbolically kicked the ball back to the Spirit World. If that was to become Phase Two and my next mission, then they would have to manifest it. This was something that I knew could happen and I knew if it was meant to be, that it would happen, much in the same way as The Sir Arthur Conan Doyle Centre had come to be. But it prompted thoughts of Shiel and Lady Ann Clyde. Had she been influenced to offer me her country retreat for this purpose? Had Arthur Conan Doyle influenced her before I had had any knowledge of this next phase? I had been aware of the presence of Arthur when I had sat together with Loretta, when we visited Shiel, but this was nothing new to me and I had thought nothing of it. Now I was revisiting those visions and the fact that Loretta had seemed to see Arthur and Lord Clyde shaking hands. As I pondered those thoughts and reminded myself that this can't be right, as Shiel was effectively on-hold now, I heard that distinct Scottish voice from Spirit saying, 'there will be other opportunities.'

These enigmatic answers were always a source of annoyance to me; I just wanted the facts. What did this mean? Did it mean that there will be another opportunity at Shiel? Or did it mean that there will be another opportunity somewhere else? I didn't have long to wait. In a strange quirk of synchronicity, I was contacted by the people who had invested in the proposed new spiritual retreat that I had initially seen as a competitor to Shiel, and possibly to the Sir Arthur Conan Doyle Centre too. They wanted my input and possibly my involvement. I arranged to visit and as I travelled in the train through towards the west of Scotland, I was again revelling in the intelligence of the Spirit Realm which always seemed to be one step ahead of us. Indeed, it was perhaps more accurate to say that they are leaps and bounds ahead of us. So, I was eagerly looking forward to seeing what this 'other opportunity' would reveal. When I got there, I was disappointed. The building had previously operated as a nursing home for the elderly and was now derelict. I was not fazed by derelict buildings, having been met with a similar scenario when the building that is now The Sir Arthur Conan Doyle Centre had also been in a derelict condition, but this one, although once a grand building, would have taken a few million pounds to put right. More importantly, it was still partly owned by a builder and as I was introduced to him and shook his hand his energy did not seem conducive to the proposed spiritual retreat. Whilst the two people who had invited me to come and visit were genuine in their aims and indeed had already put a lot of their own time and effort into the venture, I felt sure that the builder would have had plans to convert this large property into residential apartments at some future stage. I politely declined the invitation to join them, and I have heard nothing further of this venture since. As I returned home on the train that day, I was reflecting on how differently I felt on the return journey from the anticipation I had felt on the way out to the proposed venue. I had been wondering if this was it, if this was the 'other opportunity' that had been foretold. So, now I was feeling a bit deflated and wondering what that was all about and what was the point. Again, that very familiar voice from Spirit said to me, 'there will be another opportunity.' That's up to you, was my response and once again kicked the ball back, frustrated at the waste of time as I went back to The Centre and focused on the day job.

As we moved into 2017 and Arthur had continued to make further public appearances at various open circles and demonstrations of mediumship, each time telling me via the Medium that I had to get the message out and each time I would find a discrete way to accept the message without divulging whom the message was from. I knew I had to find someone to replace me as Chair of The Centre before I could find time to write the book, but as far as 'getting the message out' I felt I had done quite a good job of this as The Centre was now the premier venue in Scotland for Mediumship Demonstrations and Training Courses. We had a very active and well - respected Tuesday Talk Programme and we were attracting students internationally. Although I did concede that this hadn't really reached the mainstream, where the real change of attitudes and opinions and the winning of hearts and minds was required. Hmm, I thought, how do I do that?

Once more that familiar voice spoke silently to me in my head and said, 'I'll help you do that, but you'll have to go back to your business roots.'

No way, I thought. There was no way I was going to go back to my business roots. I had escaped that life long ago and had no intention of once again re-entering the rat race. Also, I couldn't quite see the connection. Surely this was wrong? How on earth could the business world have anything to do with getting the message out on spirituality? Again, the answer came – 'You've got to influence the influencers.'

I recognised this saying. It was one I was familiar with and had regularly used myself when trying to win hearts and minds of my own managers. It was a simple philosophy used when trying to change the culture in an organisation. The culture is set by the man (and it usually is a man) at the top. Whether that is the Chief Exec or the Business Owner or Managing Director, the business that he manages will reflect his character, his management style and his attitudes towards his people and how they do business. Some examples of this would be Invar Kamprad from IKEA, Richard Branson from Virgin and more recently Elon Musk, Tesla and Jeff Bezos, Amazon.

I have over many years in my business life seen expensive consultants brought in from 'the big four' (PWC, Deloitte, KPMG and Ernest & Young), who have been tasked with changing the culture in what is usually an old, hierarchical organisation and invariably they are given access to the branch network or the various internal departments. They will then produce a report as to how things could be changed for the better and usually this is accepted by the Executive Management or Board and a directive will be issued down the line telling those in the branches or departments that they have been consulted and this is the result, but invariably the culture stays the same. If the staff are demoralised, disincentivised and not feeling valued then this is usually reflected in the business results. I was well aware that it is only by changing or influencing the man at the top – the Chief Exec/Business Owner – that you can influence the whole organisation, and that such figures can achieve that far quicker and more effectively than spending months and in some cases years of intervention around the periphery. I realised that this indeed would be a very effective model to use to disseminate a spiritual message to a great number of people in a large organisation and I also knew what the message would be and how I could convince a CEO of the benefits. But how would I get access to him? And did I want to re-enter this arena – no. I promptly disregarded this message from Spirit as this was something that I definitely did not want to do. Further, I could see no good reason for the message. I no longer had any connection with the business world; it didn't make sense.

In March of that year, I was assisting Gordon Smith run a workshop at The Sir Arthur Conan Doyle Centre. Gordon remarked to me that when he was instructing the students in sitting in silence and talking them into an altered state, he had noticed that one man was not complying at all and had just sat with his arms folded looking around the room and out of the window as if he was bored. Gordon seemed concerned, so I suggested he pair me up with this man for the next exercise which involved students working together in pairs, and in this way, I would try to find out what the problem was. As the next session started, I sat opposite this big man. We had been instructed to try to tune-in to each other psychically, to see what we could pick up or sense about each other. After we had introduced ourselves to one another by exchanging first names, I asked if he wanted to go first.

'You'll have to go first because I've no idea how to do this. I don't really know why I'm here.' Knowing that he had booked and paid for his place on this course, I enquired further, 'so why *are* you here?'

'I don't really know. I just happened to see this course advertised and knew that I had to be here on this particular course, and it had to be here in this building. And I don't know why.'

I had heard this same scenario many times before from people who had felt drawn into the building somehow and there was always a reason for it. Sometimes, it was something they needed for them- selves but more often than not it was something they could do for me; so this was my cue, to find out a little more about this man and why he was here. 'What do you do?' I asked him.

'I'm Chairman of the Scottish Institute of Business Leaders, SIBL we call it.'

I couldn't believe it. I had chosen to ignore the message from Spirit to 'go back to my business roots' and now here was not just a businessman but the Chairman of Scottish Business Leaders sitting in front of me; the mountain and Mohammad came to mind. I tried not to show my surprise as he continued talking.

'It's a forum for Chief Execs, business owners and leaders because they are often too busy running their businesses to take time out to think and plan, to develop new strategies and also for their own self-development. So, we ask them to commit to dedicating one day per month for their own development by attending our meetings. We also use it as a sort of think-tank where we explore new ways of working and they can debate these strategies in a group of their peers – other Chief Execs from other non-competing industries'. He went on, 'I started the organisation in 2003 and we have gone from strength to strength with some of the top companies represented as well as the Police and now the Fire Service also coming on board, as some of the public sector monoliths try to streamline their operations and become more efficient and perhaps learn some of the lessons from their private sector colleagues.'

Listening so intently to what he was saying it brought back memories of some of the restructuring processes I too had experienced in a number of the financial organisations where I had worked, as they had undergone that same need to restructure. I also had some experience of working alongside the public sector and remember distinctly the clash of the different cultures that I'm sure was just as frustrating to both parties at the time. So, I said to Drew, 'That's inspired thinking to have both private and public bodies working together.'

'And learning from each other,' he said, 'let's face it, these are their top people, the bosses, the Chief Execs and they have egos to match, so you can't teach them anything – they know it all – but they *will* listen to their counterparts and so that's what we do.'

I had completely forgotten about Spirit and the fact that this man had no doubt been put in front of me for a reason. I had been instantly transported 'back to my business roots,' as he spoke.

'And there's something else that will interest you,' he said, and that is when he told me his story.

'In October 2004, I was diagnosed as having myasthenia gravis. It's a breakdown of the immune system, which is triggered by anti-bodies in the bloodstream and is incurable. Initially it was controlled by medication but after about nine months the disease became immune to the medication and so I started to explore the possibilities of alternative therapy and specifically vibrational medicine. In October 2005, I went on a two-day vibrational medicine workshop in Nairn in the north of Scotland but at the end of the second day my condition was extremely acute. My eyelids dropped, I was seeing double, and I couldn't move my jaws, so I couldn't speak or eat or swallow, and then the myasthenia started to close down my lungs. My first thoughts were to get back to my family and to Ninewells, the Hospital in Dundee where I had been diagnosed. But thankfully there was a doctor on the course and she said, 'Drew, I'm afraid you are too ill to travel. You will have to come home with me and stay with my family and I will treat you.'

At this stage of the condition the only orthodox treatment available to me was steroids or blood transfusion. However, I started to receive three or four vibrational medicine treatments per week from this same doctor, Dr Helen Petrow, but no medication. This process was repeated for 50 days during which time I lost about 60 pounds through being unable to chew and swallow. Then on Christmas Eve 2005 the Doctor took me to an afternoon service at Pluscarden Abbey near Forres. The monks were conducting a service in Gregorian chant which is in itself a form of ancient vibration. And as I sat in a pew, I listened to the singing and suddenly my eyelids lifted. I could see and also move my jaw freely and, hey, I could speak! All my symptoms just fell away! They returned shortly afterwards but at that point I knew that I would be healed.

My healing and recovery continued over the next few weeks, and I was able to return to my family in Fife in February 2006. Throughout all of my three months in healing I had total faith in my doctor, the treatment, the visualization and that one day I could and would be well.

Between that February 2006 and the following January, I had 11 months of blood, muscle and eye tests as an outpatient before being fully discharged by the Head of Neurology at Ninewells Hospital who said, 'Mr Pryde, you are the only person that I have heard of who has fully recovered from myasthenia gravis.'

What came with my experience of healing from an 'incurable' disease was a deeper inner understanding of myself. On returning home friends felt that I was a different person in some profound way. Indeed, I felt reborn. I don't mean this in an evangelical way, but it did leave me asking myself the question, why me? And what now? And so now I use this knowledge and experience in SIBL to try to influence others and in particular the business leaders who in turn can influence others. I focus my energies on personal learning and encouraging the continuous quest towards new leadership that will make a real difference in an increasingly challenging world. My case has subsequently appeared in Dr. David Hamilton's latest book, 'How Your Mind Can Heal Your Body'.

Wow! If at first I had been surprised by the synchronicity of having the Chairman of the Scottish Institute of Business Leaders sit in front of me at a time when I had been told to go back to my business roots, now I was aware that he too had encountered some esoteric intervention in his life that like me had changed his life. But in his case he had chosen to stay in that environment and try to influence from the inside (or from his new organisation SIBL), whereas in my case I had chosen to escape that life, feeling that it was not conducive to the more spiritual side of life. Now I was being instructed to get back to it and here was a man who was presenting the perfect opportunity; this couldn't be simply coincidence, could it? I hadn't yet revealed anything about myself. He would have known that I was Chairman of the charity which ran The Centre, but he would not have known that I too had encountered a dramatic esoteric intervention that had caused me to change my whole path in life, nor did he know that I too had been a Chief Exec or Chief Operating Officer as the Americans like to call it.

I explained in my last book *Arthur and me* how I had left the financial world behind after the dramatic premonition that had changed my life. It had been the catalyst to leave the corporate world. Not right away, as I had been traumatised by the event and had to seek out help and that had introduced me to The Scottish Society for Psychical Research and Psychical Investigations. Over the next few years, I had studied this strange new world and began to feel that far from being supernatural this was the real world and our physical world was just a manifestation, so much so that when my organisation too was going through a restructure I decided the time was right to resign from my job and follow this new path.

So, I certainly had the credentials to join his 'club', but did I want to? I contemplated that thought whilst realising that Spirit had clearly orchestrated this whole 'chance meeting'. I decided if they had indeed brought the mountain to Mohammad I should at least reciprocate. I took a first tentative step. 'That is an amazing story Drew, and also that you're now fully recovered from what was an incurable disease. I also encountered a transformational event in my life which caused me to re-evaluate what I was doing in life and eventually to leave the business world behind and do this.' I raised my hands to indicate the surroundings of the workshop at The Sir Arthur Conan Doyle Centre.

'What was it?' he sounded intrigued.

'It was a premonition, and it was traumatic, it had a profound effect on me.' I felt the emotion rising in my throat and the tears developing in my eyes as they always do when I recall that event. I decided to keep my account short. 'It was the Dunblane Massacre.' Everyone in Scotland of a certain age remembers the Dunblane Massacre with horror and I could see in his reaction that same revulsion. 'I saw it before it happened. In my mind's eye, I suppose you would say, and I confided in a colleague so she too I'm sure must have felt that same sense of guilt and responsibility for not having done anything to stop it – not that we ever spoke of it. But I didn't know it was a school and I didn't know where it was going to take place, I just knew it was in Scotland and that a gunman was shooting everyone.' That was as brief as I could make the summation without going into all the gory details I had seen in my premonition.

'Well, that certainly tops my story,' he said.

'No, I don't think so. Yours was life-threatening to you, mine only threatened my career and that was one of the reasons I chose to leave that profession and eventually do this.' I again indicated our surroundings at The Centre, but just as I was speaking we were all called back into the main lecture hall as the time had finished for that exercise, although all we had done was chat and now we had come to the end of the course. Drew handed me his business card on the way out of the door and told me that he would be in touch as we needed to speak more.

I was happy that I had just given enough information and so if this 'chance meeting' really had been manifest by Spirit and further action was to come from it, then they, or he, would have to make the next move – I'd just wait to see what happens next.

I didn't have long to wait, the next morning there was an email from Drew giving further information on SIBL – here's an extract from that email:

At the risk of overloading you, this is to provide some background to The Scottish Institute for Business Leaders as promised...

- We are a not-for-profit Community Interest membership Company (CIC). Any surplus is donated to a Scottish mental health charity.

- We have been organising all day invitation monthly events for MDs and senior partners for the past 14 years without missing a heartbeat. We now operate from four SIBL Regional Learning Centres in Edinburgh (Central), Glasgow (West) and Dundee / Dunfermline (Tayside & Fife) plus Tulliallan (*We are joint-venture partners with Police Scotland re leadership development*).

- The SIBL model is designed to offer senior executives, in all three sectors, a total support package in respect of their business and personal development.

It is essentially experiential, and the model is much more than just a series of speakers' events but includes the highly rated Tri-sector peer group collaborative problem-solving sessions, one to one coaching and a 24x7 helpline.

His email also invited me to the next SIBL meeting to represent the third sector – the charities sector. I hadn't considered charities as being part of a business model or in participating in strategic trans-formational thinking, but as I reflected now, why not, some of them are the size of major conglomerates with world-wide coverage and huge financial resources. When Drew and I had been speaking earlier we were discussing the bringing together of public and private sectors, but now I could see that he had covered all angles with his tri-sector strategy and I was being invited as Chairman of The Sir Arthur Conan Doyle Centre, not as a previous CEO in the finance sector. I accepted the invite. Here's part of my email in response:

So, looking forward to it - with some trepidation - it's 15 years ago since I gave up the corporate sector to develop my spiritual life - the two were not conducive at that time. So, now I've been prompted back in that direction, I hope they are now!

However, its only by taking the risk and going out there will we know.

See you on Thursday.

Thanks for the invite.

Ann

That first meeting and indeed many of the subsequent SIBL meetings were held at Tulliallan, the Police Training College in Scotland where I found myself surrounded by some of their senior officers, who were keen to see changes within their organisation. And I was also able to discuss the use of psychics in policing and forensics amongst other topics. Through Drew I met some of the top business people in Scotland, particularly in the engineering and petrol-chemical industries, something I would never have had access to otherwise. I remember being introduced to and speaking to one of the top execs from one of the largest oil and gas companies represented in Scotland and him telling us that the world had only about 10 years before it reached a tipping point, when nature could no longer counteract the effects of global-warming. That was in 2017, when the Paris Agreement(COP21) was still in its infancy and it was enlightening to hear of how these polluters were taking strident steps in their quest to find answers and literally clean up their act. It was refreshing to find how many of these top execs were seeking new ways of working, exploring new frontiers and were open to hearing and discussing energy, consciousness and working in a kinder world.

Of course, I had now confided in Drew that I had been instructed by Spirit to 'return to my business roots' and that I had to 'influence the influencers' and that it appeared that he had been put in front of me for this purpose. He responded by email:

Good Morning Ann,

As you are aware I didn't know why I went on Gordon's course; I just had to be there.

And as we have discussed the "out there" purpose of SIBL as a Community Interest Company is to advance wellbeing in people and profits. But the simpler and personal purpose is to advance spirituality in business. What in turn this means is to offer and advance "healing" for organisations and individuals.

"Healing" has several meanings and occurs in various forms - even "*peer group coaching*" can be one form of a "healing" process.

So, the aspirations that you shared in bringing spirituality and healing to the world of business seems to be a match with SIBL CIC as we have been working on that theme continuously for more than a decade.

I had become aware that Drew had gathered a small team of trusted individuals together who were all already aware of the power of the unseen world and some, like Drew, had had their own personal epiphany and felt driven to help change the way we do things in this world. In this inner sanctum, I met Jim Bennett who had produced, 'The Spiritual Leadership Handbook' which was channelled from Ascended Masters, and Robert Yarr who had spent much of his time travelling and learning from indigenous tribes around the world. And then Drew surprised me again by divulging his experience of going with a friend to visit a Medium back in April 2010. The date rang a bell with me as this was the year that I eventually found the building which Arthur Conan Doyle had directed me towards, and which would become the Sir Arthur Conan Doyle Centre. Drew sent me a transcript from his session with the Medium who claimed to be channelling ACD. Drew's friend, Dave, had arranged the session as he had written a book in memory of ACD and had wanted to find out what Arthur thought of it and hence had sought out the two Mediums (detailed below) for this session. Here is an excerpt from the transcript:

Dave: Well, Arthur, I know you have taken a great pride in the fact that I've done the book [THE VIEW] in your memory, and at a later period I doubted my ability to take things forward. I'd really appreciate some guidance,......

ACD (through the Medium): Dear boy, you should not worry so much, you have done incredibly well with everything that has been asked of you so far. And just as it fell into place and was easy the last time, so it shall be this time, too.

The key focus with you going ahead is to bring this more mainstream. My mission was always to prove to those doubters and sceptics about the spiritual community and also that we do still exist once our physical body has gone.

I have chosen, however, to reincarnate, you must know. The date for reincarnation is not yet set, but it is important for you to know that my soul shall return to the Earth Plane once again.

I do not want you to panic, however, about this news, for as the Medium knows it is possible for one to channel even when one is still incarnate. The Human Mind has capabilities beyond your current comprehension and people are still able to channel from lifetimes in the past as ultimately the Higher Self has all the knowledge contained within it.

Dave: Arthur, you've mentioned the fact that we as a group must work more closely together with these two Mediums. Can you say a little bit more in practical terms how this might be achieved?

ACD: You will find people are brought into your lives at certain times and often these people are brought to be teachers, and also to learn and be taught.

What these Mediums can teach you is knowledge of which they do not disseminate to the world at large. You are being introduced to two people who have an understanding of spirituality and also the different realms and dimensions that are within it.

I wish for this information to be disseminated at large within the Spiritualism community. This information may not be for all, and you may have to find that the Spiritualism Churches have to change their structures and ways of working.

You can still have people visiting just to hear the stand-up mediumship and receive messages from departed loved ones; but, as the planet evolves and the vibration speeds up and transcends as we move into the higher frequencies, then people need to start to have an understanding themselves of their place within the whole and also their abilities which must be encouraged.

The days of proof being required are now gone, my son, and that is what we are trying to convey to people incarnate at this time.

Lead Spiritualism forward, take the next step, and do not be afraid of what this means. Many people are becoming awakened and now is the time for you to start to allow them to flourish.

My messages may appear coded. However, it is important for you to understand these basic concepts within yourselves first before you can then see the clear path that is ahead.

For if I was to give you the information now you may reject or refuse it, as it may seem too far-fetched.

Trust me with this and work with the knowledge that I am giving you at this time.

I am going to leave you now for I wish you to ponder over what I have said. But I am around often and watch over you always, and still behind the scenes try to influence and help pave the way for there to be a greater acceptance of the fact that Spirit lives on.

Dave: Thank you.

This transcript really was intriguing as it mirrored a lot of the direction and information I too had been given by ACD. This reference about getting the message to the 'mainstream' and that 'people are brought into your life at certain times either to be teacher or to be taught' was certainly something that was familiar to me, as well as the need to be more progressive within Spiritualism and to move the message forward beyond simply 'stand-up mediumship'. That was something I had already been doing in The Centre. Also, the paragraph that starts, 'My message may appear coded' was well understood as this indeed was how he first appeared to me – by giving various clues. That paragraph goes on to suggest that Dave and Drew were perhaps to be taught 'the basic concepts' before they would be able to understand the path ahead. This resonated too with the instruction to my Group (which is outlined in *Arthur and me*) when we were told we would be taught in various concepts before we could disseminate it to the wider world.

When *Arthur and me* was eventually published and I was being interviewed about my experiences I always maintained that I did not consider myself to be special. I believe that Arthur Conan Doyle was still on his mission to get his message out to the mainstream public and was using any means he could to do so; in this case, my own mediumship. And I felt sure there would be others. The transcript above is one example of where ACD was allegedly communicating via another medium to Dave and Drew and it is interesting that this was at the same time as he was in regular communication with me and my Group. When I was invited to give a talk to the Society of Psychical Research in London in 2017, I made the same comment about not being special and that I suspected there would be other groups around the country (and possibly further afield) receiving a similar message. There were three people who came up to me individually afterwards to tell me that their group had received a similar message. All of these people were well-respected members of the SPR, one of whom was their chairman.

And last but not least, as far as that transcript is concerned, the reference to reincarnation was intriguing. But I was not to find out more about that until the following year, for now it was clear to me that the message to 'get back to your business roots' did indeed have a greater significance than I had given it and from the time that Drew had appeared at that workshop the connections and synchronicity just kept coming.

The next SIBL meeting was due to take place on 5th April (2017). I was told it was being held in Kilgraston near Bridge of Earn, as this venue had been used before. But I was also told that it was now closing down, as it was due to be sold; so, this was the last opportunity to use this venue – The Garden Cottage. Drew had expressed disappointment that the place was to be sold as he said it was a lovely place and most conducive to their activities. He told me that it was actually run by Carmelite Nuns as a spiritual retreat and that SIBL hired the space for their meetings but as the nuns were all getting on in years a decision had been made to sell it.

What I had picked up from that exchange was 'spiritual retreat;' my ears pricked up as I had been informed by Spirit that Phase Two of my mission was to find another spiritual Centre somewhere in the countryside. But I quickly dismissed any coincidence, since this one was clearly run by a devout religious order of nuns. But it would be interesting to see it nonetheless. Then a few days before the due meeting, I received an email from Robert Yarr who said:

This popped out of the ether this morning...'
    I see a coalescing vision of a Scottish-based, international spir-
    itual Centre of excellence. It would develop world class healers,

leaders, teachers and human beings for our collective next chapter and be deeply connected with the world's best peer Centres. What better way to raise the collective energy on the planet?

Best Wishes

Robert

It was intriguing to me to see that some of the inner sanctum of SIBL seemed to be picking up on an opportunity that this sale presented but maybe it was more to do with the fact that they were subconsciously picking up on 'Phase Two' and Arthur Conan Doyle's desire for a second Centre in the countryside. Afterall, if this was the case it would be the third such opportunity presented to me; the first by Lady Clyde, the second by the group with the derelict Care Home in the West of Scotland and possibly now this one. No-one knew about Arthur's wishes or of Phase Two, so I decided to keep it that way and just wait and see what happened, although there were interesting similarities with what Robert had said in his email. I was aware that this second Centre in Phase Two would have a more prominent focus on healing, amongst other things, and whilst this is mentioned in Robert's email it went on to suggest a tie up with a QiGong Master to achieve these objectives.

On the day in question, I drove northwards towards Perth and soon found Kilgraston and the Garden Cottage. I turned into the walled estate and parked the car. Although the entrance to the venue was through an old stone-built façade, when I walked inside I was suddenly in a very modern purpose-built conference Centre complete with auditorium with audio-visual equipment built-in, a large café/restaurant area, various offices and toilets. This is not what I was expecting at all. Clearly, it had all been upgraded very recently to provide these state-of-the-art facilities, but housed within a beautiful walled garden from which I could see various out-buildings around the perimeter. The place had a beautiful feel of tranquillity and peace.

I was shown into the conference room which had floor to ceiling windows along one side out of which was a lovely view of the garden and the fields and hills beyond – beautiful. Drew made special mention of the venue in his opening remarks and then handed over to the speaker of the day. At lunchtime we were invited to take a seat in the restaurant for lunch. I walked to a vacant seat and sat down. Very shortly thereafter a smartly dressed woman asked if she could sit next to me.

'I'm hoping you'll be able to help me', she said.

'Well, yes, if I can.'

'I'm Carmel, one of the nuns that run this place and I don't know if you know or not but it's about to be sold.'

'Yes, Drew mentioned this.'

'We have spent many years building up the spiritual energy in this place. It is such a special place to us, and it's used as a spiritual retreat. We would like to keep it like that, but we're worried if it is sold it will probably go to a developer to turn it into residential property and all our good work will be gone.'

I could hear the hurt in her voice and the urgency in her quest. 'How can I help you?'

'I hear that you are the Chairman of The Sir Arthur Conan Doyle Centre?'

'Yes, that's right.'

'You could buy it and run events from here and create a holistic healing Centre?' she suggested.

That was some straight talking; there was clearly no messing with this woman. She was on a mission. I heard my own thoughts and realised that I too was on a mission; could it be the same one? Could it converge in some way? Or was she just picking up the signal too that I was to find a second Centre, in the countryside. However, my response was immediate, 'I don't have the money to buy this place – I wish I did, it's lovely.'

She looked despondent. 'Oh, I thought you could help us.'

I felt immediately sorry for this woman and her fellow nuns. Although I had not met them before, I could tell this place had been a labour of love and I knew exactly how that felt. I decided to divert her from my answer and instead ask her to tell me about the place and what they did here. Apart from their actions of prayer and contemplation, I was surprised to hear that some of the rooms had been rented out to alternative therapists; the conference room was clearly already rented out to businesses and other functions but what surprised me most of all was to hear this nun talk about mindfulness training, the Labyrinth in the grounds and the fact that she had just undergone a croning ceremony.

For those who don't know what that is, here's an excerpt from www.learnreligions.com:

In early cultures, the female elder was considered a wise woman. She was the healer, the teacher, and the one who imparted knowledge. She mediated disputes, she had influence over tribal leaders, and she cared for the dying as they took their final breaths. For many women in Wicca and other Pagan religions, reaching the status of Crone is a major milestone. These women are reclaiming the name of crone in a positive way, and see it as a time to joyfully welcome one's position as an elder within the community.

Any woman can have a croning ceremony, although traditionally most choose to wait until they are at least 50 years old. This is partly because of the physical changes in the body, but also because five decades of learning is nothing to sneeze at! In some traditions of Wicca, it is recommended that you wait until after menopause to become a Crone. However, some women in their thirties no longer have periods, and some women continue menstruating into their 60s, so the timing of your ceremony will depend on the guidelines of your particular path.

A croning ceremony may be performed by a High Priestess, but can also be performed by other women who have already attained the position of crone. The ceremony itself is typically performed as part of a women's circle, a coven's Esbat, or a Sabbat gathering.

Some of these rituals were clearly Pagan or indeed Wiccan in their origin and I was very surprised that an order of Carmelite Nuns was practising them; but impressed too, it showed me that they were open to different forms of spiritual ritual, healing and meditation.

'Why is it being sold?' I asked.

'There are only three of us left now – nuns – and we are all getting older and don't have the energy to continue running this place. It also needs someone with a bit more foresight to try to make it more popular and try to find a way get more people to come. We thought this was something you could do.'

We only had the briefest of conversations over lunch, but we seemed to hit it off, this nun and me. I wondered if this was it; was this to be the second Centre that ACD had outlined as Phase Two? It certainly felt like it could be. I wondered, was this 'third time lucky? Spirit had once told me that before, when I was about to give up on setting up my own circle. Try, try, try again they had said, and this had resulted in the formation of my Group, The Thursday Group, who had received all the pertinent instructions and direction from ACD that had resulted ultimately in the formation of the Centre in Edinburgh. I decided I'd have to investigate further and asked Carmel if she could show me round the place. As the SIBL meeting was due to re-convene, we agreed to meet up at a later date when the place would be empty, so she could show me around the grounds and the other property on the estate.

Two weeks later, I returned to The Garden Cottage to meet Carmel and we walked around the grounds. There was the labyrinth in the walled garden, there was an ancient, small, private graveyard which somehow seemed significant and most of the rest of the grounds were covered in large mature trees. There were three cottages on the estate, which were currently occupied by the nuns and one which was used to accommodate visiting nuns.

There was only one stumbling block I could see; like Lady Clyde's home at Shiel, if this was to truly function as a spiritual retreat it too would require additional accommodation, and I said that to Carmel. She agreed, as they too had come to that realisation. And then she surprised me by telling me that there had previously been an application for planning permission to build an accommodation block next to the car park, which had been granted. This seemed too good to be true. All the elements seemed to be coming together and it certainly had the spiritual sanctuary feel that clearly had been built up by the nuns through years of devotion. I was beginning to get excited about the prospect. And again, like Shiel, I suggested to Carmel that if her desire was that it should continue to function as a spiritual and holistic healing Centre and retreat, then I could make that happen but without the necessity of owning it. I would just manage it, like the ACD Centre and pay them a rent or income from the events and activities. 'It depends if they really do want to sell it and realise the capital, or if they're happy receiving an income from it so that it can continue to function as a sanctuary?'

I could see the conflict in Carmel's eyes as I explained how that might work. 'You'll need to do a business plan. And then I can forward it to the Mother Superior.'

There was the stumbling block that I hadn't considered. This was owned by the Catholic Church, and I was a Spiritualist; I couldn't see how the Mother Superior would be very happy with that combination. Undaunted, Carmel said that if I presented my case well and she was to back it, then this potential problem could possibly be overcome if there was a true desire to maintain the sanctuary for the purpose it was intended.

I did my research, presented my case, and pushed the fact that I was brought up in a Christian family, albeit Protestant and not Catholic, but having considered it, the news eventually came back to me from the Mother Superior that the property was going on the market and would be sold.

I was deflated. It had seemed that all the indicators were in alignment. It had been brought to my attention by indeed going back to my business roots, as I had been told. I had also engendered the support of Drew Pryde and Robert Yarr of SIBL, so there was the potential to raise funds for additional accommodation, and there was planning permission. It already was operating as a spiritual sanctuary and had the beautiful walled gardens, labyrinth and woodland walks of a retreat, yet was just minutes off the main M90 motorway in central Scotland, so was well placed for commuting from the airport or indeed Edinburgh or Glasgow. Yet it wasn't to be. Why, I wondered, and what was the point of all of that effort, if it wasn't meant to be?

'There will be another opportunity.' I heard that message from Spirit again, but this time it annoyed me. I was already pretty exhausted running the ACD Centre. I was told there was to be a second Centre – a country retreat, yet for the third time these 'opportunities' came to nothing. In frustration I said, 'Where is this second Centre?' not really expecting anything back in response. After all, when I went through a similar scenario when we were told to find the building that would become The Sir Arthur Conan Doyle Centre, we were told, 'you'll know it when you find it', and other such enigmatic responses. I was much too annoyed and frustrated to go through that again, and so I think that might have been why this time I was given a response. I was shown the exact location of this proposed second Centre, not only the geographical location but the actual building where it is to be housed. I was also shown its purpose (much along the lines already outlined to Carmel) but also where the funds would come from to buy and transform this building into a new spiritual retreat, healing sanctuary and place of learning and contemplation. There would be no more wild goose chases. I would know when this place became available and when the funds were made available that this was the place it was to be.

I have chosen not to reveal that location here for reasons of commercial sensitivity and to preserve the sanctity of that message, but the members of my Group and two other trusted individuals know of this location, and we await it coming into fruition. For now, and in order to move on from the ACD Centre, I had to focus on finding someone to take over from me as Chairman and to get the book out. The plan for Phase Two had begun.

Chapter 18

The Scientists

In March 2018 the Sherlock Holmes Tartan was launched. The Scottish Field reports:

This is the first time that a literary character has had their own tartan approved by the Scottish Register of Tartans. Holmes was created by Sir Arthur Conan Doyle who was born in Edinburgh and gained his medical degree from Edinburgh University.

Appropriately, the official launch party took place on Thursday, 22 March, at the Royal College of Physicians on Queen Street in Edinburgh.

And it is a Conan Doyle descendant who has highlighted these Scottish links through the creation of a uniquely Scottish textile for his most famous character.

It was designed by Tania Henzell, a great-great step granddaughter of the author, who worked with weavers at the House of Edgar to finalise the design and have it registered.

Tania had attended my Fringe Show the previous year and I remember being a bit perturbed when our receptionist had told me just before I was due to go on stage that there was a descendant of ACD in the audience – his great, great granddaughter. Firstly, I felt very nervous, thinking I hope I don't say the wrong thing or anything that may upset this person, and then I remembered that ACD did not have any grandchildren. None of his four children had had children. So, how I wondered, could his be; maybe this was a crank. I didn't have time to concern myself with that; the show was due to start and so I stepped up on to the stage. Afterwards Tania came to introduce herself and she was lovely, but I was still a bit confused by the connection and as she had given me her email address I wrote to her afterwards and she responded:

Hi Ann

It was lovely to meet you too and thank you so much for a very interesting talk! So much that I didn't know about my step great great grandfather.

Jean was my step great grand mother, and yes, Jean and my great grandfather had no children, but my grand father did from his first marriage.

It would be lovely to meet you .....; I am free Wednesday, Thursday of next week, and all of the following week except Wednesday and Friday!.

Look forward to seeing you again at the Centre.

Kind regards,

Tania

Tania and I kept in touch, as she developed the new tartan which we now show at The Sir Arthur Conan Doyle Centre. I was also delighted to be invited to the grand launch at The Physicians Hall where I was also introduced to Richard Doyle, great nephew of Arthur Conan Doyle via his brother, Innes' son and his second wife, Angela.

Tania and I met up from time to time. One such time was when we were both separately invited to speak at the same event at Undershaw, a previous home of ACD in Hindhead, Surrey. Another interesting coincidence is that a number of ACD's previous homes are all involved in some sort of caring provision; Liberton Bank House, Edinburgh where he lived as a small boy is now a school for children with learning difficulties, as is Undershaw, where Tania and I were invited to speak to help raise funds for their school, Steppingstones; and Windlesham Manor, Crowborough, Sussex, where ACD died and was buried (in the garden, before being re-interred in a church graveyard in the New Forest) is a care home for the elderly.

Following the launch of the tartan, we had a visit from another family member of ACD who had attended the launch and was staying in a hotel just around the corner from us in Edinburgh. The hotelier contacted us and asked if they could bring them to see The Centre; we were pleased to oblige. Cathy Beggs is great niece to ACD and sister to Richard Doyle, referred to earlier. She and her husband Mike visited and seemed very impressed with what they saw and made a kind donation to our charity. Remember, still, at this time I had not revealed that ACD had been communicating with me and my 'cover story' was that we named the building after him because he was a Spiritualist and born in Edinburgh. In meeting Richard Doyle the evening before at the launch of the tartan, I could tell that he didn't have much interest in Spiritualism so kept my comments focused on the tartan. But it was from Mike that I learned a most interesting fact.

'Have you seen the picture of The Old Horse?' he asked as we walked around The Centre.

'No, I haven't seen that.'

'It's a sketch that Arthur did himself almost on his death bed and it suggests that he is going to reincarnate.'

'Really?' I said, 'I'd be really interested in seeing that'. Mike said that he was sure that he had it somewhere at home and he would send me a copy by email, once he returned home, which he did.

On 24 March 2018 at 22:06 Mike Beggs wrote:

Dear Ann,

Meeting you yesterday was very much appreciated on our visit to Sir Arthur Conan Doyle Centre.

Many thanks for your kind welcome and illustrating to us the history and activities of the Centre.

As promised, I attach a photo of the cartoon by Sir Arthur. It would seem to illustrate the 'load' he carried throughout his life.

As the last illustration shows him in bed and is dated 1930 it would seem it was drawn as his own 'cartoon obituary'.

With best wishes,

Mike Beggs

And my response:

Hi Mike and Cathy,

It was a real pleasure to meet you both at The Sir Arthur Conan Doyle Centre on Friday and thanks too for forwarding the cartoon of the Old Horse, it is indeed fascinating. I particularly like the prognosis that within 6 weeks it will be back on the road again - I might have some indications that this might just be the case!!!........

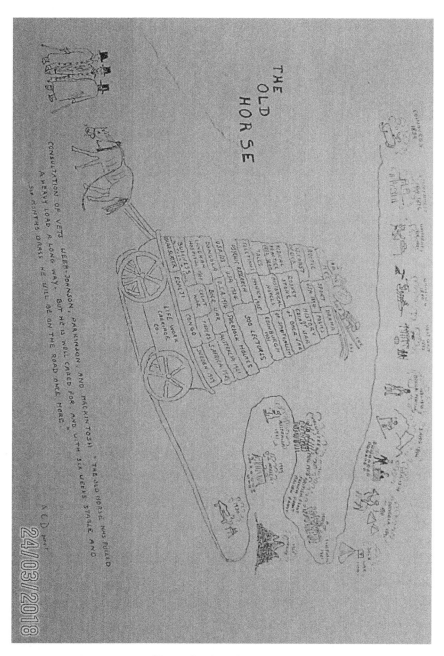

Here is the photo they sent me

As you can see from this image, ACD has outlined the many aspects of his life from his birth in 1859 to him appearing to be on his deathbed in 1930. But for me what is the most interesting element is the paragraph he has written at the bottom of his sketch, which says: 'The old horse has pulled a heavy load a long way. But he is well cared for, and with six weeks stable and six months grass he will be on the road once more.' This might mean that he did not expect to die but to recover, but his relatives, Mike and Cathy Beggs, suggest this indicates reincarnation, something I hadn't considered before in relation to ACD especially since he was in communication with my Group. But it is interesting too that the transcript already presented in this book, (in Chapter 17) where Drew Pryde and his friend Dave Patrick visited a medium also suggested that ACD was about to rein-carnate; the transcript states that if he does, Arthur would still be able communicate, even when incarnate. An intriguing theory.

Something much more intriguing happened around the same time in 2018. Through my regular monthly meetings with the Scot-tish Institute of Business Leaders, I had already met and got to know Robert Yarr. Robert's background was in Electronics and Electrical Engineering but like me, he had previously worked with one of the aforementioned 'big four' consultancy firms and now he had set up his own consultancy business. His main interest however was not in the corporate world but in the esoteric and in particular visiting the various indigenous tribes throughout the world. He was already aware of the non-physical world and realised that the indigenous tribes had maintained their connectivity with this unseen world, unlike the Western world who had poo pooed it as nonsense. Some of these tribes used it for communication with each other and some to connect with their ancestors for advice and learning. There was also an innate knowing about the land and nature and a concern over the future of the planet and Robert was keen to learn from this ancient wisdom. He has visited, sometimes lived with but very often communicated and learnt from the Dogon, in Africa, the native

American Indians both in the US and Canada, the Amazonian tribes and many others. This inspired him to look for ways to help the planet as this was the major concern from many of these tribes. They knew how to take care of their land but it was the vast swathes of land further afield that was of concern. It was being stripped of its forests and being turned into desert by de-forestation and farming with chemical fertilizers that was poisoning the land. An initial website called, 'Treetobe' was set up to deliver the message. Then, a very impressive downloadable e-book was created to bring the message home. The book went beyond the more typical carbon-based discussion by addressing how reforestation at scale might work to restore the water cycle thus averting mass water shortages, reduce CO_2 levels, and how the economics might work. It also encouraged everyone to get involved without waiting for inter-government agreement that would slow everything down.

This was all conceived over the previous couple of years after gaining the insights from planting 25 million trees in tropical and rain forests in three continents, a collaboration between the Tree To Be founders and the leading climate scientists who have studied these natural cycles for decades. From this early beginning this morphed into a new foundation called UnifyingFields.org, of which Robert was a co-founder. I am pleased to say that he included me in those early discussions, when the foundation was in its infancy, sending me many versions of green papers to review and comment upon and being included in meetings with interested parties. It was during this time that the conversation moved on towards not only looking at the problems with agriculture and deforestation but also the need to find clean energy sources. I already alluded to some of the conversations we had had with some of the top oil and gas executives in our SIBL meetings, but they were going to take some time to 'turn the ship' - if they decided to do so - and especially when government agencies get involved.

As Robert and Kees Hoogendijk, one of the original co-founders, both have engineering backgrounds with senior corporate experience, they both shared a long passion for the trailblazing field of 'New Energy'. Sometimes called 'Free Energy', it is commonly associated with the inventor of the technologies that launched the 20th century, Nikola Tesla. Facing the huge funding requirement to address the real human causes of climate change, Robert and Kees recognised that if they could bring Tesla's dream of 'abundant energy for all people' to life, then this would provide the transitional income to heal the climate.

Their plan was to introduce a 24th century energy paradigm in just over a decade.

After years of funding the most likely 'New Energy' scientists around the world, their key lesson was that what separated those with promise from those without, was consciousness.

These rare few scientists would suddenly report that they would be working and researching various solutions sometimes for many months or years when suddenly the answer would drop into their heads. Sometimes the answer would come as a dream, sometimes they would autonomously scribble it down and other times they would see it as a sort of vision in their minds eye.

As well as this, more scientists would somehow get in touch and report similar happenings or report that they simply felt compelled to make contact, and many of those scientists were already working on new sources of clean energy.

When Robert mentioned this to me, I said, 'they've downloaded it. Someone, somewhere, up there, has given them the answers or is trying to help.' It was incredible that scientists from various parts of the world, all working independently, would suddenly make contact with Robert and his team. It was as if they had all been given a small part of the jigsaw; this was a phenomenon I recognised. My Group had been through this scenario many times when we were downloading information about the building that would become the Sir Arthur Conan Doyle Centre.

I also became aware through discussion with Robert that some of those scientists who were particularly close to finding an alternative energy source and were at the point of trialling it disappeared. Some of this was quite sinister and this was quite well-known in this particular field of research, that there were many accounts of some scientists/inventors trying out new energy sources in their own homes as a sort of prototype only for them to disappear without a trace. It was apparent that there were powerful agencies who had a vested interest in keeping things exactly as they were. This meant that many were wary about collaborating and sharing their findings.

'We need to get them to meet', Robert said. 'Or at least some of the main thinkers on this subject. You see they're all around the world – they've never met – we need a safe place to meet.'

Without really thinking I said, 'Well you can always meet here?'

Robert looked at me as he thought through that proposition. 'That would be good and then I could take them over to see Liam too.'

Robert had found a manufacturing company that could tool some of these new components that some of the scientists had designed and the owner of the company was already well versed in healing and alternative sources of energy, so he was already on board.

'Well, if you think they'll come, I'm happy to provide a venue for a meeting place?', I said. And so it was that in May 2018 a small group of scientists from around the world met together for the very first time at The Sir Arthur Conan Doyle Centre. Prior to that, when the meeting was being arranged and I was liaising with Robert over the itinerary and at what time each person would arrive, Robert asked me if I would make an opening speech to them to kick off their agenda.

'I'm happy to do a 'Welcome to the Sir Arthur Conan Doyle Centre', if you wish?'

'No, I want you to do an opening presentation'.

'Me? What am I going to talk about to a group of scientists; I don't know anything about what they're doing,' I said.

'You need to talk about your experience in manifesting things. You've had the experience that they're just experiencing now and you are the living proof that it can be done, as you're standing in the very building that *you* 'downloaded'.

And that is exactly what I did, and surprisingly they were all very interested and intrigued and wanted to know more. I showed them around the building, the photo of the vortex and allowed them to feel the energy of the place. Their questions meant that I had already overrun my one-hour slot on the agenda and was concerned that the other more pressing issues, as I saw it, that they were really here to discuss, was being squeezed in terms of time. I reassured them that if they wanted to know more they could come back anytime and further if they really wanted to feel natural earth energy, they should go to Roslin; as I've mentioned before, this was my old stomping ground and I was always aware of the special energy of the place, from being a very small child, long before the chapel was made famous by Dan Brown and his book 'The Da Vinci Code'.

I'm not sure why I mentioned Roslin as this was something I had not really discussed outside my own Group but somehow it seemed important to tell these scientists, who were experiencing the meta-physical for the first time, questioning whether it was real or not, whilst trying to do their bit to save the planet. And so, it was agreed that we meet up again six months later in Roslin. I hired Roslin Castle for our meeting and by now they were all much more relaxed and confident in each other's company, since they had been sharing their findings over the intervening six months. The castle was not large enough to accommodate them, so they stayed in a nearby hotel. We would simply use the castle during the day for our discussions. We were surprised then when we turned up on the Saturday morning to find not only that the castle had been broken into the previous evening but that the burglar was still there – he had decided to stay overnight – and was still in bed when we arrived!

After this inauspicious start and having dealt with the police in various degrees of seniority we settled down to our meeting. We had already had dinner together the previous evening, so there was no need for any introductions or opening speeches this time. Robert was up on his feet with his flipchart, as they brain-stormed their technical and scientific ideas and theories. As this was going on, I realised I was totally superfluous to this discussion. There was nothing I could add; I didn't have the technical know-how and as my mind drifted off to other things, I suddenly became aware of a man (a Spirit man) standing next to me. This was hardly surprising since we were sitting in a 14th century castle which was steeped in history, so it would have witnessed its fair share of happenings and no doubt had an obligatory ghost if not residual energies. I was not tuning in. I am not accustomed to going about with my senses open and being a 'leaky medium' as some would call it, who feel compelled to give messages to unsuspecting bystanders. One of the first things to learn in mediumship is how to open up and close down, so this man had been quite determined since he had impressed his presence on me when I was 'closed'. As I now tuned into him, I realised he had longish collar-length hair as I could feel it on my own collar as he overshadowed me with his presence. I could feel that he was wearing a tailcoat, which had a short waistcoat front which he kept pulling down as if to straighten himself up. He was wearing an evening shirt with butterfly collar and bow tie. In his hand he held a baton, and he showed me himself tapping the baton on the top of a music stand as if to bring the orchestra to attention before they started to play – he was a conductor! Now that I had understood that part, he then showed me his white gloves, and these seemed to be important in some way as he kept showing me how he would put them on and make sure that his fingers were pushed right to the bottom of the fingers in the glove. He did this by placing one hand on the other and pulling up the fingers of the glove by placing the fingers of one hand through the other. I wasn't sure why he had spent so much time carefully showing me these gloves and demonstrating once again that he was wearing white gloves by showing me his hands with fingers outstretched. As I automatically pondered what he was trying to convey, these gloved hands were now holding a black top-hat and from this he pulled out a rabbit. A rabbit out of a hat – aha, he was a magician! But why was he here? And for whom? I couldn't understand it, but just at that moment Robert must have noticed that I had zoned out of the discussion, 'What's wrong?'

I relayed the information I had just gleaned and had just finished telling him about the rabbit out of the hat, when the man from Spirit reverted back to the music stand and the baton and laughed. He was making a joke; he was letting me know there was a double-meaning to what he was conveying. He was a conductor but not of music, of electricity. I hadn't yet had time to mouth this recent revelation, when Robert shouted, 'That's Tesla.'

'Tesla? I don't know about that but he's laughing about the double-meaning of being a conductor. He's showing me himself as a musical conductor tapping the music stand to bring the orchestra to attention but he's really trying to bring this gathering to attention, and he wants you to pull the rabbit out of the hat. He wants you to focus, get on with it and get it done. He is laughing at trying to convey to me who he is and that the white gloves meant nothing to me, so he was showing himself as a musical conductor when what he was trying to say was that he was actually a conductor of electricity. He found that amusing. Does any of this make sense?' I asked.

'Tesla wore white gloves.' Robert exclaimed.

I didn't know that and clearly the others didn't either, but Robert did and he was pleased that the pioneer of wireless electricity had made a visit to the group.

Tesla developed a form of wireless electricity which he had intended to distribute freely to the world but his backers who had financed his experiments had different ideas. He was ahead of his time with his wireless communication and energy inventions, but he eventually died in poverty in New York.

A healer had also been invited along for the day at Roslin and her task was to give each person a healing session to allow them to experience the energy individually. She had set herself up to use one of the upstairs bedrooms for her sessions and was now patiently waiting downstairs for their discussions to conclude. As the debate showed no sign of abating, I suggested that she could take me first as I had little to contribute to their discussions and wouldn't be missed and this would at least tick one of us off her list. She agreed and we went to the upstairs room. I lay down on top of the bed and she had placed tiny little notepads and pencils on the bedside table which she said could be used should anything come to me whilst I'm in the healing energy. I had never seen anyone do this before and I was in two minds as to whether this was a good idea or not.

It is not uncommon for communication from Spirit to come to both the healer and the recipient when the healing energy is being channelled, as a connection with Spirit is being established. But it is usually something that is just retained in the memory rather than one or other person stopping to write something down. As I reflected on this, I didn't think it was a good idea, but the healer was unknown to me and she had clearly established her own way of working, and as it turned out I was glad she did. She suggested that before we start, I set my intention. She suggested that since I didn't really need healing of any physical ailment that instead I might be looking for help with a specific issue or have some other question that I needed resolved or an answer to. Aha, I thought, that explains the notepad and pencils. I couldn't think of anything so I simply and silently asked Spirit to help those downstairs with their endeavours in whatever way they could.

As I relaxed into the bed, soft music played in the background, and she began her healing routine. I could feel the energy around me and surrendered to this overwhelming sense of peace. I could feel my whole body relax and the tension just disappear; it is at times like this that you don't realise how busy you have been and how much I had been running around trying to organise this event and hoping that all went well for everyone. Here was a short period of respite and sanctuary and I was in Roslin after all, somewhere I've always felt at home. As I luxuriated in this thought and peace, suddenly an image dropped into my head. I could see this image quite clearly; it was a diagrammatical drawing of some sort of contraption and it was for conducting electricity. Although I have no technical knowledge of these things at all, for some strange reason I knew what I was being shown and I knew what all the various elements were composed of and how they worked together in a specific order. I grabbed the notepad and pencil. I had to get this down on paper, for I knew this was not from my own knowledge and I couldn't have remembered or retained this very complex drawing and all its component parts. I made a sketch with arrows to indicate what each element was and a few notes of explanation, until I was satisfied I had captured everything. I sank back into the duvet, partly with relief that I had managed to capture everything – thanks to the little notepads – and partly with satisfaction and a smile that once again Spirit comes through when one least expects it.

I chose not to share my 'download' until all the others had had their sessions, thinking that they too might receive something and if so they could probably make much more sense of it than I. These healing sessions stretched on into the evening, as each person got their turn and whilst this was happening the others had started socialising and we enjoyed a lovely dinner with wine. This was not the time to start a debate all over again; they had been working on it all day.

The following morning, we were back in session. This was to be the wrap-up session as everyone would be returning home later in the day, so Robert was keen to capture what had been learned and achieved. He stood again with his flipchart and pen capturing all the relevant points, as each person shouted out to him. I was again feeling that I had nothing to contribute when I was suddenly reminded of my wee notepad which I had stuffed into the back pocket of my jeans for safe keeping. Dare I mention it? I was feeling very self-conscious. How could I possibly contribute to the discussion of these top scientists who had flown in from around the world to share their expertise. I felt that prompt from Spirit and knew I had to speak up. I waited until the contributions had ceased and then said, 'I got something from Spirit when I was in the healing session yesterday. It might mean nothing at all to you or might be a lot of nonsense but if I just tell you what I got then you can decide?' There was a lot of nodding of heads and so I pulled the tiny notepad from my back pocket and started explaining my diagram.

'Come up here, Ann,' Robert said, 'draw it out on the flipchart.'

I gingerly walked up to the flipchart and accepted the marker pen from him. With my little notepad in hand, I copied the diagram on to the flipchart. Before I could add the arrows pointing to the various sections, someone shouted out, 'I know that', [he did name what the contraption was, but I don't remember what he called it; it wasn't something I recognised.] He went on, 'I've been working on that, but I can't get the right combination of elements. I've tried various things but can't get it to work.'

Without thinking and losing all my inhibitions, I said, 'I can tell you what all these elements are and the order in which they should be set.' I started drawing arrows pointing to each element in turn and writing alongside what each element was. There was another exclamation, as he repeated what I had just written; confidentiality, prevents me divulging more here.

'I never thought of that. Of course,' he said, with a look that was like the cat who had just got the cream. He seemed excited and keen to get back and try it, he said.

I was pleased too. The diagram had been accepted. Robert carefully wrapped it up in his flipchart to save for future reference and soon afterwards they all returned to their various homes.

I too returned to my day job of running The Sir Arthur Conan Doyle Centre and revelled again at the intelligence of Spirit. Arthur had said that you will find that some people are brought into your life at certain times to be teachers and sometimes to be taught. My simpler analogy is that people are put in front of me for a reason; either they need something from me or I can gain something from them. Once again this had proven true and through a strange series of synchronicities, I had found myself in the midst of a group of international scientists trying to save the planet. I hope I have helped in some small way.

The reader can view the website UnifyingFields.org and see the good work and the extent of this organisation now and may also note that they state:

> 'Furthermore, we are developing and introducing a new class of energy technologies beyond fossil fuels, traditional nuclear fission, water, wind and solar power.
>
> UFF has a subsidiary company Restoration Power, which works with inventors all over the world, to validate their inventions and uses conscious capital to develop and implement these technologies in our society in collaboration with aligned partners.'

At the time of the 10th Anniversary of The Sir Arthur Conan Doyle Centre, I wrote to Robert to invite him to attend. His response is below:

Hi Ann,

How are you?

Thank you for the invitation to your 10th Anniversary.

The New Energy programme that was birthed with you in Roslin and the Centre is now a fully funded network of

European scientists. Unifying Fields has also created a pilot initiative to fund rapid ecosystem restoration in all communities.

Then there's the real stuff ...

Let's catch up sometime 😊

Best Wishes

Robert Yarr

Unifying Fields

www.unifyingfields.org

Notes from Robert Yarr

'When Ann suggested Roslin Castle as the location for the world's first conscious New Energy conference, I immediately sensed it was ideal. Not only did that ancient place evoke the right atmosphere for our collective work but it worked overtime on us overnight too. I experienced my first lucid dream, where I was looking at the birds nesting in the eaves outside my window at noon before realising this was odd. Then I noticed my eyes were closed yet all around me was broad daylight. After 20 minutes or so, when I finally opened my eyes it was pitch dark and 4am. Later at breakfast, a colleague explained that she had had exactly the same experience.

When Ann described the man who seemed to have dropped in on our meeting from the non-physical realms, I instantly recognised Tesla from her description. I was aware of his germophobia, which drove him to constantly wear gloves along with his formal attire. His amusing use of the double meaning of the word 'conductor' was interesting too, as he appeared to be bringing us all to attention as a conductor would do with his orchestra. But he was also known to amuse his celebrity friends such as Mark Twain who would frequently join his experiments and they were often seen conducting electricity through their bodies to light up the earliest neon tubes.

The diagram that Ann received has been acknowledged and recorded, and is seen by the team as Crystal Technology.

All New Energy technology is conscious.

The conference crystalised the 'conscious container' that Unifying Fields uses to birth its portfolio. It now has three laboratories and is on track to release the New Energy paradigm in 2027. It has now engaged the world's First Nations network to regenerate the climate from the bottom-up.'

— Robert Yarr, Unifying Fields
www.unifyingfields.org

Chapter 19

Consciousness

Whilst staying on the subject of scientists for the moment, when the Centre first opened and I wanted to have a lecture programme, which I called, The Tuesday Talks, there were many top names and well-respected scientists and academics who supported us and were keen to talk on their chosen subject. However, those enlightened individuals would often run the gauntlet of their compatriots as there were many in their chosen discipline (whether that be science or academic research) who had a vested interest in keeping the status quo – many had built their reputations on it and didn't want to see their past papers being usurped by some New Age thinking. Often our chosen speakers would report that they were the subject of verbal and on-line attack because of their views and this would often result in search engines like Wikipedia and others being re-written by their detractors to discredit the speakers and their research.

Whilst that still continues to this day, I'm happy to report that for many years now there is a growing band of those enlightened academics/scientists who have been researching this subject of the non-material world which they simply call consciousness. In this regard I must make special mention of Prof. Chris Roe, Professor of psychology at the University of Northampton, and Prof. Gary Schwartz, Professor of Psychology, Medicine, Neurology, Psychiatry, and Surgery, The University of Arizona, as both of these luminaries have been studying mediums and mediumship directly; both, by setting up labs specifically for this purpose and both have made considerable advances in the recognition of this faculty by the wider world and of its acceptance. Both are to be commended in taking their labs out to the experiencers and working together with those mediums and psychics in their own environment. Others prominent in this area are David Lorimer, and his *Thinking Beyond the Brain: A Wider Science of Consciousness* and some of his uTube videos give a good representation of the subject and the difficulties in understanding exactly what it is. Jeffrey Kripal's book, *The Flip*, claims the entire universe is a single vast mind, and Pim Van Lommel, the cardiologist who is best-known for his studies into near-death experiences that led him to believe that consciousness does not always coincide with brain functions and can be experienced separate from the body (*Consciousness Beyond Life, The Science of Near Death Experience*). There are many physicians, philosophers, psychologists and others too numerous to mention here that I am pleased to report are studying this phenomenon. To most researchers, consciousness denotes the relationship between the mind and the world. To the religious or spiritual it refers to the relationship between mind and God or the deeper spiritual meanings that are thought to be more fundamental than the physical world.

The experiencers, that is the mediums, psychics, sensitives and healers who work with this energy, call it the Universal Consciousness, or the Source, or the Spirit World/Realm – it is the metaphysical, non-material world which we know surrounds us and is intelligent, conscious and communicative.

As always it is the experiencers who lead the way in the exploration of this unseen world and naturally as with any venture into unfamiliar territory we will be wary and sometime fearful of the unknown. In the past many of our mainstream, traditional religions have tried to control this access into the Spirit World or access to God/Source by claiming it is only available through their channel and in particular via the Priest, Minister, Padre, etc. And where parishioners have taken this into their own hands they have been warned about raising the dead, demons, possessions, etc and told not to dabble in this area. However what we find now is that it is some of the scientists and researchers (most of whom have no religious background) who are doing the 'dabbling'. And to do this many are reverting to hallucinogenic drugs to achieve an 'altered state' – something which is usually taught in mediumship and psychic development but is achieved in a natural and controlled way and without the need of drugs.

Unsurprisingly, some of those researchers have been experiencing some strange phenomena on their 'trip' and as a past tutor and practitioner of Awareness Training, Psychic and Mediumistic Development, I have been asked to comment on this aspect of consciousness and how my views and experience differs from those of the main religious bodies.

Firstly, I come from a Christian up-bringing so I have some experience and understanding of the church's views; and I started my journey into this spiritual world by studying the paranormal and becoming a psychical investigator. So, my main approach rests on psychical research and my own experience in mediumship and in psychical investigations. I'd also restate the fact that the Centre proudly proclaims that we welcome all religions and none at all so I have no religious bias.

In my humble opinion and from my own experience, I sense that there is some form of hierarchy to the Spirit World. Some religions claim there are seven stages to the soul's progression in the afterworld. I don't know, but what I sense is that when people die their entry level to the Spirit World is nearest to our physical world before moving on and 'into the light'. I believe this is why they are easiest to contact by mediums who will gladly attest to the fact that 'they are all around'. And they will stay around as long as there is someone alive who remembers them. That's not to say that they are trapped or that they don't move on, but it is as if they retain an interest in us on the physical plane for as long as we may need them or maybe even to help our own transition in due course.

I don't believe that Spirits get 'trapped' on the earth plane or that God has forgotten them. In all of my experience, when investigating haunted houses, I found that where there is a Spirit-Being remaining in a house (and not just a residual energy from some traumatic event) that Spirit-Being is there for a purpose. There can be many purposes. I used to call it 'unfinished business.' This can take the form of some piece of pressing information that wasn't imparted before death, or for some who have lived in a place for so long they just cannot bear to leave it or leave their family – particularly their children. Others, who die suddenly and traumatically, don't know they are dead. Then there's a category who stay on this earth plane for their own devilment or gratification. This latter category is by far the smallest. If you consider that those in the Spirit World are by definition a representation of the population here on earth then the majority are just like us, ordinary, everyday people. Just like society, however, there will be a small malevolent element too. These might be the serial killers, murderers, rapists, paedophiles and just gener- ally the lowlifes of society. They have the opportunity to progress in the Spirit World too and learn the lessons of their ways, but some by their very nature will opt to continue to exert their will and/or terror on their victims on the earth plane.

Then there are the categories of the angels and fallen angels; the latter being the demons who are deceiving us by wearing different masks to hide their real identity, at least according to the Bible. For me, the most important point here is having the skill to be able to distinguish the difference. César Truqui, who is an exorcist of the Diocese of Chur, Switzerland, and who was a speaker at the 11th course on "Exorcism and Prayer of Liberation" at the *Regina Apostolorum* Pontifical Athenaeum in Rome (the course which inspired the Anthony Hopkins movie *The Rite*) was asked in an interview how he recognises if a person is possessed and what he does to perform the exorcism. He is asked specifically, *'How many of the people who have turned to you were really possessed?'* and the answer, *'Very, very few.'* Source: *www.Aleteia.org*

This is not to undermine what the priests do in performing exorcisms. Indeed, I agree with much that is said in that interview (although obviously I cannot comment on the procedure). The important point here is that these cases *'are very, very few'* and that the majority of people will never come across them. This may be why – and naively in my opinion – the Spiritualists say that these things don't happen and that everything is 'love and light'. I believe this does not follow the eternal flow of yin and yang, black and white, good and evil; for every action there is an equal and opposite reaction. But I do agree that there is a natural barrier that somehow seems to keep everything in its rightful place and so those mediums operating in the spiritual world of love and light, where our Spirit friends and relatives reside, are unlikely to ever encounter anything other than that. However, in my experience there is also a dark side to this astral plane, which is continually probing for openings and weaknesses that would allow entry to the physical world. These openings and weaknesses can occur in some people whose natural barriers have been compromised in some way e.g., through drink or drugs, illness, malnutrition, some forms of mental illness and of course from the uncontrolled use of the Ouija Board. I've seen many people fall foul of a malevolent entity that has gained access through one of those means and they have had to call for help. It is for this reason that I too would warn people against using the Ouija Board. In my first book *Arthur and me,* I told of how my Group were instructed by Spirit to use the Ouija Board and how I was very much against doing so, because I knew from my psychical investigations of the dangers of doing so. Our trust in our Spirit Team was being tested and so we did as we had been asked and got some tremendous results and information that we could not have gotten by any other means, but we also experienced a 'drop-in' communicator purporting to be one of my relatives. I shut down the session immediately, as I could sense that the entity was not what they claimed to be. I believe we were allowed to communicate with both of these beings for our own development so we could sense and determine their differences. It was a learning curve and after all we had been told by Arthur Conan Doyle that he would take us through the various stages of our spiritual development so we could experience and understand such things. For the same reason I think we were allowed to experience the manifestation of Aleister Crowley. It was no coincidence that we just happened to be sitting in his room in the Theosophical Society. And this also makes me wonder if the entity in the basement of the ACD Centre that had the power to lift Iain off his feet and bodily throw him in the air was indeed a demon. I too encountered it up close and personal and could sense that it was not human and had never been human. It seemed to have no skeletal frame and instead seemed like a moving mass of pure evil. It possessed unbelievable power. Was I allowed to experience that too as part of my development - so I could experience and sense such things that I had never encountered before – and hopefully never will again?

The other point I would address here is the more recent commentary about UFO's and ET's. There is a claim that these too are demons masquerading as ET's and UFO's [now called UAP's[1]]. I am the first to admit that this is not my area of expertise at all, but I do attend weekly, on-line discussions with a group of fellow paranormal investigators from around the world and many of those are experts in this field. When I hear of their testimonies and the statements from witnesses and abductees, what stands out for me is the fact that those who experience this type of phenomenon receive communication telepathically, so the same faculty of psychic or mediumistic contact is being utilised. The other interesting factor for me is that I too have experienced a vision of an ET in the past whilst sitting myself for my normal meditation. I discarded the image as nonsense. It returned a couple of more times during that session, until I eventually managed to dismiss the image all together. Because I was curious as to why that should happen and because at the time I had access to the top mediums of the day all working at The Centre, I was able to ask them if they had ever encountered anything like this. I was most surprised to hear that most of them had, but didn't want to talk about it, probably for fear of ridicule. Now that time has moved on, there is actually a protocol that has been developed by Dr Steven Greer for making contact with Extra-terrestrials. It is called the *CE-5 Handbook* [Close Encounters of the 5th kind – humans initiating contact with extra-terrestrials]. This handbook uses meditation and telepathic communication methods to make contact and seems to have resulted in mass UFO sightings. Before leaving this subject all I would say is that there is so much information now that can verify the existence of ET's and UAP's that their presence is undeniable. What they are and what their intention is, is another matter. For more information on this subject see MUFON.com and SETI.org

In summary, I believe that all of the mainstream religions are doing much the same thing, just under a different name. It was man who set up these exclusive 'clubs' and claimed that 'my club is better than yours' and then entered into years of wars and persecution to prove their superiority with everything from The Crusades to the witch-hunts. If we look however at the origins of these mainstream religions, you will find that they all start with someone having a psychic or paranormal experience. Someone has a vision or a visita-tion and during this encounter they experience some sort of divine intervention and wisdom. These prophets then tell others of their experiences and develop a following of believers. Someone then writes it down and what is written is believed and becomes sacrosanct – like the Bible, the Quran or the Zohar – and then the book is distributed throughout the world. So, whether the prophet is Mohammad, Buddha, Jesus or any of the others, they all receive their visitations whilst being in the silence i.e., sitting under a tree or going into the desert for forty days and forty nights but it is in this period of contemplation that they receive their wisdom. The same is true of Spiritualism and mediumship; it is in the silence that one can become aware of the other world and a universal consciousness. The majority of religions believe too in some form of life after death. Whether that be heaven, nirvana or even reincarnation, the main principle is that you do not die but live on in some other form. Just like atoms in the science labs, energy does not die it just changes and continues in a different direction.

When I see these similarities and realise that most of these religions are doing the same thing, just under a different guise and adding their own variations to it as rules or guiding principles, I can see that there is a common denominator here, a common purpose and a common experience. That being the case, I would simply posit that there is a greater power directing operations. Whether that be God, the Source, the Universal Consciousness or even ET's, those prophets already mentioned were all experiencing the same thing just interpreting it differently. This suggest that there is an omnipotent power and intelligence that governs this universe that we are all part of. When we die, we shed our physical body but our Spirit survives, sometimes staying around and in touch with others still on the earth plane but otherwise we progress through those spiritual planes, eventually shedding all need of the material and memory of ourselves as individuals as we merge into the oneness of the source. Just as it is easy for mediums to access those Spirit-Beings nearest to the physical, it is possible for some mediums to fine tune their vibration still further to access those higher planes and make contact with angels and those highly evolved Spiritual Beings. In this realm there is no need for protection or for fear of those lower-level entities, as they simply cannot penetrate this higher vibrational level. Conversely, just as I've had to go into a few haunted locations and prepare myself to make contact with some of those in the lower realms that persist to wreak havoc [the lowlifes] I'm sure it is possible for those demons that the churches talk of and which Aleister Crowley dealt with, to infiltrate our world wherever they find an opening or weakness. Thankfully I've not had to deal with those and I am perfectly happy to leave this to the priests and the exorcists, who are specially trained to deal with them.

Once again, I state the importance of being able to determine the difference. Indeed, the Bible tell us, "Test the Spirits to find out if they are of God" (1 John 4:1), and Paul says that we should be "discerning of the Spirits" (1 Corinthians 12:10). In mediumship this skill is learnt through experience and builds upon your natural sixth sense and your fight or flight response; your body will often tell you when to stay put and when to run. And so it is entirely reasonable to advise others not to dabble in areas that they do not understand or cannot control, like the Ouija Board. Mediumship training on the other hand is usually done with the training and supervision of an experienced medium and in those environments those lower levels are unlikely to ever be encountered.

So I would encourage the experiencers to explore further; to be discerning but to be the pioneers of the future and push the frontiers of this exciting unseen world. Like religion, this will begin by the experiencers reporting a phenomenon. The more people who report having this experience, the more likely it is to be researched and examined – and the scientists and academics will follow.

Notes

Interesting that the Vatican has held their own Seances and the Catholic church now endorses psychic abilities, provided you're a church member. On 16th May 2016, the Vatican released an important letter indicating that those parishioners with 'charismatic gifts' were to be welcomed, and this shows how the church has changed their perception. An excerpt from that letter is below:

The charisms are particular gifts that the Spirit distributes "as He wishes" (1 Cor 12:11). In order to give an account of the necessary presence of the diverse charisms in the Church, the two most explicit texts (Rm 12:4-8; 1 Cor 12:12-30) make use of a comparison with the human body: "For as in one body we have many parts, and all the parts do not have the same function, so we, though many, are one body in Christ and individually parts of one another. Since we have gifts that differ according to the grace given to us, let us exercise them" (Rm 12:4-6). Between the members of the body, this diversity does not constitute an anomaly to avoid, on the contrary, it is both necessary and productive. It makes possible the fulfilment of diverse life-giving functions. "If they were all one part, where would the body be? But as it is there are many parts but one body" (1 Cor 12:19-20). A close relationship between the particular charisms (charísmata) and the grace of God is affirmed by Paul in Rm 12:6 and by Peter in 1 Pt 4:10.[13] The charisms are recognized as a manifestation of the "multiform grace of God" (1 Pt 4:10). They are not, therefore, simply human capacities. Their divine origin is expressed in different ways: according to some texts they come from God (cf. Rm 12:3; 1 Cor 12:28; 2 Tm 1:6; 1 Pt 4:10); according to Eph 4:7, they come from Christ; according to 1 Cor 12:4-11, from the Spirit. As this last passage is the most insistent (it mentions the Spirit seven times), the charisms are usually presented as "manifestations of the

Spirit" (1 Cor 12:7). *It is clear, nonetheless, that this attribution is not exclusive and does not contradict the preceding two. The gifts of God always imply the entire Trinitarian horizon, as theology has affirmed from its beginning, both in the West and in the East.*[14]

Source: https://www.vatican.va/roman_curia/congrega tions/cfaith/documents/rc_con_cfaith_doc_20160516_iuve nescit-ecclesia_en.html

Chapter 20

2019, Still Traveling

I had already been travelling quite extensively, having previously worked frequently in Frankfurt as well as Munich in Germany and Basel in Switzerland amongst other UK and international venues then in 2018 my travel plans extended further, to Asia and especially to Hong Kong, where I was invited to speak and teach in that city. I was proud and a little nervous to be invited to speak to The Royal Geographical Society in Hong Kong. At last, I thought I have been invited to speak to a mainstream organisation, this being one of my aims. The venue had sold out quickly and there were people standing at the back to hear me speak about Arthur Conan Doyle, Edinburgh and The Centre. I was relieved it was such a success and the Chairman immediately invited me back, as his phone continued to ping with positive feedback from his members as we sat and had dinner afterwards. I also spoke at The Asia Society in Hong Kong and conducted a two-day workshop in the city. Buoyed with this success, I decide to take up an earlier invitation I had received to come and teach and speak in Lilydale, New York. For some, such an invitation is regarded as the ultimate accolade, since it is the home of Spiritualism. I planned a visit for August the following year, 2019, and linked it up with other invites to Toronto, Vancouver and Nova Scotia in Canada.

When 2019 arrived, the Thursday Group had another retreat arranged, in Roslin. We had been to Roslin as a group before for a day visit, and also in 2017 when we hired the castle to stay for four days. This had enabled us not only to sit regularly and in this special place of mine but also to stay overnight in situ as we worked with Spirit in the Group. The castle is very atmospheric, but it does not have the best layout, as some of the bedrooms are accessed through another bedroom and none of the bathrooms had locks on the doors. We joked about the fact that we'd have to sing or whistle when we went to the toilet, so as to let others know it was occupied. Gill did the catering and always had tasty dishes for us to look forward to in the evening in the castle's dining hall, which was complete with hanging tapestries, candelabra and squeaky doors. Of course, no self-respecting castle would be complete without a dungeon and the one in Roslin Castle is several floors down into the bowels of the earth or that's how it felt. But for the most part, we sat in the cosy lounge in front of a roaring log fire and reconnected again with each other and with Spirit.

One example of the playfulness of Spirit came during that visit. As we sat together in circle in the castle, I heard very distinctly, 'when the student is ready the teacher will emerge.' And I was also shown a specific grave that I was to find, that would provide more information on this point. I was shown the actual position of this gravestone in my mind's eye, so I knew it was in Roslin Graveyard and near the back wall. The Group members were very interested in this latest revelation and wondered whether it could be someone connected to the Knights Templar, which had figured regularly in our sittings. Or could it be someone connected to Arthur Conan Doyle or some other great luminary? We knew that William Wordsworth, Rabbie Burns and Sir Walter Scott had all visited Roslin, but as far as I was aware none were buried in the graveyard.

When we finished our sitting, we all set off to visit the graveyard. We walked along the lines of graves with me signalling to the others that it was 'along here,' only to come to the actual grave and find that it was that of my old primary school teacher!

The Group laughed at the irony of it, as I explained who she was; clearly the message being that the student was *not* ready and had only just begun. It was also a check on our expectations. We did have great expectations as we had received so much in the past that we probably expected more. I think the lesson we were being shown was one of patience and restraint, and perhaps a reminder of who was in charge.

As always, the main reason to plan a retreat was to allow us time to sit more regularly and in a focused way. This was becoming more and more important to us as it seemed that the physical phenomena that had been promised to the Group by Arthur Conan Doyle were happening spontaneously in the main part of the building, and being witnessed by others in the building rather than within the confines of our Group. What did seem to be happening in the Group was that Spirit was working much closer with us. Tricia would often connect with the angelic realm, so we could feel this highly-evolved spiritual-being shower us with unconditional love. George was working more with Shamanic energies and some of the visualisation and animal Spirit guides were very physical. Jim would have familiar Spirit communicators that would speak through him that were readily identifiable. Evelyn tended to render profound philosophy from her Spirit contacts, whilst Gill would always keep a watchful eye on everything, forever the teacher and her guidance was very much appreciated. As far as I was concerned, for some time I had been aware of being moved by Spirit – literally. It started with a swaying motion, both side to side and back and forward but now it was as if there was something inside me. As I sat, I could feel as if something inside was walking their fingers up my spine at the joint of every rib but from the inside. As I sat in the Group, I could feel this little push of my spine as each vertebra one by one was pushed into the back of the chair, but from inside my body. It was a weird feeling.

After setting up the Group in 2006, I had been told by Spirit that it was going to be a physical group and that we were going to be taught about different forms of energy and communication for our own development and that at some point we would be required to speak out about this to the public. During that time, apart from not wanting to do physical mediumship at all, I was always of the opinion that if the physical phenomena were to take place then it would just take place in the Group spontaneously rather than via any one individual. Jim used to always challenge me on this point and would regularly ask, 'Who do you think will be the Physical medium?'

I would always reject this point and tell him that it would be a group thing. Now I was beginning to wonder. The physical movement continued to increase week by week, so that now when I sat I would feel as if there was something inside me struggling to get out. The Group would talk about seeing my stomach ripple uncontrollably and often I would feel as if I was going to be physically sick and would look for something to throw up into. The best way to describe it is as if the 'fingers' that had previously been tiptoeing up my spine had now moved to the front of my body and turned into 'fists' that were fighting to get out. I realise that this all sounds very dramatic but what I think was happening was that Spirit was trying to take control of my body and I was resisting and retaining control. This continued for the next few years until a smoother merging could take place, so much so that when I was sitting very recently (2023) Fredrik Haglund a medium from Sweden who had briefly sat with our Group exclaimed:

'I saw Arthur Conan Doyle with different faces through your face, Ann. When everything stabilised, I saw his face clearly in your face with a moustache like the picture in The Centre. It was fantastic and mind blowing. I don't remember if there was move-ment, but I do remember the smell of tobacco, like a pipe or cigar. I've never seen anything like it.'

And another Spiritual medium who also witnessed this said:

'I had never seen Ann work as a medium although I was aware of the connection between Ann, the others in the Group, the Arthur Conan Doyle Centre and the inspiration for her previous book. While observing someone in an altered state, I like to keep an open mind as I have witnessed some mediums who say this great pioneer, or other great pioneers influence their mediumship, so I tend to sense or feel out more for the power of Spirit and simply ask 'show me you are there,' just as I did on this occasion. While observing Ann in the altered state, clairvoyantly I was aware of the figure I recognised through photos I have seen of Arthur Conan Doyle come from her right-hand side and stand directly behind her. He then looked at myself and wagged a finger towards me. I was made aware as he stepped forward and blended more with Ann and at this point the power became very intense. Only once before I have felt that intensity. Suddenly there was a strong overshadowing taking place with Ann, as I could see the strong male features as the power became so much stronger and it was as though Ann was disappearing in this power. I was drawn to Ann's hands and at that point, the same finger on the same hand shown clairvoyantly in my mind by Arthur Conan Doyle slowly started wagging in the same manner as shown before. There was no doubt in my mind, I was sitting in the presence of someone special and had the pleasure of meeting Arthur Conan Doyle.'

— John Seely, Spiritual Medium

Back to 2019 and our repeat visit to Roslin. This time we hired College Hill, which is an old coaching inn and now turned into a cottage that is situated right next door to the new Visitor Centre at Roslin Chapel. This venue is far better laid out for our use, with no need to access one bedroom from another and no need to sing in the bathroom. This time we had another visitor with us, Peter [pseudonym]. I have mentioned before that Arthur Conan Doyle once said that some people are brought into your life to teach you and others to be taught. We had had a few examples of this during the lifetime of the Group when we would realise that someone had crossed our path for a reason and when we sensed that we would invite them into the Group as a visitor on a temporary basis. They would usually get what they needed, and we too would learn from the process and things would progress from there. Peter was one such person. He had come to my attention when he was in the audience listening to my Fringe Show and had come up at the end of the show to ask me some questions. As it turned out, he too had a financial background and had worked in the city, so we had common ground between us. But also, like me, he was searching for something different, and his world view had changed. He was starting to explore the non-physical world – we brought him into the Group.

Strangely enough we had had a previous incidence of doing this with someone else when our goodwill was tested to the full. We had invited someone into the Group on the basis already outlined, and shortly after this Iain and I went on holiday. We were on a cruise to New Zealand from Australia and just as the cruise-ship was leaving Sydney I got a message from Spirit, 'There's a Judas in your camp.' I was concerned to receive this message and I knew exactly to whom the message referred, but I was on the opposite side of the world and had left this person in the Group back in Edinburgh. Later that same evening, using the ship's internet I accessed my email account with the intention of sending some sort of warning to my Group, only to find that I had actually *received* a warning. This time from Mayumi.

She had sent me an email to tell me that she needed to speak to me urgently because I had a problem in the Group and that someone had infiltrated the Group with negative intention that was specifically targeted towards me. (As a reminder to the reader, Mayumi was one of the original members of the Group – a founder member – and she had left to emigrate to Canada. So, here she was still picking up information about the Group and from the other side of the world too; just the opposite side from me in Australia.)

I had no such concerns about Peter. He was searching and questioning and that was perfectly okay, although he did still have his corporate persona which raised a few eyebrows in the Group from time to time. But he came with us to Roslin in 2019 and like us, this helped him to focus on his own development and he went on to study comparative religions at New College, Edinburgh University's School of Divinity. But whilst he was with us in Roslin, he and I went for a walk after one of the sessions just to get some air. As we walked, we were talking about 'Phase Two' and how that might manifest itself. I remember Peter being quite keen that I take more decisive steps towards achieving this next objective. Although I was explaining to Peter what I thought was intended by Spirit as the way ahead, it had to be made clearer for me. If what I had been shown was indeed what was intended, then Spirit would have to do more to make it happen. I also guessed that the timing wasn't quite right. My Group had received messages from Spirit over a five-year period about finding the building that would become the ACD Centre and when we eventually found it and I asked why we couldn't have been there before (since it had been empty during all of this time), I was told it wasn't ready. I guessed that Phase Two wasn't quite ready yet, since it was only me who had had this vision and no clues or signposts or messages had yet been received by the others in the Group.

As Peter cogitated on this, I could see he was not sure whether he accepted this scenario as the urge to take a more hands-on approach was upper most in his mind. I too understood and resonated with his thinking, as it most closely resembled how I would do things in the past but I felt if I took the steps myself then it would be my initiative rather than that directed by Spirit.

Our walk had come full circle and we were now on our return journey back towards Collegehill Cottage to re-join the others. We walked uphill towards the graveyards; two of them straddle the path that leads towards the castle and the third one is separated by another path that leads towards the road and the Powder Mill (another walk in the area). We were on this latter path and as we were approaching the graveyard, I saw in the distance a gravestone that looked as if the top of it had been broken off. It looked as if the gravestone had been in the shape of a cross, but the top part of the cross had been broken off and the gravestone now resembled a sort of lopsided 'T' shape.

'What a shame,' I said, 'someone has broken that gravestone,' and we proceeded towards the stone to have a closer look. As we got there, I was most surprised to find that the grave was actually that of Canon Roland Walls, the monk or hermit that I had spoken of with Lady Ann Clyde as well as Patty Burgess, and I found that she too shared this grave with him. There was something more too. I found that the gravestone had not been broken as I had suspected but it was in this 'T' shape, which I instantly knew was significant in representing the Tau. Was this the sign that I had just spoken of?

Here are some extracts from www.seiyaku.com:

The Tau is an ancient symbol and also known as the Crux Commissa, the Franciscan Cross, the Anticipatory Cross, the Advent Cross, the Crutch Cross, and the St. Anthony's Cross.

Dive into heraldry and we see naming conventions often have profound meaning. The heraldic term for Tau is Crux Commissa, which transliterated means a 'commissioned cross'; that is, a cross that has been assigned a mission (the Crucifixion) by a higher authority (God).

The Tau is an emblem of immortality, of life in general, and sometimes a phallic symbol. It is a pagan sign of the mystic Tau of the Chaldeans and the Egyptians, where it represented the Roman god Mithras, the Greek Attis and their forerunner Tammuz, who was the Sumerian dying and rising god, consort of the goddess Ishtar. Conveniently, the original form of the letter 'T' was the initial letter of the god of Tammuz. During baptism ceremonies, this cross was marked on the foreheads by the pagan priest.

Today in India and elsewhere, marking the forehead (at the point of the Ajna Chakra - the location of one's conscience / third eye) with a sacred tilak mark, is a custom practiced by Hindus and others, signifying that they follow Brahma, Vishnu, Shiva, Devi or Shakti.

Much later, the Tau cross shape attributed to Moses as an instrument of healing was adopted by the Egyptian Fr. Anthony as an ascetic in the Egyptian desert. Although his lifestyle was simple and hermit like, he was admired for his health (he lived to be 105) and wisdom. His fame spread - even reaching Emperor Constantine. The Tau cross then took on an additional name: the St. Anthony's Cross.

St. Francis adopted St. Anthony's Cross after meeting monks working at a leper house in Assisi and at the hospital of St. Blase in Rome (now the church of San Francisco a Ripa) where Francis stayed.

He used this cross as an amulet for protection against the plague and skin diseases, just as the Egyptian claim that the symbol aided immortality and general well-being.

Ann Treherne

Monk's habit, arms outstretched, forming a Tau

Stretching out his arms, St. Francis demonstrated to his friars that their habit was the shape of the Tau cross. They must go out into the world, wearing this cross like an incarnation of Christ. The monks were Antonines from the holy Order of Hospitallers of St. Anthony.

The tour to Canada and New York in August 2019 would be my swan song, since it would be my 60th birthday that September and I had previously given my Board of Trustees a year's notice of my intention to retire then. I felt I had achieved all that I had been tasked with doing by Arthur and our Spirit Team; we had found the building, set-up The Centre and in the name of Arthur Conan Doyle. It was very successful and well-known both at home and abroad, and we were getting the message out to the wider public. The one remaining thing I had to do was write the book, but as I decided I wouldn't have time to do that until I had retired another action point became more pertinent: i.e. to find someone to take over from me as Chairman.

There were two things that changed that plan. Firstly, I was encouraged to have the book available for Lilydale or even to launch the book while I was there so that it was available to the American market as well as the Canadian one. Just as I was considering that that couldn't be achieved in the timescale, when considering my duties as Chairman to The Centre and all my other speaking and teaching engagements, I received the second and more important reason why the book had to go out sooner rather than later. Jim, the patriarch to our Group, took me aside to tell me he had been diagnosed with prostate cancer. This was a bitter blow. Although Jim was now 82, he was a very sprightly and active octogenarian. He was still actively helping me at The Centre whenever we needed him and was an anchor-man in our circle. Because of this, I had already decided that I was going to dedicate the book to him when I had time to write it. Now it seemed that time was running out and I needed to make a huge effort to get the book out.

I started writing furiously whenever I could. A couple of years before this in 2016 I had taken myself off for a week of solitude in a cabin in the woods, so I could think about what would go into the book and how I would structure it. I had taken a flipchart with me and opened it out like a double page spread so that it covered the whole of the large wooden table. With marker pen in hand, I started doing a brain dump of all the things I could think of that should be included in the book and to help me with that I had taken the tapes and transcripts of our recorded session with the Thursday Group as we had sat each week from 2006 until we found the building in 2010.

So, I already knew what I was going to write about. I had the bullet-point headings. I just needed to write it now. But how long was that going to take; I had better get my head down. By the end of 2018, I had managed to write ten chapters of what I envisaged would be around 23 chapters, so less than half way; the pressure was building. As we entered 2019 and The Centre re-opened for business after the Christmas and New Year break, Iain and I were due to head off to Mexico for some R&R as we usually did at this time of year. I was also secretly thinking that this would enable me to do more writing whilst I was away, when Violet a frequent visitor to The Centre asked, 'And have you got someone to edit your book?'

'*Edit* my book,' I said indignantly, 'it's all I can do to get it written.' I hadn't had time to even think about it being edited let alone consider who might do this. But as always, as soon as that thought goes out it gets answered. Just the next day Lance Butler was attending one of the first Tuesday Talks of the year. He had written to me previously telling me that he was moving from Perth to Edinburgh and since he would now be living close at hand he asked if I needed any volunteers. I had previously met Lance as he had attended one of the Gordon Smith workshops, but I hadn't had any opportunity to speak to him then. But now, as he walked in to take his seat at the talk, I went over to greet him. 'Good evening, Lance, nice to see you here.'

'Nice to be here, now that I've settled into Edinburgh, and I can get on with writing my book.'

'Oh, you're writing a book – so am I.' I had said it without thinking and was now wishing I hadn't. How could I possible talk about my book in the same sentence as his book, a Professor of English Literature. And just as I was trying to hide my embarrassment, he said,

'If you ever need an editor for your book, I'm your man.'

'Really?'

'Yes, of course,' he said, as he sidled along a row to take his seat for the talk, and I walked to the podium to introduce the speaker. I didn't see Lance at the end of the talk, as there were the usual questions to the speaker from people who had waited around at the end to ask them. But I went home that night thinking, did he mean what he said? Was he just being polite? Had I stupidly put my foot in it? I decided I had to ask him as it was too good an opportunity to miss. At the next meeting I asked if he meant what he said about editing my book.

'It would be a pleasure,' he said.

'Really? It's not an academic book - far from it, it's just popular, hopefully, light reading.

'I can do that', he said.

I had found my editor. I paid tribute to Lance in the book, for amongst other things meeting my ridiculous timescales. I explained to him the two reasons for the urgency in getting the book out and when I said I needed it published in time for me to take the books with me to Lilydale in August, he told me that that would be a tall order, but he would do his best and he certainly did. On 14th January 2019, two days after I had sent him the first ten Chapters, he wrote back to me:

Dear Ann,

It has been a pleasure for me to take what I imagine is one of the first looks at your manuscript. You have quite a story to tell and you tell it well, especially considering your trepidation about writing a book at all. Of course, Spirit commanded you to do it, so you must feel you have no option. But well done you.

Reading your MS, I have been left with an even greater admiration of your talents than before. And of course, left also with the feeling that just as so many things have been *meant* in your life perhaps you have been *meant* in mine.

I look forward to the next instalments.

Let us get together after your return from Mexico, perhaps in early February.

With love,

Lance

We agreed that I would keep writing and shovelling chapter

after chapter to him until I had got the book to its natural conclusion and then I would go back and attempt to include his edits. We almost made it. By August I had uploaded the manuscript, photos and front cover ready for publishing but there was just no time left for printing and delivery of books, so I opted just to publish as an e-book at this time which was sufficient to launch in New York and Canada. I had also purchased branded USB sticks so that the link to the book and some pictures could be downloaded by my students. [I must thank Betty-Jane Ware for her help with this and her assistance at Lilydale.]

I was away on this tour of New York and Canada for a month, and I called home every day to ask about Jim who was in hospital by this time. But he rallied and made it home and by the time I got home Iain had printed off the book in large print (as Jim also has macro-degeneration of his eyesight) and we bound it and took it to him at his house. He was quite overcome to see the dedication.

September was my 60th birthday and Shereen had organised a lovely wee celebration in The Centre just with a few friends and colleagues. But it was also Board Meeting month, and I had approached Lance as a potential trustee in April that year and asked him to sit in on the September meeting to get a feel for how we worked and to allow the other Trustees to meet him. He was appointed as a Trustee at that meeting. When we got to the item on the agenda concerning my retirement, despite the years notice nothing had been done to appoint a replacement. I pointed out that I didn't consider it appropriate for me to appoint my own replacement since I would no longer be working with that person in the future but that I thought in due course Lance might make a good Chairman but for the moment he was just joining us for the first time. Lance was absent during that part of the discussion as he had to leave early because of an emergency at home but it was agreed in his absence that I would approach him about potential Chairmanship and if he agreed I would stay on till the end of the year to allow him to shadow me before I retired. He agreed.

Just a month later Shereen asked Lance and me for a meeting in which she informed us that she was pregnant and expecting her first child. I still remember the look on Lance's face as he said to me afterwards, 'You've got to stay – you can't leave.'

I realised too that I couldn't handover the Chairmanship to a new person who had only been a Trustee for a couple of months, whilst at the same time the Centre Manager would soon be off on maternity leave. I agreed to stay on for one more year; and that year was 2020, the year of the pandemic.

In January it was clear that the UK was about to shut down as Covid 19 traversed across the world from China. Europe had shut its doors country by country and now this nasty illness was in the UK. I got our staff together and urged Scott and Natalie to work together as fast as they could to put as many of our activities on-line as possible in preparation for this eventuality. I remember Scott asking, 'How much will we charge?'

'Make it free', I said, 'we have to do our best to keep our customers and give them something to keep coming back to us for, as we don't know how long we will be in this situation.' Scott and Natalie worked diligently to achieve this; Scott doing most of the technical stuff and Natalie working on how we would market this to our database of customers. The country locked down on 23rd March 2020, but we were ready. We had purchased 'Zoom,' an internet-based software system that allowed for meetings and group chats etc. When purchasing it, we had to opt for the plan that would accommodate the size of the audience that would be attending our events online. Since we would normally have in-person audiences of around 100 attending our demonstrations of mediumship, we opted for the next category up which would allow us up to 500 attendees. This was a generous margin above what we would normally expect, or so we thought. At our first Tuesday Talk we were oversubscribed and had a number of complaints from people who couldn't get access because we had exceeded our 500 limit. The limit was duly increased. We were one of the first organisations to offer our services online and for free.

As the pandemic was now very much upon us, I put our staff on furlough; the government scheme that allowed them to be paid while being 'locked-down' at home. As if this wasn't tough enough, a series of challenging obstacles were thrust upon us. Just a couple of months before Shereen was due to take her maternity leave, the person who had been recruited to cover her absence decided that he could no longer do this and we were left wondering how we were going to re-fill this position at such short notice and during lockdown. Lance came up with a suggestion that his wife Pauline could possibly step in and provide cover since it was just for a short, temporary period. I thought this was a great idea since Iain and I had previously run The Centre together and I know how much commitment is needed to do so, and a husband-and-wife team together will usually rise to that commitment more so than any individual employee. No sooner than that had been agreed, Shereen's baby decided to come early – very early – so we suddenly lost Shereen to her maternity leave, before she had had any time to prepare a handover for Pauline. And most worrying of all, Lance took a stroke and was rushed into hospital. All of this took place in July, and I remember that day well as I had stepped in to try to provide the hand-over to Pauline that Shereen hadn't been able to do when the phone rang and Pauline took the call from Lance that an ambulance was on its way. Of course, Pauline rushed to be by his side and I was left alone in The Centre real-ising that there were no staff (they were at home on furlough), the Manager was on maternity leave and her temporary replacement had just left to be by the bedside of the proposed new Chairman who had just suffered a stroke. I felt very alone and was feeling that I had suddenly been thrust back to the time when there were only Iain and I running the place together, but this time without even Iain.

Shereen delivered her new baby girl and both mother and baby were well. Thankfully Lance had managed to call the ambulance himself and they treated him quickly, and Pauline returned to work almost immediately which was a great feat of fortitude given that her husband had just been rushed into hospital. Lance understandably he was recuperating for some time afterwards. And I just knew during that time that he would be contemplating whether he would indeed take over as Chairman after such a life-threatening incident. Thankfully he seemed to make a remarkable recovery and by September Lance was encouraged to return to The Centre, initially to help chair the Tuesday Talks as I was aware this was his favourite part of our portfolio of activities, and to my surprise Lance asked if I thought we could run these talks once a week instead of the usual monthly meetings. He has continued to do this successfully since then.

When Lance initially came home from hospital, my Group met at his house and sat with Lance and Pauline and gave healing both directly and remotely. Lance felt that this aided his recovery and they continued to sit with us whenever the covid rules allowed us to get together in our wee room in The Centre.

As far as the pandemic was concerned, by August the rates of infection had dropped sufficiently for the government to lift the 'lock-down' rules and encouraged the public to 'eat out to help out'. This was designed to help the hospitality sector get back on its feet but there were still restrictions on gatherings and social distancing rules meant that the public had to maintain a two-meter distance between one another, so there was no opportunity to open The Centre's activities under these restrictions. By October the infection rates were climbing once more, and I just knew we were heading for another lockdown, so Iain and I decided to grab a quick break away before that happened. We managed to secure a self-catering lodge for 5 nights in Ballater, Royal Deeside and that gave me the space to have some thinking time. As I contemplated handing over the running of the place that had been founded after five years of my Group sitting each week receiving messages and clues as to the building that was to become the Sir Arthur Conan Doyle Centre, I looked for some confirmation that the information I had received about 'Phase Two' was correct. I asked for a sign, a signal of some sort that I was on the right path. Iain and I went for a walk in this lovely part of the country, and as we walked alongside the River Dee with the trees in their autumn colours, I was thinking to myself no wonder the Queen has chosen this place as her country retreat; it was simply stunning. There were little pedestrian bridges over the river leftover from Victorian times, as Queen Victoria too loved this area. And there on the parapet of the bridge was a red admiral butterfly sitting in the autumn sun. I took a picture of it before it flew away, as I was so surprised to see a butterfly at this time of year and in Highland Scotland. As I was thinking about the strangeness of this event, I wondered if this was my sign, the signal I had asked for. So, I silently said to Spirit, 'I need more confirmation – I need a clearer signal'. Iain and I walked on along-side the river and into the trees and hills beyond. As we walked up a track, we saw a ruin that was over in the field about a hundred yards away and I felt immediately drawn to it. 'I want to go over there,' I said to Iain as we climbed over the dry-stone dyke and walked across the field in the direction of the ruin. This looked like it had been two farm cottages built of rough stone with only the outside walls and one internal dividing wall still standing, the roofs had long since gone. As we got nearer, I could see that there was a plaque that announced this place as Tullich:

'Tullich's first church was probably a chapel built by or for St Nathalan in the 7th-9th Centuries AD. The church was given to the

*Knights Templars in the 1200's AD and to the Knights Hospi-
tallers in the 1300's AD, who built a fort around it.*

I could understand now why I was drawn to the place from the
path on the far side of the field; the Knights Templars had figured
quite regularly in our sessions in the Group and clearly they had left
their mark here, but what I was about to experience was even more
impactful.

Iain was walking round the gravestones that still stood in the old
graveyard around this ancient site, whilst I walked into what
remained of the building. As I crossed the threshold under the old
stone lintel where a door must have once stood, I immediately felt as
though I had stepped into a whirlwind. It was as if there was a mini
tornado spinning inside this part of the old building. I could hear the
sounds and the force of the wind, and it felt as if it could have lifted
me off my feet. I wondered if this was a strange weather event being
created by the building because it had no roof, but soon realised that
this was not a physical phenomenon but a psychic storm. I acknowledged that I had stepped into a powerful place of some significance
and knew instantly that something was about to happen here. I felt
drawn to walk through the adjoining open doorway into the other
half of the building and when I did so the place was calm, exception-
ally calm. The contrast was remarkable. This second part of the
building felt like an oasis of tranquillity. I stood there enjoying this
sanctuary but still knowing that something was about to happen.
There was nothing remarkable about the four stone walls that
surrounded me and with an open roof I lifted my eyes skyward. The
sky was partly cloudy, and the sun was peeking through the clouds
causing some rays to escape through. As I watched slowly, the ray of
sunlight seemed to intensify and focus towards a spot near to me. I
was still looking up at the sky and thinking that I had never seen
anything quite like it; it was like a laser beam. I was just wondering if
I could capture it on my camera, when I realised that I was supposed

to be looking at the other end, the end which was directed towards the ground. As I did so, I was equally amazed that this beam of light did not dissipate as expected in the broad daylight of the afternoon but could quite easily be seen as it hit the ground. *X marks the spot*, I heard. I realised that I was being directed to stand on this spot and so I slowly walked over and stood in the spot so that the 'laser' was now hitting my feet. As I did so, I was made aware that I was standing on a grave. There was a knight buried under my feet and he was under there with his shield covering most of his body. There was no stone marking the site, which was strange given there were other ancient stones in the vicinity. I just stood on the grass in this laser-light feeling perfectly comfortable and at ease in this energy that seemed to convey a greater power than you and I, when a little orb appeared on the ground by my side. I silently acknowledged the burial site of this once proud knight who seemed to have been buried secretly and in the sanctity of this ancient chapel. Then I quietly left, re-joining Iain in the graveyard outside.

We left Ballater and headed home having enjoyed a peaceful and renewing experience in this wonderful countryside. On the Tuesday of the following week, I re-joined an online group that I had previously set up to try to help a BBC2 journalist with her development (so this group was completely separate to my own) and during our session one of the guys said, 'You asked for a signal to let you know you were on the right path?'

'Yes,' I said, 'that is true.'

'You'll know you're on the right path when you see the Red Admiral Butterfly.'

It is always amazing and reassuring when you get a message that no-one could have known but yourself. This group was completely separate to my own Group, and no information was shared between the two. Whilst I was hoping for some confirmation or insight into what I had experienced in Tullich, I realised that it was much easier to give me confirmation of the butterfly than the strange events that took place in the ancient chapel there.

Tullich Church in ruins.

The beam of light from the sky with the orb on the ground.

The beam of light hits the ground without dissipating.

Lance was back in situ now and beginning to feel more confident in taking over as Chairman and I was preparing to retire in just
a few weeks' time at the year end. Ever since receiving the instruc-

tion from Spirit about 'Phase Two' and knowing I'd have to leave if this next mission was to happen, I had been following a plan to make it easy for whoever would be taking over from me to do so. Earlier in 2020 I had agreed a proposal from The Theosophical Society in Scotland to lease our basement so they could build their library and study room on site. This secured considerable and regular income and it was guaranteed for the next five years; at the same time agreeing the terms of our rental of the building with our landlords over the same five-year period. Our other room-renters had been retained throughout the pandemic by giving them incentives to stay on and most of all I was pleased to have been able to retain all our staff and welcome them back into The Centre. As well as that, somehow I had managed to protect the funds in our bank account so I could handover a 'cushion' of funds to help maintain our charity for the future. I had successfully steered The Centre through the pandemic, and we had emerged relatively unscathed through the other side. I had done my job and now I could leave satisfied that I had put all the elements in place to help the new Chairman and the future of The Sir Arthur Conan Doyle Centre.

I handed over the Chairmanship to Prof. Lance Butler on 1st January 2021.

Let Phase Two commence!

~

Addendum

Is the energy still in the building?

As already mentioned, I was aware that the energy of the building – both that in the basement and the vortex in the stair – would change in intensity. The more people in the building the more the energy was diluted. I had also questioned why it had taken my Group five years to find a building that was being foretold to us during all of this time and I was told that it wasn't ready yet. Did it have to be empty for the energy to form or strengthen? From my own knowledge of the criteria that aids the formation of psychical phenomena, I knew that a building that had been empty for all of this time, before we took up occupation, would fit the criteria perfectly. Subsequently of course we've had a pandemic to contend with, where the building once again has been quiet; indeed, deserted over the whole lockdown period and throughout furlough etc. I was aware during that time that a few strange things had taken place, namely that a large plate glass mirror that had been fitted to the wall and secured with silicon had suddenly detached itself somehow and crashed to the floor shattering completely and having to be replaced. Just a few months later, the replacement mirror did the same thing.

Prior to this, one of the glass doors in the library had shattered overnight. This was caught on the CCTV cameras; there was nothing near the door and no apparent reason for it to shatter the way it did.

Then Pauline wrote to me:

Hi Ann.

I wanted to write to tell you about a potentially strange thing that happened today. We've been having issues with the boiler recently. Sometimes it works, sometimes it doesn't. It's due a service in December so I thought I'd bring it forward and got a guy in this morning. He came in at 8.15 and after about 30 mins everything in the boiler room (only the boiler room) switched off as though the switch had tripped. 15 minutes later it switched itself on again. The guy was very confused - as were Billy and I, as none of us had located an isolation switch to turn it on again. He worked for a further 15 mins and the same thing happened again. Off then on again after 15 mins or so. It seemed fine after that until I left around 11.15am. As far as I'm aware it's been fine for the rest of the day. The gas engineer was a very down to earth Glaswegian and I think even he was a bit spooked by it. 'A've never seen anything like it in ma life...'

Could you please have a word with the Spirits this evening if you can and politely ask them to play with something else in the building - other than the boiler. Everyone complains to me when it disnae work!

Thanks

Pauline

And finally, I handed over the Chairmanship of the Centre to Prof. Lance Butler at the beginning of 2021. Just a few months later, he informed me that he was considering appointing a new Trustee and that he would like me to meet her. She was Lady Hilary Menzies, wife of Lord Menzies, Judge of the Supreme Courts in Scotland. And she was lovely. A very enthusiastic and positive character with a real interest in the holistic and energetic disciplines. However, as our conversation developed she told me that her one problem in accepting a Trusteeship was that she had become very unsettled by the energy in the building during her first visit to meet Lance. And as she was telling me this, once again she felt that the energy was so strong that she had to leave the building; we went to the garden. Here is her statement of 5th August, 2021:

First occasion -

Shortly before I arrived at the Centre I had a clear image of two faces, both Victorian gentlemen, and I heard the word "beware".

As a result, I redoubled my protection, and all was fine until we started going up the stairs. As I got to the top of the building, I began to feel really uncomfortable, unsteady, shaky, fearful. At the top of the main stairs, I had a quick flash image of somebody having fallen over the top of the stairs and lying dead on the floor. As we went further and further up, I just felt more and more uncomfortable and I couldn't wait to get out. I felt awkward as this was my first meeting with Lance, so I did not say anything. I left the building, but the feeling remained and on my return home I worked hard on clearing my energy field. However, I didn't feel it was totally successful, I still felt extremely uncomfortable and fearful. I had to ask for more help from another psychic friend to fully clear my energy and that was successful.

Second occasion -

Again, I went into the Centre with my protection very firmly in place and I felt fine at the beginning, but then despite all my attempts at creating a barrier I gradually began to feel uncomfortable in the same way as before and felt I had to get outside. We went outside into the little garden, and I felt much better there, but had a feeling of being trapped although the sun was shining and the energy was much lighter. We then all went back into the building into the sanctuary. (I don't know if you remember but there was great difficulty unlocking the door, first there were no keys and then the key would not work.) In there I felt much better and then Ann said to me "Do you know someone who has committed suicide? Is this not triggering something in you?" A friend of ours had recently committed suicide. I wondered if it was him trying to get my attention. Anyway, I assumed that it was a Spirit so I treated it as a moving on (my word for a ceremony for Spirits who have become stuck) and asked whatever it was to leave me and go and wait. I then felt completely clear, and I was then able to go up and go to the top of the building on my own with no difficulty. I felt the presences of several people clearing a way for me and indeed one of them giving me a namaste. When I left the building, I felt absolutely fine. I came home and I did a moving on ceremony, which was successful, but I am not sure who it was for. It may have been to help our friend who had taken his life, but my feeling was that it was more to do with the energy of the Centre.

— Lady Hilary Menzies, www.Leaston.co.uk

So, is the energy still in the building?
Probably!

Appendix 1

Profile of Bill McGregor:

Bill left the Royal Military Police in 1974. He re-trained and qualified as a Papermaker in the border town of Duns but unable to settle moved to Guyana, South America with his wife, Paula (who is Guyanese) and their three sons. Here, he became Motor Transport Officer in charge of mechanical workshops and Safety Officer for transport - carrying road and rail bridges in the north west region of Guyana, near the Venezuelan border.

His outspoken views of the poor Human Rights Policy in that country made him a target of the government and he was advised to get himself and his family out of the country immediately – which he did with the assistance of the British Consulate who returned him to London. There he gained employment at The Science Museum and at The Victoria and Albert Museum until his wife, Paula gained promotion in her work and took up a new post with HSBC, in Edinburgh.

Back in Edinburgh, Bill was employed by the Royal Dick Vet College in Summerhall until transferred to their Medical Research Dept at George Square and joined the team looking for a break-through in Diabetes treatment. (Here he was interviewed by the Daily Record – see photo below).

He subsequently re-trained once more to attain an SVQ 2 certification for care of the elderly, dementia and stroke victims as well as being a skilled Phlebotomist at the Royal Victoria Hospital, Edinburgh. He has also been an active volunteer for Marie Curie Cancer Care, Care in the Community and Erskine Edinburgh Home for Military Veterans. And of course, at The Sir Arthur Conan Doyle Centre.

My flight into the unknown

Bill's story

LIFE has changed for the better for Bill McGregor since his near-death experience.

Bill, a technician at the University of Edinburgh, was a young military policeman attached to the Parachute Regiment when he suffered a serious motorbike accident.

His memories of those next few hours remain as clear now as they were in 1964.

Bill, now 58, recalls: "I was only 21 and was racing off on my motorcycle, but missed a pothole and was thrown violently into the air, suffering serious head and back injuries.

"The first thing I remember is floating upwards into the far right hand corner of a military helicopter and looking down on myself strapped to a stretcher below.

"The image is as clear as a bell today and, at the time, it was like a sudden burst of enlightenment.

"It was a marvellous moment, an experience so bright and warm and beautiful. I was genuinely surrounded by colours so vibrant and overcome with a feeling of well-being and love for my fellow man.

"I was aware of the noise of the engine and the rotor blades and I was looking down on a crewman sitting with his legs dangling over the edge of the cargo bay. Around 1000 feet below him, I could see the countryside, fields and roads.

"Suddenly I was hit by a jolt of realisation that my friends were not in the helicopter with me. It was then I was pulled at incredible speed back towards my body. After that, only blackness.

"I did not regain consciousness until several days later when I awoke in a military hospital. A nurse told me I had been brought in by helicopter.

"I later spoke with the crew and they told me they thought I was dead until they saw me join in the stretcher. I hold no strong religious convictions, but that experience strengthened my belief in the afterlife.

"It was such a wonderful experience I want to share it with as many people as possible. It changed my life."

Above: Further info on Bill McGregor.

Appendix 2

The Sir Arthur Conan Doyle Centre appoints Artistic Adviser

The Sir Arthur Conan Doyle Centre is delighted to announce the appointment of Terry Johns as Artistic Adviser to The Centre.

Terry Johns has enjoyed a distinguished career as a member of the Royal Philharmonic Orchestra, and the London Symphony Orchestra. A composer of music for studio, television, instrumental groups and brass bands. He formed an early passion and flair for jazz that was to influence many of his own compositions. In the early years he played with many of the "greats" of the day -The Tubby Hayes Freddie Logan Afro Cuban big band, the Kenny Wheeler octet and bands led by Graham Collier and John Dankworth.

He is renowned as one of the world's finest French Horn players and played on the sound tracks for the films "Star Wars", "The Empire strikes Back" and "Superman" and with television appearances on Andre Previn's music night, with jazz through the B.B.C.'s "Jazz in Britain" broadcasts, and by special request to the Royal Ballet at Covent Garden.

His own composing continued when he wrote the theme and incidental music for Harlech TV's The Pretenders. He also played for many opera recordings with Richard Bonynge, Joan Sutherland and Luciano Pavarotti and film sound tracks by Jerry Goldsmith, Jerry Fielding, Elmer Bernstein Lalo Schifrin and Henry Mancini; and on many pop records with Paul Simon, Paul McCartney, Chicago and Gilbert O'Sullivan and toured Britain with Barry White and his "Love Unlimited" Orchestra and for "Peggy Lee Entertains" for London Weekend T.V.

Terry now lives with his wife Karin in Edinburgh, where he appears regularly with the RSNO, Scottish Ballet and the BBC

Scottish Symphony orchestra. He recently composed a piece of music to commemorate the first anniversary of the opening of The Sir Arthur Conan Doyle Centre, in Edinburgh and arranged for his piece to be played on the famous Conan Doyle Quartet of instruments. These instruments were crafted from the tree that grew in Conan Doyle's garden, when he lived in Edinburgh, by Scottish Violin Maker, Steve Burnett.

"Following the success of this concert, we are delighted that Terry has accepted the position of Artistic Advisor at The Centre. The Arthur Conan Doyle Centre was formed to provide for the physical, mental emotional and spiritual welfare of the community and as such, one of our aims is to re-introduce music into the building. We are a Spiritual Centre and already provide space for the creative arts but we are extremely grateful to Terry Johns for bringing all the elements together so that this concert could take place and for composing this special piece of music to commemorate our first anniversary at 25 Palmerston Place. We look forward with eager anticipation to his next selection of music and concerts which complement our beautiful building so well, in Edinburgh's West End. Thank you, Terry."

— Ann Treherne, Chairman.

Appendix 2

Time to take on Sherlock violin case

ALASTAIR Savage plays a tune on a violin made out of wood from a tree that grew in Arthur Conan Doyle's boyhood home – Liberton Bank House.

The musician is helping celebrate the first anniversary of the Sir Arthur Conan Doyle Centre, in Palmerston Place, which is marking the occasion with a string quartet concert in October.

Operated by The Palmerston Trust, the centre is also home to the Edinburgh Association of Spiritualists.

The violin was fashioned from the wood of an ancient sycamore by Edinburgh instrument maker Steve Burnett in tribute to Sherlock Holmes, who would play to relax. The violin was made for the 150th anniversary of Conan Doyle's birth.

Picture: DAN PHILLIPS

Example publicity of the first anniversary concert, Source: EdinburghNews.com

Appendix 3

Before going to print in 2023, I was aware that these experiences of Iain and I still required further investigation and possible explanation for this book. My own Group had previously sat several times in the basement to try to ascertain exactly what was going on. On one such sitting I got the impression that the owner of the house whom we met in Chapter one had descended the stairs one evening to speak to the servants about something, only to find them absorbed in a session with the Ouija Board or Talking Board as it might have been called at that time. This would have been a new invention around that time and as Spiritualism was very popular then too this scenario would seem felicitous. In our vision the home-owner was fascinated and joined in the session with the servants and this may have resulted in him organising regular sittings with other interested parties. As we are already aware, the Ouija Board can facilitate the release of lower-level entities and so this may provide one possible explanation for what was experienced in the basement, but further investigation was required.

More recently, I have been liaising with Barry Fitzgerald and Steve Mera in a paranormal investigators group in which we are all members. I have discussed with them some of the phenomena experienced at The Sir Arthur Conan Doyle Centre and invited them both to visit in order to investigate further. I was aware that those energies had dissipated since their peak in 2012, and also that the main basement rooms were completely transformed in 2021 to accommodate the Theosophical Society's Library, therefore Barry and Steve may find nothing at all, but I felt it important to try for independent witness statement from some of the best proponents in the industry. We will hear from Steve in chapter 12 but Barry's Report is below.

Barry Fitzgerald is a renowned paranormal investigator with

over thirty years' experience in this field. He has appeared on numerous TV Shows including Ghost Hunters and Ghost Hunters International. He is also a prolific author and film producer having made many documentaries about his discoveries.

REPORT ON VISIT TO SIR ARTHUR CONAN DOYLE CENTRE,
(5-6TH MARCH 2023)
BY BARRY FITZGERALD

My brief visit to Edinburgh during March 2023 was over-shadowed with the threat of snow, however, upon arriving at the Victorian styled Arthur Conan Doyle Centre on the corner of Palmerston Place and Chester Street the biting cold remained outside the welcoming spiritual embrace I encountered beyond the front door.

I was accompanied by Ann Treherne who led me through the main hall and onto a breath-taking staircase lined with red carpet that wound its way around in circles to the upper levels of the building, greeted at the top with a remarkable ornate circular ceiling similar to that seen on the lavish main staircase of the famous Titanic built back in my home country of Ireland at the turn of the last century.

I asked Ann not to relay details on any spiritual encounters she or others may have experienced till I walked through the building. The lights were on which lent a clue that others were still in the building, which proved accurate when visiting the various rooms on the many floors. Some of the other rooms were privately rented and we were unable to enter those rooms, but I felt it didn't obstruct my initial impressions.

The black and white chequered tiles of the main hall drew my attention to the doorway that led to the servant's staircase and bathrooms a half level below. I was buzzed, something approached me but it didn't hang around. I noted it, and would come back to it later.

It was amazing to see the varying stylists of spirituality and dominant right-hand hemisphere at work throughout the building, manifesting in music production, artists and even a Church dedicated to services of the Edinburgh Association of Spiritualists on the ground floor. It was like the building was built for this, or at least had a powerful past association that continued to attract. All the skills on display throughout the rooms reflected of a long past Roman belief system that suggested those attributes and wisdoms were whispered to us by our genius, a being outside our bodies, rather than the modern internal reflection the word would associate today. The Roman association with genius has a longer history stemming back thousands of years into our pre-history.

The main focus points on my tour noted the second level of the main staircase, the main hall way on the ground floor, the third step of the basement staircase, the basement kitchen, and the female consciousness higher on the servant's staircase who previously buzzed me on my initial entry to the building on the ground floor.

As dusk settled over the city, the living departed the building leaving Ann and myself alone to tune into the echoes of the buildings past and three in particular who caught my interest. Using the handle rail both of us descended the servant's staircase to the basement, pausing for a moment, I acknowledged the female presence higher between the 2nd and 3rd floors and continued to the basement.

On the third step from the bottom, I was speedily approached by a masculine presence. To say it was toxic would not correctly define its nature, more like over whelming, not in a negative nature like others I've encountered, but enough to activate my gift of discernment. Its appearance took on a slender male, that with the way it initially approached may have been construed as confronting me. His face was void of detail but he wore a black dinner jacket, black trousers with a white shirt.

Studying it in the limited time I had in its presence, I began to probe it, which it certainly didn't appreciate. It quickly became apparent this was not human, but possessed dominant masculine tendencies. Before I could get to the origin of the energy, a large orange/red lotus suddenly puffed up behind it and both were pulled back into the shadow of the basement.

Tracking the route of its departure, I was led to the direction of its escape under the floor in the direction of Chester Street, under the other Victorian houses on the row.

Remaining in the basement for a time after the masculine energy left, I was aware of a former member of the Edinburgh Association of Spiritualists who continued her duties in the kitchen. Another presence was discovered attached to a book near one of the libraries, ironically a book called 'How to become Supernatural.' Both of these were mainstream encounters and didn't demand further attention, whereas my mind continued to be puzzled by the first encounter in the basement.

Leaving the lower level, we made our way back in the direction we descended, strangely though we discovered a large button resting on the stair handrail we had previously used. How it came to be there, and why, remains a mystery as we should have come across it before.

Entering onto the black and white tiles I picked up on a memory, one of a tragedy as it pertained to a body of a Victorian era woman lying on the floor directly under the doomed ceiling. Her body lay as if she had walked in off the street and collapsed and died on the spot. Whatever the cause, it was in association with her upper chest and head. I ruled out murder and suicide as there was no blood or markings, but her purse she wore on her right wrist hid a small clear glass vessel whose contents remained a mystery.

On the second level of the main staircase, I discovered the imprinted memory of a young male child who observed the body below. Not fully understanding the events that unfolded, the child was still moved by what it saw, and was powerful enough to be recorded.
Ann and I concluded our tour and I wished to visit the spaces again to retrieve more information a few hours after she left. Returning to the scene of the body via the main stairs I was stunned to find the child's imprint gone, also on the ground floor, the memory of the body was also gone, no trace or hint remained.

The male energy in the basement was also missing, three out

of three. This intriguing coincidence seemed to suggest the three events were connected in some shape or form. The building I found was difficult to navigate, it felt like the winding staircases interfered with my sense of direction, however another culprit for this phenomenon was discovered as I chased up the masculine presence in the basement the following morning.

Climbing the servant's staircase I followed the female presence to the third floor, her anxiety was potent but once she was recognised and acknowledged she settled right away and Ann stated there was an unconfirmed rumour of the building being used as a former hotel and one previous guest took her life on the servant's stairwell.

The rest of the night passed peacefully and sleep was welcomed after the journey, but once breakfast was eaten, I descended to the basement for more clues. As it turned out, there was a strong magnetic discrepancy in the basement which in the space of twenty feet caused a 10-degree shift in the compass from a 55-degree NE to 65-degree NE, the cause of which remained unknown.

Following the escape route the masculine presence took the previous evening, I entered the Study Room of The Theosophical Society and over to the spot where it descended a set of steps under the floor and into a vaulted brick tunnel, though I've no idea where it led. The image vanished quickly and I was left staring at a carpeted floor in a modern room whose shelves were filled with old books.

Ann later confirmed there was a vent in that area that seemed to lead downward, but it was blocked in favour of modernization and nothing more was thought about it. The identity behind the presence was scrutinised over the following days. Even the notorious beast Alistair Crowley, a proficient occultism was considered, his shocking explorations into humanities darker aspects fed a mountain sized ego would not have let him appear with no face we concluded. Rather Crowley would want it known he was there and hence was ruled out.

However, a clue in Crowley's past may have presented itself, lending in some way a direction for others to look. He was a member of the Golden Dawn, a secret esoteric group founded in 1887 and run till 1903, by which time the darkness had penetrated the organisation's heart and consumed it from the inside out.

The location of the Golden Dawn's Edinburgh temple was lost to history, but a magical symbol used by the order was a lotus flower mounted on the end of a magic wand, and was known as the lotus wand. A type of colour coding was found along its shaft and the red/orange colours represented Taurus.

Arthur Conan Doyle was also a member of the Golden Dawn, so I'm left wondering if there may have been a ceremonial room at the end of the arched tunnel under the basement, used by the esoteric group. We never have enough time to explore these avenues in greater detail, besides the presence took the step after the initial contact to stay out of my reach and it would seem, even now, 120 years later, the order still like their secrets.

Barry Fitzgerald
Paranormal Investigator and Author

NOTES

Arthur Conan Doyle and the original owner of our building at 25 Palmerston Place were contemporaries, as was Joseph Bell, ACD's Tutor/Mentor and the inspiration for Sherlock Holmes. Joseph Bell lived just around the corner from Palmerston Place in Melville Street and both these houses were being built around the same time. Aleister Crowley and McGregor Mathers were also in Edinburgh– the latter, founder of The Hermetic Order of the Golden Dawn. The Edinburgh Temple was founded in 1893 and known as the Amen-Ra Temple. Aleister Crowley joined The Golden Dawn in 1898, but is thought to have been in Edinburgh before this as Mather's protégé, as they worked on the foundation of the Edinburgh temple. The site of the Amen-Ra Temple is not known.

There are many commonalities between all these men; too many to list here. But like Conan Doyle, Crowley was a mountaineer and he was a member of the Scottish Mountaineering Club. In 1899 Crowley bought Boleskin House on Loch Ness.

In my first book, *Arthur and me*, I outlined how my Group, the Thursday Group inadvertently found themselves sitting (each week) in the very room that Aleister Crowley (and McGregor Mathers) had used; a room that had previously been kept locked because of the negative energies there. I included a testimony from the then President of the Theosophical Society in Edinburgh. That statement is reproduced here for completeness:

'I arrived in the UK in 1996, having been previously part of the Theosophical Society in Krotona, California,the Head Quarters of the T.S.

When I first joined the T.S. in Edinburgh at 28 Great King Street, no-one used the room on the top floor, which is referred to in this book. I am aware however that McGregor

Mathers, founder of The Hermetic Order of the Golden Dawn met there many years beforehand and Aleister Crowley must have been there too at that time as he was Mather's prodigy.

While I was in that room myself, I experienced some kind of energy of the negative sort affecting a particular area of the room. There was also a strange sensation from the floor where the energy seemed to manifest from.

There has been various attempts over the years, by a Bahai Master, Lama Rinpoche from Samye Ling Centre and various other spiritual masters, to close down these negative influences, therefore I am not surprised to hear that when a group such as Ann's sat to do spiritual work in that room, that they would encounter Aleister Crowley and some of the same energies I had experienced in that room myself.'

— Margot D Elliott President,
The Theosophical Society, Edinburgh

Barry's report also refers to a possible underground tunnel in the basement where he tracked the masculine energy to. This is the same spot from where I felt the entity which attacked me in the basement had emerged. This also pricked my memory to the time when I was researching the history of the building (see Chapter 11) and I had a vague recollection of seeing or reading something about an underground tunnel.

In searching the website of Historic Environment Scotland for 25 Palmerston Place, the property is merited a 'Statement of Special Interest' in which I found this quote, '*The house is now in use as a hostel and is connected internally to 1 Douglas Gardens (see separate listing). (2008)*'

Source:
http://portal.historicenvironment.scot/designation/LB51340

   Clearly their information from 2008 refers to when the building was in use as a hostel but I was intrigued to find out more about the separate listing they referred to as the source for this statement. When Historic Scotland wrote back to me they too could not find the source of their reference and so I have undertaken to do some more research – the game's afoot!

   See below an excerpt from Googlemaps showing the location of the two buildings and the distance between them both (around 245mtrs). Interesting that it forms a straight line to a slope in the road which leads down to Rothesay Mews. (1 Douglas Gardens is the property immediately above the termination of this slope but up at road level). Rothesay Mews was the original location of the stables for these grand Victorian houses. Could it be that an underground tunnel was built for access to the stables by the stable-hands? (The servants would have been stationed in the rooms in the basement of 25 Palmerston Place.)

Appendix 3

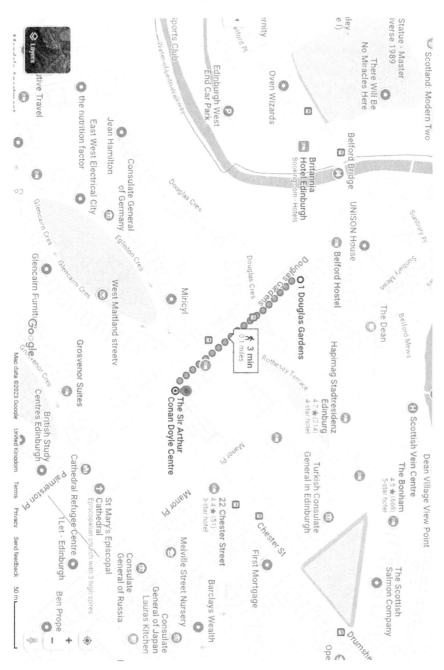

Source: Googlemaps.com

Appendix 4

Photo of the top floor bedroom showing the items as they were in place.

Photo of the top-floor bedroom showing the items removed – in an instant.

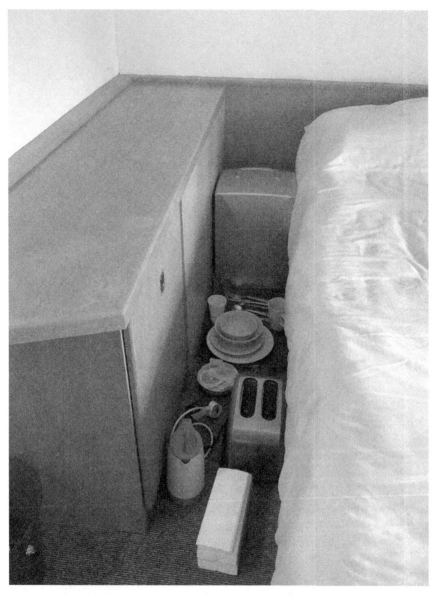

All the items were placed on the floor – without making a sound!

Note: The fridge and the tray of cutlery and crockery only just fit between the cabinets and bed!

The same movement of items happened simultaneously on the other side of the room.

This bowl was full of fruit at the time and there was a free-standing mirror also on the counter-top (not pictured).

How this side of the room looked when the items were moved – in an instant.

Appendix 5

Elementary decision to show works by Conan Doyle's dad

Picture: JANE BARLOW

Illustrations taken from scrapbook he kept while in asylum

■ JEN LAVERY

ILLUSTRATIONS created by the father of Sherlock Holmes creator Sir Arthur Conan Doyle as he languished in an asylum have been brought back to Scotland for the first time in over a century.

The drawings and paintings are part of a scrapbook kept by Charles Altamont Doyle during his incarceration in a number of different institutions around Scotland where he was treated for alcoholism and depression. He died in 1893, while still a patient in Crichton Royal Institution in Dumfries.

Ann Treherne, a trustee of the Arthur Conan Doyle centre on Palmerston Place, who will be giving talks over the author, said the painting were an important part of the author's relationship with his father.

"Conan Doyle's youth was marred by his father's "episodes" – his early acceptance to university at the age of 16 happened around the same time his father lost his job and his graduation was also shadowed by his father's first incarceration," she said.

"However, in later life he felt that his father had been an unrecognised genius and was said to have felt guilty about how his life had turned out."

He decorated his first office as a writer with his father's work and apparently playwright and political activist George Bernard Shaw declared that they deserved a room to themselves in a national gallery.

Workers at the Arthur Conan Doyle Centre have now tried to bring that idea closer to being a reality, by hanging some of the paintings in the centre. This is the first time the works have ever been put on public display in Scotland.

"Some of the drawings are quite wild and scary, depicting the things he saw on the hospital wards where he was kept, with notes alongside them saying he was a prisoner," said Ann. "Fairies were an obsession of the Doyle family. Conan Doyle's grandfather and uncles were also artists, and every one of them painted fairies. And of course Conan Doyle himself wrote a book about his belief in the five Cottingley

Fairies photographs, which were revealed to be a hoax decades later."

Sir Arthur Conan Doyle was also a fervent Spiritualist, and wrote a two-volume history of the religion.

Ann, who is a practising Spiritualist and medium, said: "The centre is a hub for Spiritualism in Edinburgh, though all are welcome to come along and see what we have to offer."

The Arthur Conan Doyle

Experience will run on August 13, 15, 20 and 22 at the centre at 25 Palmerston Place. For more information visit www.25palmerstonplace.com. jen.lavery@edinburghnews.com

IMPRESSIVE: Ann Treherne with the collection; left, a pen ink and watercolour titled A Contention; below, Charles Altamont Doyle with six-year-old Arthur Conan Doyle

Source: Edinburgh Evening News

333

Appendix 6

Excerpt from the Edinburgh News showing ghostly image.

The actual photo taken by the tourists from which the above excerpt was taken.

The photo taken during our investigation by David Deighan of Edinburgh Ghost Hunting Society

Note the distortion to the picture around the head area and also the black shadow on the floor around the position of the feet/legs. She would also appear to wear a watch! Interesting?????

Upon writing this chapter in 2021, I could recall vividly what had happened in this case and that Frances had reminded me about the lady in red whilst on the phone to me – this was something that she had mentioned in her earlier investigation with Archie that had been televised by the BBC. That fact is important as it would appear that the later photos would substantiate her vision. However, in reviewing the TV footage no lady in red is mentioned. I phoned Archie but he could not remember this either. I was disappointed, as I always look for corroboration for each of my cases and don't just expect the reader to believe me but in this case sadly Frances is no longer with us and I was struggling to find someone who knew what she had witnessed back in 2003. However, a little more digging produced the evidence and from none other than Frances herself, confirming via Facebook that she indeed was the medium who had seen the lady in red. This is what she said:

> 'Hi I'm Frances Ryan medium and I was involved with BBC Scotland for the investigation of the white Hart inn and saw the lady who was killed in the basement and wore a red dress'

The above comment was lifted from the Facebook Page of Edinburgh Ghost Society. Below is a copy of their page showing that post by Frances Ryan re Woman in Red.

Appendix 6

Facebook post by Frances Ryan re Woman in Red.

And, here is a link to the Scotsman newspaper's account of White Hart Inn (inc. both photos): https://foodanddrink.scotsman. com/drink/6-of-the-scariest-haunted-pubs-in-edinburgh/?fbclid= IwAR2LU3x---LZeWucWY2MwVWaFoXXWciWW-xred3owLm Tq8-tDD3H4tT_fck

Appendix 7

An excerpt from the notes for Edinburgh Doors Open Day 2014:

The property was built in 1881 for William McEwan and he took ownership on 23 May 1882 and he had a hand in its interior design, as it is by far one of the grandest and most impressive buildings in the street. Indeed, we believe that the faces carved above the doors are of McEwan and his daughter Margaret, who would have been 18 at the time.

Margaret was his illegitimate daughter. There are 2 stories concerning this.

William McEwan wasn't married but was having an affair with Helen Anderson the wife of one of his porters at The Fountainbridge Brewery. It is said that McEwan arranged for William Anderson to work nights so that he could be with his wife Helen.

The other story – the true version, is this. Because McEwan wasn't married he lived in boarding houses. And he got his landlady pregnant. Her name was Miss Helen Anderson. Coincidentally he had an employee in The Fountain Brewery named William Anderson (no relation). Whilst trying to save-face in Victorian Edinburgh, where he was a well-known and respected statesman, he arranged for William Anderson to take McEwan's pregnant girlfriend to London where McEwan rented a house for them to stay for appearances sake as husband and wife until the baby was born. Then Helen Anderson returned to Edinburgh claiming to be Mrs Anderson with a story that her husband had died. And William Anderson returned to his wife and children in Fountainbridge, presumably having been paid handsomely for the privilege.

But McEwan must have loved her, for he married Helen Anderson in 1885 after his mother and sister had died, as they would not have approved of him marrying beneath himself.

McEwan and his wife were both in their 50's by the time they married (McEwan 58 and Helen almost 50) and Margaret was 18 when they moved in here together as a family. This was the first house McEwan had owned and he clearly was preparing it and lavishly finishing the interior for his new wife to be, when he bought it in 1882.

Whilst both Arthur Conan Doyle and William McEwan were **not** keen to accept titles from the monarchy even although they both moved in these prominent circles, the same cannot be said of McEwan's illegitimate daughter Margaret. She married the Hon. Ronald Greville, elder son and heir to the second Baron Greville.

She was first cousin to George Younger and Robert Younger who were both raised to the peerage in 1923, and as a rich brewer herself (*after her father died*) she was created DBE during Robert's chairmanship of the Unionist Party in 1922.

Margaret became a self-styled society hostess and friend of royalty, entertaining Edward Vll and other titled dignitaries. She was given the impressive Polesden Lacey Estate in, in Surrey, 1906, bought for her by her father as a wedding present and when he died in 1913 she inherited all his wealth – some £1.5m. This gave her the means to continue her quest to befriend the royal family. She was friends with Queen Mary and Queen Elizabeth (the late Queen's Mother). Indeed, the future King George VI and Queen Elizabeth (then The Duke and Duchess of York) spent part of their honeymoon there in 1923. When she died, she left jewellery that had once belonged to Marie Antoinette to Queen Elizabeth II, £25,000 to the Queen of Spain and £20,000 to Princess Margaret. She bequeathed Polesden Lacey to the National Trust.

Her jewellery remains in the Royal Family collection to this day – there is a photo of Camilla wearing the Greville tiara and necklace. (The late Queen's Mother first wore the tiara in 1947 and then gifted it as a wedding present to her daughter, Queen Elizabeth, the same year).

Coincidentally, the association with Camilla introduces an interesting connection with Polesden Lacey. Mrs Greville's husband Ronnie was a close friend of George Keppel and very close to the royal circle of Edward VII. Alice, George Keppel's wife was amongst Mrs Greville's friends and became the favourite mistress of Edward VII from around 1898 to the end of his life. One of Alice's daughters, Sonia, married Roland Cubitt, a descendant of Thomas Cubitt (the architect of the previous house at Polesden Lacey). Mrs Greville was godmother to one of their daughters, Rosalind Cubitt who is the mother of Camilla, Duchess of Cornwall. And now we see Camilla wearing part of Mrs Greville's jewels!

Source: '*Mrs Ronnie, The Society Hostess who collected Kings*', by *Sian Evans.*

Further information about Conan Doyle running for the Central Edinburgh Constituency:

He writes to his mother from the Old Waverley Temperance Hotel:

'Day of rest! Thank God! Though I must work at the history all day. This contest is going to be historical. If things go on I shall not only carry the Central Division but all Edinburgh for the other candidates. That is really a fact for it is a delirium of excitement. It is curious but I am as cool as ice myself. The people for two nights have followed me – a thousand at least – from my meeting, and block Princes Street until I wish them goodnight. They crowd round me to touch me. It is that my words have found their higher feelings and that they respond. It looks as if I were sweeping all before me – but there are still 3 days. May there be no contretemps. It is religion, I fear. But if it rises I shall be as straight as a die...'

And then he lost. The night before the election, allowing no time to react, a bitter anti-papist named Plimmer papered the district with bills accusing Conan Doyle of being a

Roman Catholic and agent of the Jesuits, plotting to subject Scottish Protestants to the Pope. "It was very cleverly done, and of course this fanatic alone could not have paid the expenses," Conan Doyle wrote in Memories and Adventures. "My unhappy supporters saw crowds of workmen reading these absurd placards and calling out, 'I've done with him!' when just a few hundred more votes would have sent him to Westminster."

— Arthur Conan Doyle, A life in Letters by
Jon Lellenberg, Daniel Stashower & Charles Foley.

Interesting that he tells his mother, 'It is religion, I fear' when this is exactly what led to his failure to win the seat – did he have a premonition?

Appendix 8

In contacting John Martin, Chairman, Scottish Brewing Archive Association, for permission to use his name in this book prior to publishing, he happened to hand me a copy of his annual journal, which just happens to have an article about water:

> *The salts dissolved in water, particularly well water, were significant in the brewing process and contributed to the development of different types of beers. An aquifer is a body of porous rock saturated with groundwater. The water can move through the aquifer and resurface through springs and wells. For example, the water drawn from the aquifer in the Edinburgh area had dissolved gypsum (calcium Sulphate) derived from the rock it had flowed through.*

> *This is why the most suitable water obtained from wells formed a pattern of the locations where breweries developed. This is sometimes described as the 'charmed circle'.*

Source: From an article in the Annual Journal of the Scottish Brewing Association, entitled: *Water: an essential ingredient of beer,* by John Martin and Les Hutcheon

Appendix 8

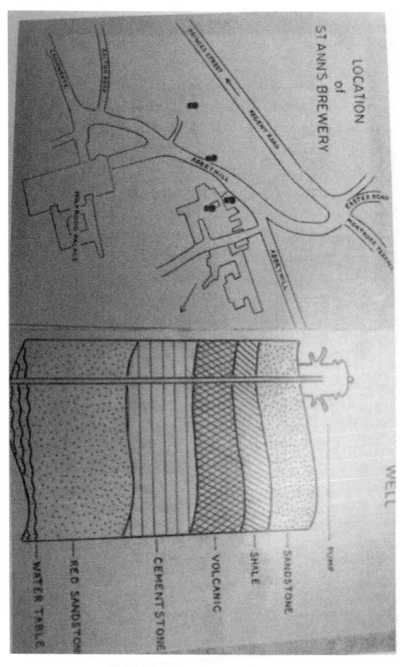

An extract from the above article showing the sub-strata of a well at one of Edinburgh's breweries and the layers of rock present.

Note: There were 3 breweries within walking distance of Palmerston Place and each had several wells providing their water, the nearest location being at Roseburn, just a few streets away. So, the 'Charmed Circle' was very close by and may provide some more factors to contribute towards Steve's point about underground water becoming charged – either by passing through the rock or by the cathedral's electricity conductor.

William McEwan's Fountain Brewery was located just a few streets away from Palmerston Place and it was said that one of the reasons to choose that site was because it was served by underground water.

William McEwan's uncle, John Jeffrey (who gave McEwan his apprenticeship) lived just a few doors away in Chester Street and his other uncle, who was also involved in the brewery lived in Melville Street, just around the corner. This is where Joseph Bell lived too, on Melville Crescent.

John's article lists 55 breweries in Edinburgh. If each of these had at least 2 wells (to provide a continuous source of water - some with four or more), it would seem Edinburgh was acting like some sort of inverted colander with water rising through the volcanic rock and other substructures to reach the surface – would this have added to the recognised paranormal nature of old Edinburgh, recognised as the most haunted place in the world?

Addendum

When I relayed this latest information to Steve Mera, he agreed, 'yes, water does seem to play a part in possible generated disturbances, especially underground running water, these I refer to as Hydrological Associated Phenomena (HAP).' He then directed me to a study by Lindsey Danielson, Department of Resource Analysis, Saint Mary's University of Minnesota, Winona, MN 55987 entitled, *Using GIS to Analyze Relationships to Explore Paranormal Occurrences in the Continental United States:*

Abstract:

According to a poll conducted by Gallup, 37% of Americans believe houses can be haunted (Gallup, 2005). There are also hundreds of paranormal research groups and societies in all 50 states who investigate and research paranormal activity. Within the last decade, paranormal activity has become increasingly popular in the media, with numerous television shows that follow paranormal investigators or share personal paranormal experiences (Hill, 2012).

However, interest in the paranormal is not new; people have believed in Spirits since biblical times. Many hypotheses have surfaced as to why paranormal activity manifests at a particular location; some locations of which are related to the geology and hydrology of a location. These hypotheses include tectonic strain, stone tape, running water, and magnetic anomaly theories. This research attempts to spatially analyze variables that may promote and increase manifestation of paranormal activity. This research will also use alleged haunted locations to analyze correlations between the locations and individual geological and hydrological features. Results of this study indicate one or more geological or hydrological features are suitable for paranormal activity to manifest.

Further extracts from above report:

It is also hypothesized running water can be used as a source of energy much like a battery for paranormal activity. In The Other Side: A Paranormal Blog at Rapid City Journal.com,

*Mark Rowland, the lead investigator for the Black Hills Para-
normal Investigations summarized this theory by explaining,
"because paranormal activity is believed to be electrical in
nature and water is an electrical conductor, water can
conduct paranormal activity" (Rowland, 2009). Further-
more, Rowland suggests because running water produces
energy, and paranormal activity requires energy to manifest,
it can draw the required energy from running water (Rowland, 2009)*

.....

*The tectonic strain theory is one of the most popular
hypotheses linking geology to reports of paranormal activity
(Townsend, 2006b; McCue,2002). This hypothesis suggests
stress less than what is required to generate an earthquake,
within the Earth's crust, may result in piezoelectricity in sub-
surface rock due to highly localized surface electromagnetic
disturbances (Persinger,1985; Townsend, 2006b).*

Unfortunately this study takes place in the US and not the UK
but using GIS (Geographical Information Systems) she raises other
factors which may well contribute towards the incidence of paranormal activity particularly water and tectonic strain which is
described as not sufficient to cause an earthquake but she too agrees
that further research is required.

Is it just coincidence therefore that Edinburgh is situated on an
extinct volcano!

Appendix 9

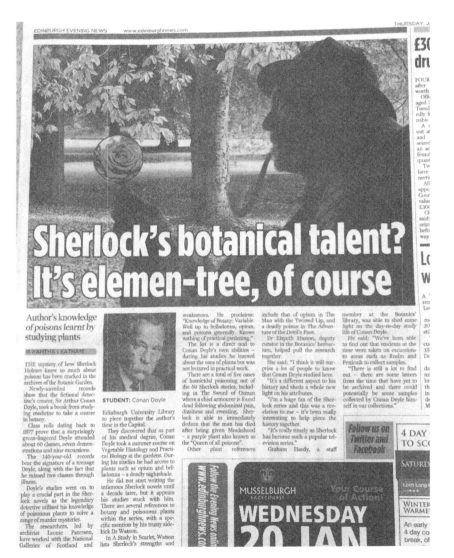

Sherlock's botanical talent? It's elemen-tree, of course

Author's knowledge of poisons learnt by studying plants

■ KANTHA LEATHAM

THE mystery of how Sherlock Holmes knew so much about poisons has been cracked in the archives of the Botanic Garden.

Newly-unveiled records show that the fictional detective's creator, Sir Arthur Conan Doyle, took a break from studying medicine to take a course in botany.

Class rolls dating back to 1877 prove that a surprisingly green-fingered Doyle attended about 60 classes, seven demonstrations and nine excursions.

The 140-year-old records bear the signature of a teenage Doyle, along with the fact that he missed two classes through illness.

Doyle's studies went on to play a crucial part in the Sherlock novels as the legendary detective utilised his knowledge of poisonous plants to solve a range of murder mysteries.

The researchers, led by archivist Leonie Paterson, have worked with the National Galleries of Scotland and

STUDENT: Conan Doyle

Edinburgh University Library to piece together the author's time in the Capital.

They discovered that as part of his medical degree, Conan Doyle took a summer course on Vegetable Histology and Practical Biology at the gardens. During his studies he had access to plants such as opium and belladonna – a deadly nightshade.

He did not start writing the infamous Sherlock novels until a decade later, but it appears his studies stuck with him. There are several references to botany and poisonous plants within the series, with a specific mention by his trusty sidekick Dr Watson.

In A Study in Scarlet, Watson lists Sherlock's strengths and

weaknesses. He proclaims: "Knowledge of Botany: Variable. Well up in belladonna, opium, and poisons generally. Knows nothing of practical gardening."

The list is a direct nod to Conan Doyle's own abilities – during his studies he learned about the uses of plants but was not lectured in practical work.

There are a total of five cases of homicidal poisoning out of the 60 Sherlock stories, including in The Sword of Osman where a chief armourer is found dead following abdominal pain, dizziness and sweating. Sherlock is able to immediately deduce that the man has died after being given Monkshood – a purple plant also known as the "Queen of all poisons".

Other plant references

include that of opium in The Man with the Twisted Lip, and a deadly poison in The Adventure of the Devil's Foot.

Dr Elspeth Haston, deputy curator in the Botanics' herbarium, helped pull the research together.

She said: "I think it will surprise a lot of people to know that Conan Doyle studied here.

"It's a different aspect to his history and sheds a whole new light on his attributes.

"I'm a huge fan of the Sherlock series and this was a revelation to me – it's been really interesting to help piece the history together.

"It's really timely as Sherlock has become such a popular television series."

Graham Hardy, a staff

member at the Botanics' library, was able to shed some light on the day-to-day study life of Conan Doyle.

He said: "We've been able to find out that students at the time were taken on excursions to areas such as Roslin and Penicuik to collect samples.

"There is still a lot to find out – there are some letters from the time that have yet to be archived and there could potentially be some samples collected by Conan Doyle himself in our collections."

Confirmation that ACD visited Roslin – Source: Edinburgh Evening News.

Appendix 10

One example of the press coverage of the newly found ACD book. Source: Glasgow Herald

Appendix 11

One example of the press coverage of Stewart Lamont's appointment:

Source: www.dailyrecord.co.uk/news/scottish-news/holy-ghosts-church-scotland-minister-9454546

The Daily Record report continues:

Stewart Lamont's first experience with the other side was not a great one. It was 1964 when he spotted a seance advertised in the local paper. He enlisted two other teenage lads and headed off.

"It was in a housing scheme in Broughty Ferry," he recalled. It was all conducted in the dark. Unfortunately the medium was helping things along."

When the seance trumpet tipped over and began to float, one of Stewart's pals intervened.

"It rose in the air in the dark of this room. My friend reached out to grab it – and touched the wire that was raising

it. He pulled it. "*The medium pretended he was ill and had a coughing fit. We left soon after.*"

Five decades on, Stewart is still fascinated by things that go bump in the night.

Now a semi-retired Church of Scotland minister, he has joined the board of the Sir Arthur Conan Doyle Centre, a spiritualist organisation in Edinburgh.

His role is to head up the centre's Psychic Investigation Unit and help people who experience mysterious phenomena and unexplained visitors.

He said: "If somebody has had things that go bump in the night, their hair pulled by a ghost, if they are being terrified, they can phone.

"People here are trained to go out in twos and threes. We try to put their mind at rest and tell them something about it."

Stewart has been on six home visits since starting his new role. Each one has been different.

"Some see figures in their house. Others have their hair pulled. One was being pushed. A number could be described as poltergeist phenomena, silly little tricks played by mischievous people.

"If you are living on your own and your life's in a bit of a mess, you get more anxious about that.

"You want somebody to come and send it away or explain it."

This requires all the tact and compassion that Stewart developed in his day job. Some people just need reassurance and an injection of common sense.

He said: "People say their situation is better, that it's calmed down. Just talking to someone who is aware such things are reasonably common is a help.

"We approach it with an open mind but in a scientific

manner. We tell them this is not something to be feared, it does happen from time to time.

"You could have someone with mental illness, or who is attention- seeking. Someone else could be genuinely troubled, they have never had anything like this happen to them before.

"Sometimes it's people whose lives are in a mess, who might be a little bit psychic. There might be something in the house. It all gets mixed together."

Stewart doesn't wear his dog collar, or tell people he is a minister, when he's on psychic duty. He's not ashamed of his calling – he just doesn't want to give anyone the wrong idea.

He explained: "Some people might say, 'That's wonderful, you've come to exorcise me.' Well we don't do that. The dog collar would build resentment in some and expectations in others.

"We're trying to look objectively at what's going on here, to study it. As well as helping people."

In fact, other people's ideas about what he does are one of the biggest barriers Stewart faces.

He said: "There are a lot of preconceptions, some people within Christian churches think this is all dabbling with the devil, which I don't believe it is at all. It's fascinating and it's where science and religion are in a no man's land."

Popular culture has not helped the serious side of psychic investigation.

Stewart is not a Ghostbuster. He has no psychic abilities, although he works with people who do. And there is no common ground with the "mediums" who fill concert halls.

He said: "I'm not terribly excited by public demonstrations of mediumship. One to one sessions, where the sitter is unknown and doesn't give anything away, that's much more interesting. Charlatanism – let's call it what it is – is soon found out."

He sees no contradiction between his work and his Christian belief in the afterlife.

"When people die, I think they do not always go to a better place. People who were nasty, selfish, even evil - and there is evil in the world - these people would intend to inhabit the sewers of any world that existed afterwards.

"That's why people are a little bit wary of folk dabbling in the occult. They go to ouija boards, they end up tuning in to the sewers rather than the higher spheres."

Stewart acknowledges that there are various explanations as to why these sewer-dwellers pull the hair and hide the belongings of some folk and not others.

"One theory is that, when people die, they are bound to their surroundings. They hang about where they were unhappy and that unhappiness is transferring itself psychically to the person who lives there."

Stewart is a scientist as well as a minister, with a degree in physics. The more the physical universe is explained, he believes , the less we know about how it sits with the spiritual world.

He said: "In the 21st century we are coming to science with quantum theory and dark matter. We know more about what matter is and what constitutes life. Consciousness is a fascinating interface between the two.

"In my lifetime, there has been an enormous explosion in sub-atomic particle physics, genetics and bioengineering, huge advances, but it has created more mystery.

"The older I get, the more I realise how little we do know."

Appendix 12

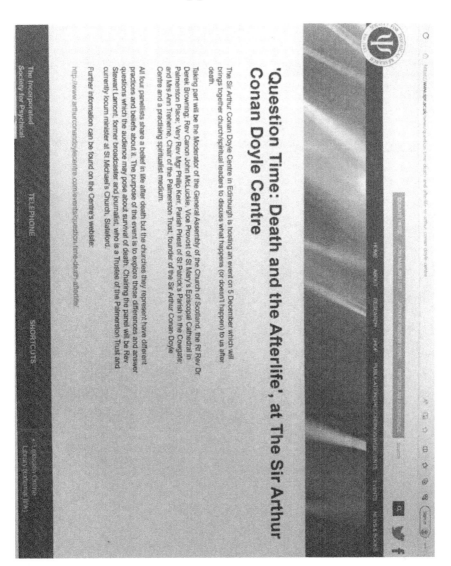

'Question Time: Death and the Afterlife', at The Sir Arthur Conan Doyle Centre

The Sir Arthur Conan Doyle Centre in Edinburgh is hosting an event on 5 December which will brings together church/spiritual leaders to discuss what happens (or doesn't happen) to us after death.

Taking part will be the Moderator of the General Assembly of the Church of Scotland, the Rt Rev Dr Derek Browning; Rev Canon John McLuckie, Vice Provost of St Mary's Episcopal Cathedral in Palmerston Place; Very Rev Mgr Philip Kerr, Parish Priest of St Patrick's Parish in the Cowgate; and Mrs Ann Treherne, Chair of the Palmerston Trust, founder of the Sir Arthur Conan Doyle Centre and a practising spiritualist medium.

All four panellists share a belief in life after death but the churches they represent have different practices and beliefs about it. The purpose of the event is to explore these differences and answer questions which the audience may pose about survival of death. Chairing the panel will be Rev Stewart Lamont, former broadcaster and journalist, who is a Trustee of the Palmerston Trust and currently locum minister at St Michael's Church, Slateford.

Further information can be found on the Centre's website:

http://www.arthurconandoylecentre.com/events/question-time-death-afterlife/

SPR promotes Question Time. Source: https://www.spr.ac.uk/news/ question-time-death-and-afterlife-sir-arthur-conan-doyle-Centre

Notes

1. The man on the stairs

1. Spirit – This word is both singular and plural and refers to a single spirit that may be communicating or a host of spirits communicating as one.

3. The Volunteers

1. I'd like to take this opportunity to thank, Nick Kyle and Innes Smith for also volunteering and coming through from Glasgow to help with the cleaning up process and preparing the building for opening after the refurb. Thanks to Nick Kyle and Janet Parker for their kind donations and to Bob Pitketley for his help with the joinery work

4. We're Open

1. Synchronicity - Jung understood psi phenomena in terms of his concept of synchronicity, the occurrence of a meaningful coincidence in time.

6. Iain's Experiences

1. Residual Energy – an imprint of past events. This imprint can be a vision, a smell, a feeling that remains in a place and can be repeated regularly over time. The imprint is usually created from a highly emotional state where a traumatic event has taken place e.g. a death.

7. Ann's Experiences

1. There are spiritual and religious group which sit at Auschwitz and some of the other concentration camps with the intention of changing the energy from negative to positive.
2. *Spiritual Pilgrims by John Welch, O.Carm. Paulist Press p145.*

8. The experiences of others

1. Physical Mediumship – is defined as something which everyone present witnesses e.g. a voice is heard, a manifestation takes place, something moves or the medium takes on the image and characteristics of the communicator (transfiguration), as opposed to Mental Mediumship where the medium tells people what they are hearing, seeing, etc.

9. Meanwhile back at the Ranch

1. *Arthur Conan Doyle A Life in letters*

13. Where there is evil

1. Psychometry is the art of divination through contact with an object where the medium is able to sense information about the owner of the object or the person whose possession it has been in.

15. People Drawn in – Arthur drawn out

1. Soulphone – See www.soulphone.com
2. Sweat Lodge – a dome-shaped tent made from natural fibres with fire pit in the centre. Used for sacred ceremonies of a shamanic nature.

19. Consciousness

1. UAP's – Unidentified Anomalous Phenomena

Acknowledgments

There are a number of people to thank who have helped in the production of this book; the editors: Dr Adam Reed, Loretta Dunn, Prof. Lance Butler and Nick Kyle. And my proof-readers Fay Hogg and Annie Broadley. To Gavin Ritchie, for formatting this book. I helped Gavin with his book, *For One Night Only*, and he has been helping me ever since. To all who have given testimony and lent their names to this book, I thank them all for their input, critical assessment and for meeting my deadlines - your help has been greatly appreciated.

Most of all I want to thank my husband Iain, without whose help, patience and understanding I would not have been able to write this book. He has enabled me to do so by taking on extra responsibilities himself and has gone above and beyond all expectations to allow me to dedicate my time to researching and writing this book.

Lastly, to Arthur, who continues to direct me and my group towards even greater achievements - he knows no bounds.

About the Author

Ann Treherne comes from a corporate background in banking and finance, having worked as an independent consultant with PWC, she found herself heading up a subsidiary company of a large international bank as CEO.

As her first book tells, she left that world behind after suffering a dramatic premonition, and its subsequent realization, which changed her life forever. She embarked on a journey of investigation and discovery of the paranormal, becoming a psychical investigator, but also setting up a home circle to develop her mediumship. it was there where she discovered that Arthur Conan Doyle was communication with her and directing the group to find a building in Edinburgh, his hometown, to be named after him for the purposes of spiritual exploration and development.

Ann Treherne is founder of The Sir Arthur Conan Doyle Centre, in Edinburgh, Scotland's premier centre for holistic well-being and a centre of excellence for mediumship training and development as well as studies into consciousness and parapsychology.

The book tells how she, together with her husband, Iain, developed a derelict building into the grand building that it is today. It also tells how she devoted 10 years of her life to making The Centre such a success - and of the strange phenomena encountered along the way.

Ann handed over the Chairmanship of The Centre on 1st January 2021, when she retired to write this book. Ann lives with husband, Iain in Edinburgh.

Also by Ann Treherne

Arthur and me

The true story of Sherlock Holmes's creator communicating from beyond the grave, culminating in the foundation of The Sir Arthur Conan Doyle Centre, in Edinburgh.

Arthur and me

Arthur and me (Chinese translation)

Chinese translation provided by Rongrong McLeod.

Arthur and me (in Chinese)